Natural Resource Co
Sustainable Development

Providing both a theoretical background and practical examples of natural resource conflict, this volume explores the pressures on natural resources leading to scarcity and conflict.

It is shown that the causes and driving forces behind natural resource conflicts are diverse, complex and often interlinked, including global economic growth, exploding consumption, poor governance, poverty, unequal access to resources and power. The different interpretations of nature-culture and the role of humans in the ecosystem are often at the centre of the conflict. Natural resource conflicts range from armed conflicts to conflicts of interest between stakeholders in the North as well as in the South. The varying driving forces behind such disputes at different levels and scales are critically analysed, and approaches to facilitate and enforce mediation, transformation and collaboration at these levels and scales are presented and discussed. In order to transform existing resource conflicts, as well as to decrease the risk of future conflicts, approaches that enhance and enforce collaboration for sustainable development at global, regional, national and local levels are reviewed, and sustainable pathways suggested. A range of global examples is presented including water resources, fisheries, forests, human–wildlife conflicts, urban environments and the consequences of climate change.

It will be a valuable text for advanced students of natural resource management, environment and development studies and peace and conflict management. The book will also be of interest to practitioners in the field of natural resource management.

E. Gunilla Almered Olsson is Professor in Human Ecology, School of Global Studies, University of Gothenburg, Sweden. Her interdisciplinary work in research and teaching is on use and management of natural resources and biodiversity involving knowledge integration in social-ecological systems in agricultural landscapes in Europe and Africa. She also worked on those issues for the Swedish government and the United Nations Environment Program. Current research is on urban resilience related to food systems and the linking of urban and rural regions within the context of sustainable development. She is a co-author to global assessments for the UN/Intergovernmental Science-Policy Platform on Biodiversity and Ecosystem Services (IPBES).

Pernille Gooch is Associate Professor in the Human Ecology Division, Lund University, Sweden. Her main focus of research is the political ecology of human–environmental relations. She has done extensive fieldwork on forest conflicts in the Indian Himalayas. Other issues of interest include environmental justice, environmental history, gender, livelihood and participatory methods.

Earthscan Studies in Natural Resource Management

For more information on books in the Earthscan Studies in Natural Resource Management series, please visit the series page on the Routledge website: http://www.routledge.com/books/series/ECNRM/

Natural Resource Conflicts and Sustainable Development

Edited by
E. Gunilla Almered Olsson and
Pernille Gooch

Routledge
Taylor & Francis Group

LONDON AND NEW YORK

from Routledge

First published 2019
by Routledge
2 Park Square, Milton Park, Abingdon, Oxon OX14 4RN

and by Routledge
52 Vanderbilt Avenue, New York, NY 10017

Routledge is an imprint of the Taylor & Francis Group, an informa business

© 2019 selection and editorial matter, E. Gunilla Almered Olsson and
Pernille Gooch; individual chapters, the contributors

British Library Cataloguing in Publication Data
A catalogue record for this book is available from the British Library

Library of Congress Cataloging-in-Publication Data
Names: Olsson, E. Gunilla Almered, editor. | Gooch, Pernille, editor.
Title: Natural resource conflicts and sustainable development /
edited by E. Gunilla Almered Olsson and Pernille Gooch.
Description: Abingdon, Oxon ; New York, NY : Routledge, 2019. |
Series: Earthscan studies in natural resource management |
Includes bibliographical references and index.
Identifiers: LCCN 2018058877 (print) | LCCN 2019006555 (ebook) |
ISBN 9781351268646 (eBook) | ISBN 9781138576889 (hbk) |
ISBN 9781138576896 (pbk) | ISBN 9781351268646 (ebk)
Subjects: LCSH: Natural resources–Management. |
Conservation of natural resources. | Sustainable development. |
Natural resources–Management–Case studies. | Conservation of natural
resources–Case studies. | Sustainable development–Case studies.
Classification: LCC HC85 (ebook) | LCC HC85 .N353 2019 (print) |
DDC 333.7–dc23
LC record available at https://lccn.loc.gov/2018058877

ISBN: 978-1-138-57688-9 (hbk)
ISBN: 978-1-138-57689-6 (pbk)
ISBN: 978-1-351-26864-6 (ebk)

Typeset in Bembo
by Taylor & Francis Books

Printed and bound by CPI Group (UK) Ltd, Croydon, CR0 4YY

Contents

Illustrations

Figures

Tables

Boxes

Contributors

Karl Bruckmeier is Professor in the Department of Sociology, National Research University, Higher School of Economics, Moscow, Russia. Formerly he was Professor in Human Ecology at the School of Global Studies at the University of Gothenburg, Sweden. His areas of research and publication include human and social ecology, rural development, fisheries management, environmental policy.

Anders Burman is Associate Professor in Human Ecology at the University of Gothenburg. Since the early 2000s, he has conducted ethnographic research in the Bolivian Andes, focusing on social movements and activist research, ritual practice, questions of indigeneity, knowledge production and decolonisation, and, more recently, environmental conflicts and climate change. He is author of *Indigeneity and Decolonization in the Bolivian Andes: Ritual Practice and Activism* (Lexington Books, 2016).

Ana Elisa Cascão is an independent consultant/researcher working in the field of transboundary water management and cooperation. She holds a PhD in Geography from King's College London. For the past 15 years, Ana has been involved in several projects (Applied Research, Capacity Building, Advisory Services) in transboundary river basins in the Middle East/North Africa, Eastern and Southern Africa regions, namely as Programme Manager at Stockholm International Water Institute (2010–2017). She is the author of several academic publications. Her latest co-authored book is *The Grand Ethiopian Renaissance Dam and the Nile Basin: Implications for Transboundary Water Cooperation* (2017). She is currently working on a collective publication on 'Water Security in the Nile Basin: Understanding and expanding the solution space' (forthcoming 2019).

Shivcharn S. Dhillion, PhD, is guest professor in Human Ecology at the University of Gothenburg and senior consultant at ENVIRO-DEV, Norway, www.enviro-dev-no.com. Of late, he has worked worldwide on the impact assessments, social and environmental safeguards, benefit sharing and CSR, due diligence approaches and measuring sustainable development.

Josefin Gooch is a senior lecturer at Lund University, Sweden, specialising in environmental law at the national and international level. She has earned an

LL.D in international environmental law, an LL.M in environmental law and has also taken a range of courses in natural science. Her main research interests are natural resource law, water law and protection of ecosystems. She is the course director of the advanced level Environmental Law in an International Context course at Lund University.

Pernille Gooch (PhD in social anthropology) is Associate Professor in the Human Ecology Division, Lund University. Her main focus of research is the political ecology of human–environmental relations. She has done extensive fieldwork on forest conflicts in the Indian Himalayas and also published widely on the subject. Other issues of interest include political ecology, environmental movements, environmental history, gender, liveli-hood, and participatory methods. She has taught critical thinking to many generations of human ecology students, but also imbued them with a sense of hope, that it is possible to make changes in the world.

Sofie Hellberg is a senior lecturer in Peace and Development Research at the School of Global Studies, University of Gothenburg, Sweden. Hellberg has recently been a postdoctoral fellow at the University of the Witwatersrand, Johannesburg, South Africa. Hellberg's water research has predominantly focused on water governance and user responses in South Africa and on global water policy. In 2018 Hellberg published the monograph *The Biopo-litics of Water: Governance, Scarcity and Populations* with the Routledge/Earthscan Studies in Water Resource Management. Her work on water also features in *Geoforum* and *Water Alternatives*.

Torsten Krause is an Associate Senior Lecturer at the Lund University Centre for Sustainability Studies, Sweden. He has a background in International Business Administration and an MSc in Environmental Studies and Sustain-ability Science. In 2013 Torsten Krause finished his PhD research at Lund University, Sweden, on the social-ecological and economic effects of a conservation incentive programme in the Ecuadorian Amazon. Since then he has continued to work on a diversity of topics on forest governance, conservation, traditional ecological knowledge, ecosystem services, agrofor-estry and sustainable development in a range of countries, such as Ecuador, Colombia, Nigeria, Scotland, South Africa, Spain and Sweden.

Staffan Larsson is an economist and independent consultant. He was with the Swedish National Board of Fisheries for 30 years, for many years responsible for Swedmar, a consultancy group in the Board working with international development cooperation within fishery and aquatic development and man-agement. He was stationed in Liberia, Angola and Bangladesh for six years. He has also been working on market issues related to fish products and in 2011–2017 he headed a fishermen's producer organisation in Sweden.

Kristina Sehlin MacNeil is a doctor of ethnology and a postdoctoral researcher in Vaartoe – Centre for Sami Research at Umeå University in

Sweden. Her research interests include conflicts and power relations between Indigenous peoples and extractive industries and international comparisons of these. Kristina has worked extensively with Sami and Aboriginal communities in Sweden and Australia.

Gunilla Almered Olsson is Professor in Human Ecology in the School of Global Studies, University of Gothenburg, Sweden. She is also Professor in Environmental Science and holds a PhD in Plant Ecology. Her inter-disciplinary work in research and teaching is on use and management of natural resources and biodiversity involving knowledge integration in social-ecological systems in agricultural landscapes in Europe and Africa. She has also been working on those issues for the Swedish government and the United Nations Environment Programme. Current research is on urban resilience related to food systems and the linking of urban and rural regions within the context of sustainable development. She is a co-author to global assessments for the UN/Intergovernmental Science-Policy Platform on Biodiversity and Ecosystem Services (IPBES).

Eileen O'Rourke is a lecturer and researcher in Environmental Geography at University College Cork, Ireland. She lectures in Biogeography and Human Ecology. Her research interests lie at the interface of natural and social systems, with particular emphasis on conservation, biodiversity and high nature value farming systems.

Olga Stepanova is a postdoctoral research fellow in Human Ecology/Environmental Social Science at the School of Global Studies, University of Gothenburg, Sweden. She holds a PhD in Human Ecology from the same university. Her research focuses on conflict analysis and resolution in natural resource management and in urban planning. The question of the role of knowledge use in conflict resolution is of particular interest.

Preface and acknowledgements

The origins of this book lie in the experiences from a master course at the School of Global Studies at the University of Gothenburg run by me, Gunilla A. Olsson and my colleague Kenneth Hermele over the years 2014–2018. The course, Sustainable Development: Conflicts, Communication and Collaboration, has retained its focus on environmental conflicts related to natural resources but changed over time to put more focus on the inbuilt conflicts in the concept of sustainable development and towards attention to power issues and political ecology. The focus on international conflicts has slightly changed to include more domestic conflicts and the food systems. The latter topic is particularly suitable since the food system hardly can be treated in isolation from its global repercussions. This became very clear when an excursion to the peri-urban fringes of the metropolitan region of the city of Gothenburg was introduced in this course in 2015 and became a famous tensile patch for the students.

The editing work has been much enjoyed by us, the editors, but also given us pain and anxiety in order to meet the deadlines for the publishing processes. It is a challenging task to edit a book in English without a native English-speaking editor. The work process has been elongated due to the inability to cancel other work tasks and the book project has been dominating our lives for a long time. We have had an inspiring working time as we have had the possibility to work together in a rural cottage at the Swedish west coast during bright summer days and dark November, always with long walks and intensive dinner discussions.

Editor at Routledge, Tim Hardwick, is an important father of this book, as the one who suggested this book from the content of the master course on environmental conflicts.

Kenneth Hermele, the co-coordinator with Gunilla of the master course on environmental conflicts, was a co-editor from the start of the book project. He soon thereafter got consumed in a personal book project. In spite of that Kenneth has provided valuable views and advice along the trajectory of the work process.

A new co-editor was luckily found in Pernille Gooch. Thank you Pernille for taking on this work and sharing the work load with me! Thanks for all the good discussions and inspiring dissimilarities!

Karl Bruckmeier is one of the fathers of the master course and has been a helpful and wise advisor in the editing efforts of this book.

Anne Jerneck, Kenneth Hermele, Anders Burman and Mirek Dymitrow have contributed dedicated work inputs as efficient and engaged external referees for the chapters. Margaret Sykes and Stuart Wright have polished the English language for chapters 2 and 14.

Photographer Hedvig Larsson has kindly provided the cover photo of a contemporary landscape in the European Alpes in 2017.

We are grateful for the excellent collaboration with Amy Louise Johnston at Routledge in processing this book.

The course was planned, developed and run by human ecologists and the book is edited by two human ecologists.

Lycke, Kungälv, December 2018
Gunilla A. Olsson and Pernille Gooch

1   The sustainability paradox and the conflicts on the use of natural resources

E. Gunilla Almered Olsson and Pernille Gooch

The conflicts on the use of natural resources steadily bring us new facets. Now, in December 2018, the world is looking towards Katowice and the ongoing climate negotiations for a possible new global agreement on measures to stop the increasing climate change. In the search for replacement of fossil energy sources there is a global surge for batteries producing electrical energy for driving all types of vehicles and also aircrafts in the near future. However, there is a challenge – the batteries demand components containing rare and precious metals like lithium and vanadium. This has led to an exponential increase of the number of exploration activities for vanadium in Sweden and intensified mining, for example, the huge lithium mines in Bolivia and Chile. Those activities have led to profound conflicts at the local level and massive protests against devastation of ecosystems, rural landscapes and local livelihoods for peoples. At the same time the mining operations are defended by governments as promoting green energy, climate smart solutions and offering employment opportunities. The battle on mining concessions in the arctic environments in Northern Sweden was recently complemented by a similar conflict on natural resources, the exploration for mining of vanadium, in the core of Scandinavian cultural landscapes, Österlen in South Sweden. The legacy of European colonialism in withdrawing natural resources from Africa is seen in the ongoing violent conflicts on minerals and oil in many locations, devastating human livelihoods, not least in Congo, and reported on in many publications, for example Eichstaedt (2011) and in other media. The mineral extraction is intensified and also driven by the exploding computer and cellphone business. This gives a thought-provoking background for discussion of the current interpretations of sustainability.

A *possible* narrative of our current planetary situation could be that the sustainability transitions that are part of the overarching global policy goal are influencing all activities in our societies. It would be logical since such development was formulated and agreed upon by more than 175 countries already in 1992 at the Earth Summit in Rio de Janeiro (UNCED, 1992). This aspiration was later reaffirmed as an overriding goal in *The 2030 Agenda for Sustainable Development*, adopted by all United Nations member states in 2015 (UN, 2015). At its heart are the 17 Sustainable Development Goals (SDGs), which are an urgent call for action by all countries – developed and developing – in a global partnership. Unfortunately the global reality is very different. The majority of activities in human societies are not only significantly non-sustainable but often outright destructive for maintenance of the ecosystem functions and thus threatening for human survival. The reality is further, that the destructive activities that have already led to trespassing some of the 'planetary boundaries' (Steffen et al., 2015), are executed by a minority of the human population while the majority make relatively small environmental imprints – simply because they are poor. This is related to the unequal access to resources as well as the unequal burden of the environmental consequences of the extraction and processing of the natural resources (Anguelovski and Martinez-Alier, 2014). *The significant inequality in human access to resources is one side of the sustainability paradox.*

The sustainability concept is highly normative as well as greatly contested, and thus opens for a number of different interpretations and even different discourses (Hugé et al., 2013). The triangular depiction of sustainable development with environmental, social and economic dimensions has prevailed for a long time and has its origin in the Brundtland declaration in 1987 (WCED, 1987). An interesting demarcation in the sustainability debate is between the weak and strong interpretations of sustainability, where weak sustainability is linked to the view that natural and biological resources can be substituted by technological products and manufactured assets. In contrast, the interpretation of strong sustainability implies non-interchangeability of natural resources based on non-substitutable ecosystem processes and functions (Neumayer, 2003). An example of irreversible processes is the extinction of biological species and the linked ecosystem services. This is exactly what is seen in the conflicts of mining for battery minerals defended in the spirit of weak sustainability, that the technological innovations will compensate the pollution and loss of waterways, ecosystems and biodiversity.

The sustainability paradox has another side. It is an increasing insight that the *economic growth based on continuous extraction of non-renewable resources is entirely incompatible with sustainable development in the strong sense,* and the idea of continuous economic growth as a motor for a good life in human societies is faulty. More accurately it is seen as the root of the environmental and socio-economic crisis (Gomez-Baggethun and Naredo, 2015). 'Business as usual' is no longer an option – and this understanding is stimulating the development of interesting and enthralling alternatives to the current economic growth model based on consumption of natural resources. Such alternatives are emerging in several contexts, often with a basis in community and grass-root actions and networks, for example, sharing economies and cooperatives, and formulated in circular economy and degrowth economy (Jackson, 2009; D'Alisa et al., 2015). It has also become evident that environmental and social sustainability and the equity dimension can no longer be separated. This was implicit already in the Brundtland declaration – 'intergenerational equity' – although most often overlooked at the praise of undisturbed economic growth. Admitting irreversibility of depletion of natural resources should lead us to implementing a precautionary principle – logically following from the intergenerational equity dimension in the sustainability discourse (Summers and Smith, 2014). Alternatives to the economic growth paradigm have been compellingly outlined by

Kate Raworth in the Doughnut Economics concept where the environmental planetary boundaries are combined with socio-economic dimensions as a 'social foundation' for activities at all scales in the global social-ecological system (Raworth, 2017).

In conventional conflict theory (Lederach, 2015), conflicts are seen as a prerequisite for development to another state, better fitting the current setting. Numerous conflicts on access and use of natural resources are shaping livelihoods and life for most humans on the planet. An example: for some peoples in the well-off part of humanity there might be a small conflict in use of economic resources for private consumption in convenient everyday life or buying a cheap weekend trip by air to some metropolitan city for shopping, while for others this action is adding drivers to the ongoing climate warming implying drought problems for mountain farmers, failed harvests and jeopardized food security.

Another scenario is possible – conflicts can be seen as opportunities for change as they open up a range of new options and demand innovations for transitions to sustainable alternatives. The ongoing environmental conflict on climate change, a conflict of lifestyle and overconsumption by the few, a conflict on where the different dimensions of equity, in space and over time, intergenerational equity, are at the conflict centre, could be our great opportunity to enter the transition towards a sustainable future. For the climate change discourse and conflict the accumulated knowledge and data is vast and we would like to agree with Duncan and Bailey (2017): '*we need a little less conversation, a little more action*'.

Many of the conflicts presented in this book have at the core a dimension of equity, in space and over time, and are directly linked to issues of participation and inclusiveness in decision making. In effect, many of the cases are examples of 'ecological distribution conflicts' (Scheidel et al., 2018) that illuminate the conflicting values put on environmental resources and the conflicts could, in a socio-political context, be used as forces for sustainability transitions.

The span of this book is global with case studies from both Global North and South. The themes elaborated and discussed are exemplified in the case studies and have the ambition to represent the major environmental conflicts – although far from exhaustive. The overriding theme of this book, 'Natural Resource Conflicts and Sustainable Development', can be sub-divided into three themes.

Theme one – human–environment relationship

Our basic epistemological position is that humans are part of the ecosystem, of 'Nature'. People have been part of, lived from and affected the ecosystem, in parallel to other animals, along an evolutionary time scale since we became Homo sapiens, some 300,000 years ago (Schlebusch et al., 2017). We have acquired knowledge from the use of the local ecosystem and its different components with a sustainability aspect which is a prerequisite for persisting use. We have learnt how to cope with ongoing changes in the ecosystem, for example floods and dry periods. Values and qualities for human well-being are linked to humans as parts of the ecosystem and it is pointless to separate humans from the global ecosystem since we are addressing our time on the planet. The demarcation between 'Nature' and 'Culture' becomes very indistinct and obscure, in fact not possible to identify since nature-culture is shifting in different environments and is pronouncedly context dependent. Opposed to this view is the interpretation that humans are external to the ecosystem and that humans have a right to exploit the natural resources in the ecosystems. This view, even formulated as an exploitation imperative for humans, for instance in the Old Testament, bears implicit the idea that the exploitation of natural resources is an engine to the prosperity of human development, and is rooted in the Newtonian world view (Merchant, 1980). A third view of the human–environment relationship is also taking the stance of humans outside of and external to the 'natural' ecosystem by applying a conservationist world view. This implies that the 'natural' ecosystem and its components are valued higher in the absence of humans. This latter world view is reflected in the numerous conservation areas, nature reserves etc., where humans have been evicted. Often the expected positive effects on biodiversity have turned out to be negative since the historical influence of human use and shaping impact on biodiversity has been neglected, both in tropical and alpine environments (Gómez-Pompa and Kaus, 1992; Olsson et al., 2004; Olsson, 2018).

The human–environment relationship and the development of voluntary self-governance instruments among Swedish fishermen and the intriguing background to the current fishery management debate in Sweden is presented in Chapter 5 (Larsson). The conflicts related to different world views and the human–nature relationships become evident and are well illustrated in several chapters. The study of reintroduction of a large raptor bird, in the grazing lands for domestic livestock in the agricultural landscapes in Ireland (Chapter 6, O'Rourke), elucidates the rift in the stakeholder's interpretation of the landscape and ecosystem, in essence the different views on nature-culture. The conflict is analysed in depth and possible conflict transformation is discussed. Some conflict traits from the Irish countryside are shared with the case study from the forested slopes of Indian Himalaya (Chapter 7, Gooch, P.). This chapter delivers a unique and personal account from the pastoralist Van Gujjars ethnic community based on periods of field work stretched over three decades. The author has been able to follow the development of an old conflict on the use rights to the forest, which is also a conflict between living in a traditional community in the forest ecosystem, shaping biodiversity, versus aiming for a forest ecosystem without people, that disables traditional resource use. The Indian conflict leads the way to the resource use conflict in Northern Sweden with the Sami reindeer herders and Adnyamathanha community in Australia in the struggle for maintaining crucial livelihood landscapes reported on in Chapter 8 (Sehlin MacNeil).

Theme two – justice and equity dimensions

The current actuality and importance of Carolyn Merchant's book from 1980, *The Death of Nature* (Merchant, 1980), was referred to by Mitman (2006), writing: 'Political struggles for the environment could not be decoupled from the struggles for economic and social justice. Ecological relationships between humans and the natural world were integral to the social relations of society'. This becomes completely clear in the chapters in this book where the recurring element in those reports is the lack of local influence and participation. Often, the resource extraction activity is enforced on local communities with the argumentation of bringing prosperity, human well-being and facilitating sustainable development. This is cynical since the development for local peoples too often takes an opposite trajectory – towards fragmentation of livelihoods and disruption of local communities and households resulting in socio-economic alienation and poverty and enforces an urbanisation trend.

The issues of land tenure, land use rights, use of commons, customary rights, privatisation of the commons, etc., are related to access and availability of natural resources – as sources for conflicts. Examples are drawn from different ecosystems with different resources such as extraction of minerals, use of forests, rangelands, mountains, water as water resource solely, or aquatic ecosystems with related resources and biological diversity including fish and seafood resources, and more. Justice and Equity dimensions are in fact relevant to all cases in this book. This holds for the chapter on water as a human right addressing power, inequalities related to water access and social sustainability (Chapter 3, Hellberg), and conflicts related to forest land tenure, legal property rights, power and state versus local communities (Chapter 4, Gooch, J.). The theme is evident in the texts on Van Gujjars pastoralists in India (Chapter 7, Gooch, P). The text on land use rights in forested landscapes in post-war Columbia has interesting repercussions for environmental justice (Chapter 9, Krause). This theme is outspoken in the chapter on land use in Sapmi and Australia (Chapter 8, Sehlin MacNeil). The chapter on benefit sharing with several examples from Southeast Asia (Chapter 11, Dhillion) also includes this theme.

Theme three – conflict resolution/transformation and pathways towards sustainability

Environmental conflicts cannot always be resolved, but there are a number of ways to transform conflicts and sometimes the process of conflict transformation can be a pathway towards transition to another state of sustainability. A local conflict can act as a seed for place-based transformation with wider repercussions. This book provides multiple examples of how environmental conflicts can be treated with the aim of conflict transformation, resolution and how environmental conflicts can trigger transition.

The challenging work towards conciliation of the conflict on water rights of the Nile river system is treated in Chapter 10 (Cascao). Conflicts around large-scale infrastructure installations (hydropower dams, highways etc.) can be mediated through shared risks and benefits (Chapter 11, Dhillion). Conflict resolution processes from three coastal metropolitan regions in Europe are central to the theme and presented in Chapter 12 (Stepanova). An in-depth survey of theories of environmental conflicts and their resolution in the framework of social-ecological systems is presented in Chapter 13 (Bruckmeier). It may be concluded that there exists more to learn in order to advance from research about conflict transformation to research about socio-ecological transformation towards sustainability. The numerous conflicts emanating from various food systems are deliberated and related to the United Nations 17 Sustainable Development Goals. It is discussed how the efforts towards sustainable food systems can further sustainability transitions (Chapter 14, Olsson).

The structure of this book

This book is structured in three parts, with an intent to offer generality of the large themes in the natural resource conflicts, offer a number of case studies and, finally, present some possible pathways of conflict transformation with openings for possible outlooks towards a sustainable future. Each chapter contains extensive and vital references which will help readers of this book to identify key and seminal publications of current discourses.

Part I: Overview of natural resource use conflicts in relation to sustainable development contains a chapter on the political context to the natural resource conflicts with outlooks towards sustainability transitions including activism initiatives (Chapter 2). There are also chapters on significant conflicts within the sectors of water (Chapter 3), forestry (Chapter 4) and fishery (Chapter 5).

Part II: Case studies presents five case studies on conflicts in very different settings such as European agricultural landscapes (Chapter 6), Himalayan mountains (Chapter 7) and the arctic environment in Sweden and the Australian drylands (Chapter 8), forested landscapes in post-war Columbia (Chapter 9) and use of water in the transboundary Nile River (Chapter 10).

Part III: Transforming natural resource conflicts contains chapters on conflict resolution and transformation as well as sections that look towards the future.

Sharing of risks and benefits arising from large-scale infrastructure installations as a way of transforming and mitigating environmental conflicts is presented in Chapter 11. The power issue in the natural resource conflicts and theoretical considerations of conflict transformation is addressed in Chapter 12. Chapter 13 gives a survey of theories of environmental conflicts and their resolution in the framework of social-ecological systems. The last chapter uses the concept of a sustainable food system as a basis for discussion on the prospects of sustainability transitions (Chapter 14).

References

Anguelovski, I. and Martinez-Alier, J. (2014) 'The 'Environmentalism of the Poor' revisited: Territory and place in disconnected glocal struggles', *Ecological Economics*, 102, 167–176

D'Alisa, G., Demaria, F. and Kallis, G. (2015) *Degrowth: A vocabulary for a new era*, Routledge, New York and London

Duncan, J. and Bailey, M. (2017) 'Sustainable food futures – multidisciplinary solutions', in Duncan, J. and Bailey, M. (eds) *Sustainable food futures*, Earthscan, Routledge, London, 1–13

Eichstaedt, P. (2011) *Consuming the Congo: War and conflict minerals in the world's deadliest place*, Chicago Review Press, Chicago

Gomez-Baggethun, E. and Naredo, J.M. (2015) 'In search of lost time: the rise and fall of limits to growth in international sustainability policy', *Sustainability Science*, 10, 385–395

Gómez-Pompa, A. and Kaus, A. (1992) 'Taming the wilderness myth', *BioScience*, 42(4), 271–279

Hugé, J., Waas, T., Dahdouh-Guebas, F., Koedam, N. and Block, T. (2013) 'A discourse-analytical perspective on sustainability assessment: Interpreting sustainable development in practice', *Sustainability Science*, 8, 187–198

Jackson, T. (2009) *Prosperity without growth*, Earthscan, London

Lederach, J. (2015) *Little book of conflict transformation: Clear articulation of the guiding principles by a pioneer in the field*, Skyhorse Publishing, Inc.

Merchant, C. (1980) *The death of nature: Women, ecology, and scientific revolution*, Harper & Row, San Francisco

Mitman, G. (2006) 'Where ecology, nature and politics meet: Reclaiming *the death of nature*', *Isis*, 97, 496–504

Neumayer, E. (2003) *Weak versus strong sustainability: Exploring the limits of two opposing paradigms*, 2nd edition, Edward Elgar Publishing, Cheltenham

Olsson, E.G.A., Hanssen, S.K. and Rønningen, K. (2004) 'Different conservation values of biological diversity? A case study from the Jotunheimen mountain range, Norway', *Norwegian Journal of Geography*, 58, 204–212

Olsson, E.G.A. (2018) 'The shaping of food landscapes from the Neolithic to Industrial period. Changing agro-ecosystems between three agrarian revolutions', in Zeunert, J. and Waterman, T. (eds.), *Routledge handbook of landscape and food*, Routledge, Oxford, 24–40

Raworth, K. (2017) *Doughnut economics: Seven ways to think like a 21ˢᵗ-century economist*, Chelsea Green Publishing, White River Junction, Vermont

Scheidel, A., Temper, L., Demaria, F. and Martinez-Alier, J. (2018) 'Ecological distribution conflicts as forces for sustainability: An overview and conceptual framework', *Sustainability Science*, 13, 585–598

Schlebusch, C., Malmström, H., Günther, T., Sjödin, P., Coutinho, A., Edlund, H., Munters, A.R., Vicente, M., Steyn, M., Soodyall, H., Lombard, M. and Jakobsson, M. (2017) 'Southern African ancient genomes estimate modern human divergence to 350,000 to 260,000 years ago', *Science*, 358(6363)

Steffen, V., Richardson, K., Rockström, J., Cornell, S.E., Fetzer, I., Bennett, E.M., Biggs, R., Carpenter, S.R., de Vries, W., de Wit, C.A., Folke, C., Gerten, D., Heinke, J., Mace, G.M., Persson, L.M., Ramanathan, V., Reyers, B. and Sörlin, S. (2015) 'Planetary boundaries: Guiding human development on a changing planet', *Science*, 347(6223)

Summers, J.K. and Smith, L.M. (2014) 'The role of social and intergenerational equity in making changes in human well-being sustainable', *Ambio*, 43, 718–728

UN (2015) *Transforming our world: The 2030 agenda for sustainable development* (A/RES/70/1), United Nations, New Yorkhttps://sustainabledevelopment.un.org/content/documents/UN

UNCED (1992) *Report of the United Nations Conference on Environment and Development. Rio declaration* (A/CONF/151/26),United Nations General Assembly

WCED (World Commission on Environment and Development) (1987) *Our common future*, Oxford University Press, Oxford

Part I

Overview of natural resource use conflicts in relation to sustainable development

2 Natural resource conflicts in the Capitalocene

Pernille Gooch, Anders Burman and E. Gunilla Almered Olsson

Introduction

The current environmental crisis begs us to rethink the frontiers of natural resource conflicts. Soils are exhausted and poisoned, species are extinct, forests recede and vital natural resources are privatised and enclosed while wealth is accumulated by powerful actors. Added to this comes climate change, which changes everything (Klein, 2017). As we write these lines, during the hot and dry Swedish summer of 2018, climate change is making itself acutely felt. Huge tracts of forests are being consumed by raging wildfires, wells are running dry, farmers are having to slaughter their animals or see them starve on withered pastures, harvests are a fraction of what is normally produced, the highest temperatures ever are being recorded, and there is no rain in sight. A traditionally rain-fed agricultural system is being hit by a drawn-out drought and suddenly, what was thought to be a problem mainly for the South is right here as a reality for a society not prepared for it. This summer offers a look into what the future might bring and an increasing number of people in Sweden are realising that 'business as usual' is no longer an option. No money in the world can buy back a living forest ecosystem after it has burned down and we just do not have the water needed to bring withered meadows back to life. This is not only happening in Sweden; from Scandinavia to California to New Zealand, trees and forests, essential for the climate balance, are going up in flames. The Anthropos of Anthropocene appears to have lost control. And what are at stake are our common natural resources. On the one side we have trees as part of natural forests, water, grass, biodiversity and fertile soil as absolutely vital components of functional ecosystems and essential for human livelihoods and survival, and on the other we have market-driven mono-cultures with ecosystem simplification of plantations and industrial farming. We have known for quite some time that radical change is needed but have been reluctant to step up to that challenge and make change happen.

Simultaneously, there are floods of information regarding activities that are impacting ecosystems at global and local scales. Messages are often contradictory. Here are some examples of current facts on natural resource use that are setting the frames for the discussion on the global challenges:

The ice sheets over the Arctic and the Antarctic have never before been so thin and their extent is shrinking (NASA, 2017). Norway is seriously discussing beginning oil extraction under the ice sheet in the Arctic Sea, which brings with it the risk of irreparable damage to the sensitive marine arctic ecosystem (The Wilson Center, 2017). Also, undoubtedly, more fossil oil on the market means more greenhouse gas emissions. The negative effect on the climate is indisputable. Despite all this, a well-known Swedish politician is encouraging more air travel since, she argues, if more people choose to fly, more environmentally friendly flying technology will be developed (SVT, 2018). President Trump is withdrawing the United States from UN climate agreements and closing down the US Environmental Protection Agency. Local people's protests against the devastation of their livelihoods are met by violence from industrial corporations protected by governments. Such examples abound, for instance, in Latin America where environmental activists protesting against logging and mining enterprises or large infrastructure installations, such as hydropower dams, or extraction of minerals for the growing battery sector, and other activities that are damaging local livelihoods, are being threatened and murdered, sometimes in full view of governmental institutions (Watts, 2018). The election of Jair Bolsonaro as Brazil's new president risks adding more official state power to the repression of environmentalist and indigenous struggles.

In the academic fora, as Neo-Malthusianism is resurrected, the issue of human population growth in low-income countries is once again identified as a major factor for understanding natural resource scarcity (Crist et al, 2017). Simultaneously, though, an overwhelming amount of undisputable data shows that most of the natural resources are being used by a small and extremely wealthy group of people in the Global North and the life style of this privileged group is also more or less directly the source of the most pressing global environmental challenges (Oxfam, 2015; Hubacek et al, 2017; Footprint network, 2018). There is no shortage of information, data and knowledge on the existing global environmental challenges, including climate change, the global resource flows and global unequal distribution of and access to resources.

Anthropocene versus Capitalocene

How, then, can the current reality be understood? Environmental change is nothing new. Ever since human beings first evolved on Earth, anthropogenic environmental changes have occurred. Fires have been lit, soils have been tilled, and mammals hunted to extinction. However, industrialisation, taking off in the late 18th century, and the subsequent 'Great Acceleration' of economic growth and natural resource extraction starting in the mid-20th century and continuing into the present, has implied, in McNeill's (2001) terms, 'something new under the sun'. Entire rivers and lakes have been drained and emptied, complex ecosystems have been simplified into mono-cultural plantations, and new synthetic substances have been dispersed into ecosystems and organisms. Additionally, but not least, millions and millions of metric tons of carbon dioxide have been emitted into the atmosphere, changing climate patterns and causing an increase in extreme weather phenomena. Thus, it is argued, humanity has become a geological force, dominating basic biogeochemical processes on a global scale (Steffen et al, 2011, p. 843).

Humanity's growing influence on the environment was recognised as early as 1873, when the Italian geologist Antonio Stoppani wrote of a 'new telluric force which in power and universality may be compared to the greater forces of earth' (quoted in Crutzen and Stoermer, 2000, p. 17). This new telluric force, Stoppani argued, had brought the planet into the 'anthropozoic era'. More than a hundred years later, biologist Eugene F. Stoermer would coin the term 'Anthropocene' and together with atmospheric chemist and Nobel laureate Paul J. Crutzen (2002) he would recognise and reformulate Stoppani's insights: human impact on the climate and the environment has reached such levels that we have exited the Holocene and entered a new geological era. They note that from the time of the industrial revolution at the end of the 18th century, humans have increasingly influenced meteorological conditions to the point that they now are principally anthropogenic. The concept of the Anthropocene has subsequently gained momentum in scientific as well as public debates (Crutzen, 2002; Steffen et al, 2007; Steffen et al, 2011; Head, 2016). The Anthropocene is a reality, Dibley (2012) argues, both as a geological epoch and as a rhetorical figure in public discourse.

Three successive historical stages of the Anthropocene have been identified (Steffen et al, 2011). The first stage is the industrialisation process and the emergence of fossil fuel combustion, starting in late-18th century England with the coal-fueled steam engine. The second stage of the Anthropocene began after the Second World War and is often referred to as the Great Acceleration with its drastic intensification of fossil fuel combustion, natural resource extraction and the emission of new synthetic substances into the biosphere. Economic growth emerged as an imperative in economic policy and 'the Economy' appeared in hegemonic discourse as an organism with a life of its own and in need of ever-escalating levels of production and consumption (Graeber, 2005). At present, we are witnessing the third stage of the Anthropocene, in which the acceleration of economic growth and natural resource extraction continues in spite of an increasing awareness of its devastating environmental consequences and in the face of (disappointing) attempts at global governance. The Anthropocene in the 21st century implies geoengineering approaches to fossil fuel-driven climate change and the creation of synthetic life while natural biodiversity is depleted.

Taken together Steffen et al (2011) argues, 'these trends are strong evidence that humankind, our own species, has become so large and active that it now rivals some of the great forces of Nature in its impact on the functioning of the Earth system.' But is this really the case? Is *humanity* as a *species* the main actor in this process?

The concept of the Anthropocene makes an important contribution to the understanding of environmental processes by highlighting the anthropogenic impact on the Earth system. Yet, the basic assumption of the Anthropocene narrative – that is, the idea that humanity at large is to be held responsible for climate change and global environmental degradation – has lately been seriously questioned, not least by pointing to the fact that ecological and carbon footprints and levels of income have proved to be highly correlated (Kuzyk, 2011; Malm and Hornborg, 2014). In other words, the more one earns, the larger one's global ecological footprint and the higher one's level of greenhouse gas emissions. The Anthropocene narrative, with its notion of a seemingly undifferentiated humanity, conceals global material inequalities and asymmetrical relations of power and thus, the differentiated responsibilities for climate change and global environmental degradation (Beck, 2010; Malm and Hornborg, 2014).

The global 'we' – humanity as a species – that unreflectively is present in mainstream Anthropocene discourse does not sit well with these figures on global inequalities since it refers to a collective that is all too undifferentiated for assessing any issue of accountability. Challenging the assumption of an undifferentiated humanity, it has rather been argued that there is no 'humanity in general' that can be held accountable for greenhouse gas emissions and environmental degradation (Malm and Hornborg, 2014; Greschke, 2015). Rather, humanity as a species is divided by asymmetrically distributed risks, burdens and privileges. Therefore, the species category in the Anthropocene narrative can be questioned.

Now, as Malm and Hornborg (2014) argue, a seemingly compelling argument against this critique of the dominant Anthropocene narrative would be that even though not every member of the human species is to blame equally for climate change and global environmental degradation, it is an undeniable fact that climate change and environmental degradation originate from within the human population. It would therefore be quite reasonable for the new geological era to carry the name of our species. Indeed, this argument seems convincing, especially when combined with neo-Malthusian notions of an increasing human population and the insight that there is a correlation between human population and carbon dioxide emissions. However, while carbon dioxide emissions increased roughly by a factor of 655 between 1820 and 2010, the human population increased approximately by a factor of seven during the same period (Malm and Hornborg, 2014). Thus, 'another, far more powerful engine must have driven the fires' (ibid.). That other motor is capitalism. At the root of our current fossil-fueled industrial society are specific investment decisions made in the 18th and 19th century by specific individual capitalists in Northwestern Europe. No global consensus, no debate involving a generalised humanity gave rise to this. Therefore, a more suitable name for our era would be the Capitalocene, since '[b]laming all of humanity for climate change lets capitalism off the hook' (Malm, 2015; see also Haraway, 2015; Moore, 2017).

The main contributors to climate change and environmental degradation in general are those who have benefitted most from the activities that cause it and suffer the least from its consequences, while the world's most marginalised and exploited populations pay the highest price for climate change even though their greenhouse gas emissions tend to be quite insignificant (Roberts and Parks, 2007; Burman, 2017, p. 924).

Naomi Klein asks in her 2015 film *This changes everything: Capitalism vs. the climate*, 'What if the real problem is a story, one we've been telling ourselves for 400 years?' This is a story of humanity as masters of the world and of nature as a machine and a pile of resources that is there to be exploited in order to satisfy human greed. On the one hand, Klein is part of the critique of the Anthropocene concept, pointing to capitalism as the engine driving climate change. On the other hand, Klein is also part of another critical discourse, one that involves an increasing number of scholars, activists and artists, who emphasise the need for new stories and representations, the need for new ways of understanding agency, personhood, being, and humanity's relation to that which we call Nature.

It is argued that much mainstream political thinking – and also much academic thinking on politics and the environment – is fundamentally flawed and that there is a lack of arguments and narratives about sustainable futures. Schulz (2017, p. 127) argues that 'a fundamental shift in the Earth System, which is at the heart of the Anthropocene concept, arguably requires an equally fundamental shift in our understanding of the human condition and its symbiotic intersections with nature, society and technology.'

We simply lack meaningful and convincing stories of desirable futures for human societies and this obstructs transformative action and collective mobilisation. Donna Haraway writes: 'There is no question that anthropogenic processes have had planetary effects' (Haraway, 2015). Haraway, then, is by no means a climate change skeptic. Nonetheless, she says, humans have affected the planet in inter-/intra-action with a myriad of other biotic and abiotic entities – bacteria, fungi, plants, animals, stones and rocks. No species, she says, acts alone. Humans and nature are co-produced. It is not only erroneous to describe the human species as a secluded entity transforming the planet in isolation; it is also dangerous to do so, since it is this very anthropocentric notion – that the human species stands outside of nature, controlling it, and that nature is there for us as a resource to satisfy our needs – that has led to climate change and the environmental crisis we are now facing. In this sense, anthropocentrism justifies and legitimises capitalist destruction of the world's ecosystems and the emission of greenhouse gases into the atmosphere.

Likewise, Schulz (2017, p. 127) asks: 'Is it not astounding that the proposed new epoch which is meant to serve as a warning against anthropocentric hubris, should, of all things, carry the name of our species?' What we need – as seeds of resistance and alternative ways of being in the world – might very well be other stories, but also other social practices, other ways of organising production and consumption and other ways of relating socially among humans as well as other-than-human beings (Plumwood, 2002).

The transition to new narratives and new realities

Resistance

Sliding between the global and undifferentiated 'we' of the Anthropocene and the local and embodied 'us', marginalised and exploited at the bottom of Capitalocene, one finds new frontiers and new alliances of resistance, entangling the social and the environmental with new groupings suddenly erupting, staying in the headlines for a short while in order to again dissolve. Examples of this are the *Attac movement* (the 'alter-globalization movement', now almost forgotten) at the turn of the millennium and the *Occupy movement* formed after the financial collapse of 2008. The Occupy movement engaged hundreds of thousands of young activists occupying public places, with the centre at Zuccotti Park in New York, and connected with labour unions at the height of its success. Both were resistance movements of the Capitalocene, seeing the capitalist system as the main culprit and attacking it head on. But when met with violent repressive force from the state and, in the case of Occupy, by internal contradictions, both lost their power of mass mobilisation and eventually collapsed (Roesch, 2012; Buckland, 2017). The Occupy movement and the *Arab Spring* that inspired it (Alessandrini, 2013) are examples of revolutionary movements of the early 21st century that left the local and became part of large global networks and repertoires of protest (Maynes and Waltner, 2016, p. 41). Suddenly Occupy movements were everywhere, as was the Arab Spring, signalling hope of something new and better, something more equal – and then they were gone. While not being primarily a movement concerned with environmental issues, the aim of Occupy was system change, the enemy was Wall Street – the head quarters of finance capitalism – and it went straight to the heart of the problem: the growing unequal distribution of the planet's resources, powerfully expressed in the catchy rallying point 'We are the 99%' as opposed to the 1% of the world's richest elite. In this case, the slogan has outlived the movement that created it with a new language, now used globally to characterise the growing divide between the haves and the have-nots and to shed light on the close connections between corporate and political power.

While the Occupy movement as such ceased to exist, its energy was funnelled into other grass-roots movements, based on people power, such as the protest against the Keystone XL pipeline at Standing Rock (Levitin, 2015). This was a conflict over water protection with Standing Rock Indian Reserve as a centre for cultural preservation and spiritual resistance. According to Steinman (2018), Standing Rock was in many ways something new. By identifying themselves as water protectors rather than protestors, the Sioux at Standing Rock affirmed their central relationship to land and water while opening up for correlations with other groups. This created a mesh of social ties that 'crossed and connected the Standing Rock Sioux, Indigenous environmentalists, other American Indians and the broader environmental movement' (Steinman, 2018, p. 14). Native American activist Kelly Hayes (2017) characterises the movement in the following way:

The Standing Rock was a complex place—an experiment in love, hope, courage, and solidarity, unlike anything our peoples had experienced. It was full of beauty and catastrophe. It was bitingly human because we are human. And, as is often the case, the magic was in the mess.

In its mixture of catastrophe and beauty, Standing Rock, as something new and a point of transition, may be seen to point towards the epoch that Donna Haraway has named the Chthulucene. After the Anthropocene and the Capitalocene, she sees the need for a third story, 'a third netbag for collecting up what is crucial for the ongoing, while staying with the trouble' (Haraway, 2016 p. 31). In the midst of spiralling ecological devastation, experiencing irreversible losses of our natural world, we have to keep going on, she says, 'in generative joy, terror, and collective thinking' while acknowledging the trouble we are in.

The state reacted forcefully to the Occupy Wall Street as it also did to Standing Rock and the Attac movement. So, met with the threat of violent confrontation and police brutality, much of the protests are going under the radar and leaving the streets while developing new networking procedures for solidarity, community building and collective action (Buckland, 2017). It is also going from mere protest to offering potential solutions.

One obvious solution is to restrain from extracting natural resources by voluntarily keeping them in the ground. Benedikter et al, (2016) see a growing movement for 'Keep it in the Ground' as a potential 'alternative future for global resource policy' and as an option towards avoiding resource-related conflicts. The main focus has been on ending extraction of fossil fuels, while also aiming at setting an example for other future resource conflicts such as the one on water (ibid.). The movement, labelled 'Blockadia' by Naomi Klein (2017), is part of the climate movement and consists of a diversity of submovements 'located at the intersection of resources, economy, politics, and climate' (Benedikter et al, 2016). At the grass-roots level, resistance against fossil fuel projects has, in many places, united indigenous people and environmental activists in civil disobedience actions. This was, for example, the case at Standing Rock. In Germany the anti-coal grass-roots movement *Ende Gelände* puts pressure on the government to stop the extraction of coal. Under slogans such as, *We are unstoppable – another world is possible* and *Stop coal – protect the climate*, more than 6,000 people came together in November 2018 for climate justice to blockade the infrastructure of a coal-fired power plant in the Rhineland and protect the last remaining forest in the area from being felled (Ende Gelände, 2018). It is likely that there will be a growing number of mass civil disobedience actions like this as the threat of global climate change becomes ever more evident.

Searching for alternatives

Today it seems almost impossible to move beyond the critique of the existing situation and to think outside the capitalist, neo-liberal straitjacket. Monticelli (2018) expresses it as capitalism's incredible *resilience* and capacity to always rise again after crisis. The result is that there are contemporary movements of dissent against the economic system and its workings are as fluid and difficult to pin down as the system they oppose. A fundamental starting point in the search for change is, however, still the critique of capitalism as a structure of power and inequalities (Wright, 2010). This was expressed by the Occupy movement and its critique of the rich and powerful 1%, by the slogan *System Change. Not Climate Change* of the Climate Justice Movement, *Another World is Possible* for the alter-globalisation movement (Buckland, 2017; Monticelli, 2018), or the Zapatista struggle for *A World in which Many Worlds Fit*. But perhaps the very fluidity in contemporary resistance strategies is what makes them possible. Under such circumstances, the aim is not for immediate confrontation and system change, rather 'the strategic problem is to imagine things we can do now which have a reasonable chance of opening up possibilities under contingent conditions in the future' (Wright, 2010 p. 327).

Conflicts are calls for change and a search for alternatives. Therefore, they may very well have positive outcomes by strengthening communities and coming up with new and more sustainable solutions. Inherent in the conflict is thus the possibility of something new and with that the hope that 'another world is possible'. But what – and where – are the alternatives to be found in the 21st century?

One strand of alternative movements may be found in an array of local individual and community activities based somehow on building communities from the grass roots while growing your own food and attempting self-sufficiency (Cattaneo, 2015). Many seek an alternative lifestyle through creating intentional communities such as eco-villages or cohousing while others again are active in re-commoning through sharing land, labour and resources (Lamarca, 2014). An example of sharing and mutual solidarity is CSA (Community Supported Agriculture) aimed at developing direct, cooperative relationships between producers and consumers of food (Adam, 2006).

Thus, in the search for land suitable for cultivation, resistance is moving into rural hinterlands and urban commons while connecting through social media. Fossil fuels are avoided – as far as possible – and techniques build largely on extensions of non-industrial cultivation methods seen as sustainable over time. Instead of tilling the land every season and planting annual monocultures, perennial forest gardens and agroforestry systems (Mbow et al, 2014; Hernández-Morcillo et al, 2018) are created based on crop diversity and different life forms (annuals, perennials) which give the prerequisites for multiple harvesting periods. Agroforestry can improve farm household resilience through provision of food and additional products for sale or home consumption. Agroforestry and other cultivation systems based on the centrality of a healthy and fertile soil, organic fertilisers and biodiversity in combination with in-depth knowledge of local ecosystems and adapted farming practices belong to the field of agroecological farming methods (Altieri, 2004). Here the combination of knowledge from local, traditional and indigenous farming practices and modern techniques can be seen as a valuable adaptive knowledge for handling unexpected situations and disturbances and responding to global environmental change. The core here is applying methods *adapted to the local ecosystem*, not seeking to homogenise the local conditions as in conventional industrial farming. This is valid in both the North and the South. This modern gardener and farmer may be seen as a new agent of change on the path towards a sustainable use of the world's natural resources.

Transition Towns (TT), founded by Rob Hopkins in 2005, is a main rallying point for many of these diverse grass-roots groups. The movement has now spread to more than 50 countries, engaging thousands of community groups, and is at present one of the largest and fastest growing environmental movements in the world (Henfrey and Kenrick, 2017). It is an optimistic reformist movement encouraging people as part of communities to imagine what kind of society they want and then together 'do their own stuff' towards getting there. When there are thousands of communities working bottom-up, it will create more resilient and sustainable societies and real change (Flintoff, 2013; https://transitionnetwork.org/about-the-movement/).

In spite of the persistence of the capitalist system, there has been a growing tendency to criticise the *status quo* in mainstream media, and to see the capitalist system as unsustainable in the longer perspective. Moving beyond merely criticising capitalism, this opens up for collectively envisioning new narratives of post-capitalist futures, not only among social and environmental activists actually embodying change in the 'real world', but also as an academic endeavour opting for the study of possibilities for progressive social or ecological change in today's world (Monticelli, 2018). Interestingly, the concept of *utopia*, long dismissed and mocked by leftist intellectuals, and used as a negative concept, is returning as a central point of radical scholarly debate, now with a positive connotation, with a sense of hope, and with an added adjective of *real, concrete, grounded* or *current* to demonstrate that the utopias in question are to be embedded in *real social change* (Monticelli, 2018). An example of a utopia, providing 'imaginaries of hope' through imagining another system to the status quo of 'capitalism's pursuit of endless growth' is *degrowth* (Kallis and March, 2014; D'Alisa et al, 2015).

Degrowth has been defined as a 'project of voluntary transition towards a just, participatory and ecologically sustainable society' (Kallis and March, 2014). It has also been defined as a *concrete* utopia (ibid.). Looking for the utopianism of degrowth, Kallis and March find 'seeds for a different future' in latent elements left over from a non-capitalist past, such as commons of urban gardens, gift economies and barter markets. Those are all elements of the alternative movements presented above. Degrowth calls for 'voluntary simplicity' as there will never be enough until we share what there is (Alexander, 2015; Mastini, 2018). Such voluntary simplicity is also what we find in Transition Town, Perma-culture and eco-village movements. Carlsson (2015, p. 182) has coined the expression *Nowtopians* about people who *exit* the economy by taking their time and technological know-how out of the market and its wage labour. They thus challenge the logic of a market society that depends on continuous *growth*. As a program of action,

'*Degrowth* is not an affirmative *imaginary* that simply signifies the opposite of growth; it is an *imaginary* that by confronting growth opens up new *imaginaries*, spaces, and key words' (Kallis and March, 2014).

While the Occupy movement would be an attempt at a transformation that did not succeed, the Transition Towns and the Transition movement can be seen as what Wright calls 'interstitial' transformation. This means using the cracks and crevices of the system as building blocks for a new, more sustainable society. An overview of published studies and cases of pathways towards sustainability was recently presented by the Intergovernmental Science-Policy Platform on Biodiversity and Ecosystem Services (IPBES) in their regional assessment of Europe and Central Asia (IPBES, 2018). It was found that the Transition movement pathways have the best concordance with the different dimensions of sustainability as indicated by the 17 Sustainable Development Goals (United Nations, 2015). Pathways of the Transition movement's narrative involve changes of values promoting resource-saving lifestyles, including food, energy and consumption, life-long learning and innovative forms of agriculture where different knowledge systems are combined with technological innovations. Often, non-GDP growth[1] is emphasised (IPBES, 2018). The transformation is achieved through participatory processes, community actions and voluntary agreements. Those actions are supported by laws and jurisdiction, as well as customary norms in combination with economic instruments (ibid.).

The ongoing Transition movement is not uniform; its tales are many and somehow contradictory, dependent on the people involved and ranging from those still acting from what may be termed mainstream positions to others strongly critical of capitalist society (Barry and Quilley, 2011; Cattaneo, 2015). Despite this, the movement holds together and in that elasticity there is hope.

The initiatives discussed here – for instance, the Occupy and Transition movements – are mainly situated in the North. Nevertheless, there are indeed vital lessons to be learnt from local and regional struggles in the South. As Martinez-Alier et al (2016) have manifested, a large part of the very vocabulary through which environmental justice activism is articulated globally today has emerged from social movements and communities in the South. Such groups are involved in concrete struggles in which social justice and environmental sustainability are inherently intertwined. Without such movements and communities, there would be no 'climate justice', no 'food sovereignty'.

Conclusion

We began this chapter by stating that the hot summer of 2018 has made people in a country such as Sweden realise that 'business as usual' is no longer an option. Above, we have searched for alternatives. At present, there are few concrete solutions, but the array of diverse actions and processes at local scales might function as radical seeds for more consistent changes on a global scale in the future (Wright, 2010; Bennett et al, 2016).

Note

1 Non-GDP growth means alternatives to the market-driven economic growth paradigm; see Whitehead, (2013).

References

Adam, K.L. (2006) 'Community Supported Agriculture – ATTRA', https://attra.ncat. org/attra-pub/download.php?id=262

Alexander, S. (2015) 'Simplicity', in D'Alisa, G., Demaria, F. and Kallis, G. (eds), *Degrowth*, Routledge, New York and London, 133–136

Alessandrini, A.C. (2013) 'Their fight is our fight: Occupy Wall Street, the Arab Spring, and new modes of solidarity today', Columbia Academic Commons, https://doi.org/ 10.7916/D8862SMX

Altieri, M.A. (2004) 'Linking ecologists and traditional farmers in the search for sustainable agriculture', *Frontiers in Ecology and Environment*, 2, 35–42

Barry, J. and Quilley, S. (2011) 'Transition Towns: "Survival", "resilience" and sustainable communities – outline of a research agenda', *Ecopolitics Online*, 1(2), 12–31

Barry, J. and Quilley, S. (2015) 'Transition Towns', in *Advances in Ecopolitics*, published online 8 March 2015

Beck, U. (2010) 'Unmapping social inequalities in an age of climate change: For a cosmopolitan renewal of sociology?', *Global Networks*, 10(2), 165–181

Benedikter, R., Kühne, K., Benedikter, A. and Atzeni, G. (2016) "Keep it in the ground". The Paris Agreement and the renewal of the energy economy: Toward an alternative future for globalized resource policy?', *Challenge*, 59(3), 205–222

Bennett, E.M., Solan, M., Biggs, R., McPhearson, T., Norström, A.V., Olsson, P., Pereira, L., Peterson, G.D., Raudsepp-Hearne, C., Biermann, F., Carpenter, S.R., Ellis, E.C., Hichert, T., Galaz, V., Lahsen, M., Milkoreit, M., López, Martin B., Nicholas, K.A., Preiser, R., Vince, G., Vervoort, J.M. and Xu, J. (2016) 'Bright spots: Seeds of a good Anthropocene', *Frontiers in Ecology and the Environment*, 14, 441–448

Buckland, K. (2017) 'Organizing on a sinking ship: The future of the climate justice movement', *Roar Magazine*, https://roarmag.org/author/kevin-buckland/

Burman, A. (2017) 'The political ontology of climate change: Moral meteorology, climate justice, and the coloniality of reality in the Bolivian Andes', *Journal of Political Ecology*, 24, 921–938

Carlsson, C. (2015) 'Nowtopians', in D'Alisa, G., Demaria, F. and Kallis, G. (eds), *Degrowth*, Routledge, New York and London, 182–184

Cattaneo, C. (2015) 'Eco-communities', in D'Alisa, G., Demaria, F. and Kallis, G. (eds), *Degrowth*, Routledge, New York and London, 165–168

Crist, E., Mora, C. and Engelman, R. (2017) 'The interaction of human population, food production, and biodiversity protection', *Science*, 356, 260–264

Crutzen, P.J. and Stoermer, Eugene F. (2000) 'The Anthropocene', *IGBP Newsletter*, 41, 17–18

Crutzen, P.J. (2002) 'Geology of mankind', *Nature*, 415(6867), 23

D'Alisa, G., Demaria, F. and Kallis, G. (eds) (2015) *Degrowth*, Routledge, New York and London

Dibley, B. (2012) 'The shape of things to come: Seven theses on the Anthropocene and attachment', *Australian Humanities Review*, 52, 139–153

Ende Gelände (2018) www.ende-gelaende.org/de/news/newsletter-36-we-are-unstoppa ble-another-world-is-possible/

Flintoff, J. P. (2013) 'Local, self-sufficient, optimistic: Are Transition Towns the way forward?', *The Guardian*, www.theguardian.com/environment/2013/jun/15/transi tion-towns-way-forward

Footprint network (2018) https://www.footprintnetwork.org/our-work/sustainable-deve lopment/

Graeber, D. (2005) 'Fetishism as social creativity: or, Fetishes are gods in the process of construction', *Anthropological Theory*, 5(4), 407–438

Greschke, H. (2015) 'The social facts of climate change: An ethnographic approach', in Greschke, H. and Tischler, J. (eds), *Grounding global climate change: Contributions from the social and cultural sciences*, Springer, New York, 121–138

Haraway, D. (2015) 'Anthropocene, Capitalocene, Plantationocene, Chthulucene: Making kin', *Environmental Humanities*, 6(11), 59–165

Haraway, D. (2016) *Staying with the trouble: Making kin in the Chthulucene*, Duke University Press, Durham and London

Hayes, K. (2017) 'New documentary remembers Standing Rock in beauty and cata-strophe' www.yesmagazine.org/planet/new-documentary-remembers-standing-rock-in-beauty-and-catastrophe-20171023

Head, L. (2016) *Hope and grief in the Anthropocene: Re-conceptualising human-nature relations*, Routledge, London

Henfrey, T. and Kenrick, J. (2017) 'Climate, commons and hope: The transition movement in global perspective', in Henfrey, T., Maschkowski, G. and Penha-Lopes, G. (eds), *Resilience, community action and societal transformation*, Permanent Publications, Hampshire, 161–190

Hernández-Morcillo, M., Burgess, P., Mirck, J., Pantera, A. and Plieninger, T. (2018) 'Scanning agroforestry-based solutions for climate change mitigation and adaptation in Europe', *Environmental Science and Policy*, 80, 44–52

Hubacek, K., Baiocchi, G., Feng, K., Muñoz Castillo, R., Sun, L., and Xue, J. (2017) 'Global carbon inequality', *Energy, Ecology and Environment*, 2(6), 361–369

IPBES, (2018) *Summary for policy makers of the regional assessment report on biodiversity and ecosystem services for Europe and Central Asia of the Intergovernmental Science-Policy Platform on Biodiversity and Ecosystem Services*, IPBES Secretariat, Bonn

Kallis, G. and MarchH. (2014) 'Imaginaries of hope: The utopianism of degrowth', *Annals of the Association of American Geographers*, 105(2), 360–368

Klein, N. (2017) *This changes everything*, Penguin, London

Kuzyk, L.W. (2011) 'Ecological and carbon footprint by consumption and income in GIS: Down to a census village scale', *Local Environment: The International Journal of Justice and Sustainability*, 16(9), 871–886

Lamarca, M.C. (2014) 'Federici and De Angelis on the political ecology of the com-mons', https://wwwentitleblog.org/2014/08/10/federici-and-de-angelis-on-the-poli tical-ecology-of-the-commons/

Levitin, M. (2015) 'The triumph of Occupy Wall Street', *The Atlantic*, 10 June 2015

Malm, A. and Hornborg, A. (2014) 'The geology of mankind? A critique of the Anthropocene narrative', *The Anthropocene Review*, 1(1), 62–69

Malm, A. (2015) 'The Anthropocene myth', *Jacobin*, 30 March 2015, https://www.ja cobinmag.com/2015/03/anthropocene-capitalism-climate-change/

Martinez-Alier, J., Temper, L., Del Bene, D. and Scheidel, A. (2016) 'Is there a global environmental justice movement?', *The Journal of Peasant Studies*, 43(3), 731–755

Mastini, R. (2018) 'Degrowth as a concrete utopia', https://www.degrowth.info/en/2018/

Maynes, M.J. and Waltner, A. (2016) 'Modern political revolutions: Connecting grass-root political dissent and global historical transformations', in Burton, A. and Ballan-tyneT. (eds), *World histories from below*, Bloomsbury Academic, London, 11–46

Mbow, C., van Noordwijk, M., Luedeling, E., Neufeldt, H., Minang, P.A. and Kowero, G. (2014) 'Agroforestry solutions to address food security and climate change challenges in Africa', *Current Opinion in Environmental Sustainability*, 6, 61–67

McNeill, J.R. (2001) *Something new under the sun: An environmental history of the twentieth-century world*, W.W Norton & Company, New York

Monticelli, L. (2018) 'Embodying alternatives to capitalism in the 21st century', *TripleC*, 16(2), 501–507

Moore, J.W. (2017) 'The Capitalocene, Part I: On the nature and origins of our eco-logical crisis', *The Journal of Peasant Studies*, 44(3), 594–630

NASA (2017), Sea Ice Extent sinks to record lows at both Poles. https://www.nasa.gov/feature/goddard/2017/sea-ice-extent-sinks-to-record-lows-at-both-poles

Oxfam, (2015) 'Extreme carbon inequality: Why the Paris climate deal must put the poorest, lowest emitting and most vulnerable people first' https://d1tn3vj7xz9fdh.cloudfront.net/s3fs-public/file_attachments/mb-extreme-carbon-inequa lity-021215-en.pdf

Plumwood, V. (2002) *Environmental culture: The ecological crisis of reason*, Routledge, London and New York

Roberts, J. Timmons and Parks, Bradley (2007) *A climate of injustice: Global inequality, north-south politics, and climate policy*, MIT Press, Cambridge, MA

Roesch, J. (2012) 'The life and times of Occupy Wall Street', *International Socialism*, 135, 28 June 2012, http://isj.org.uk/the-life-and-times-of-occupy-wall-street/

Schulz, K.A. (2017) 'Decolonizing political ecology: Ontology, technology and 'critical' enchantment', *Journal of Political Ecology*, 24, 125–143

Steffen, W., Crutzen, P. and McNeill, J.R. (2007) 'The Anthropocene: Are humans now overwhelming the great forces of nature?', *Ambio*, 36, 614–621

Steffen, W.J., Grinewald, P., Crutzen, P. and McNeill, J.R. (2011) 'The Anthropocene: Conceptual and historical perspectives', *Philosophical Transactions of the Royal Society*, 369, 842–867

Steinman, E. (2018) 'Why was standing rock and the #NoDAPL campaign so historic? Factors affecting American Indian participation in social movement collaborations and coalitions', *Ethnic and Racial Studies*, doi:10.1080/01419870.2018.1471215

SVT, (2018) 'Flyg mer för att rädda klimatet', Sveriges Television Nyheter, 30 January 2018

UN, (2015) *Transforming our world: The 2030 agenda for sustainable development* (A/RES/70/1), New York, United Nationshttps://sustainabledevelopment.un.org/content/documents/UN

Watts, J. (2018) 'Almost four environmental defenders a week killed in 2017' *The Guardian*, https://www.theguardian.com/environment/2018/feb/02/almost-four-environmental-defenders-a-week-killed-in-2017

Whitehead, M. (2013) 'Degrowth or regrowth?' *Environmental Values*, 22(2), 141–145

The Wilson Center (2017) *Opportunities and challenges for Arctic oil and gas development*, The Wilson Center, Washington, DC

Wright, E. O. (2010) *Envisioning real utopias*, Verso, London

3 Water, conflict and social sustainability

Bringing power into the water security discourse

Sofie Hellberg

Introduction

Given the manifold and vital roles of water for all manner of life, and its character as a limited resource, there will always be conflicts around water in the sense of clashes of interests in relation to different uses of water. These conflicts have the potential to turn violent and they therefore urgently need to be addressed. However, water conflicts do not necessarily have to have a violent outcome. The fact that some water conflicts remain peaceful does not, in turn, mean that they should not be attended to. Such latent conflicts are often characterised by power asymmetries and by an inequitable distribution of the water resource between actors, which is a problem in its own right.

This chapter has two main purposes. It will provide an overview of the debate on the relationship between (water) *scarcity* and *conflict* and it offers a critical perspective on how we can approach water conflicts within a sustainable development framework. As regards to the latter, two main arguments are presented. First, it is pivotal to place focus on *power* relationships regarding resource distribution in relation to conflicts over water, and second, that the concept of *social sustainability* can aid the process of analysing and addressing such conflicts and thereby create preconditions for *water security*.

The chapter begins, in its first section, by defining three core concepts: 'conflict', 'scarcity' and 'power', and then continues by outlining some of the main lines of argument as regards to the debate around the link between scarcity and conflict, both in general terms and in specific relation to water. Furthermore, the risks, identified in the water research literature, connected to water conflicts are outlined, as is the concept of water security. The second section presents how water governance is related to the concept of sustainable development and in particular the concept of *social* sustainability. This section also provides a discussion of how different populations are understood within a sustainable development discourse and what that means for water conflicts that are paid attention to in global policy. The third section presents how conflicts around water can be addressed through a focus on social sustainability and how this can aid the process of reaching a more water secure world. The chapter is then concluded.

The concepts of 'conflict', 'scarcity' and 'power'

Before entering into the debate around the links between 'scarcity' and 'conflict' and how these are related to 'power', it is of importance to make clear how these main concepts are understood in this chapter.

In this chapter, a conflict is understood as a situation in which there is a clash of interest that is either latent or manifest and which can have the potential to either be solved peacefully or escalate into violence. The concept of 'conflict' will here, furthermore, be used in order to describe different *kinds* of conflicts (international, intranational) that take place at different scales (regional, local, basin level), involving *different types of actors* (state actors and non-state actors such as communities and civil society organisations).

Another important aspect when trying to classify conflicts that involve water is to address the question of what role water has in that very conflict. Researchers who have aimed to give an account of the prevalence of water conflicts distinguish between different kinds of water disputes. The Pacific Institute, with Peter Gleick as its president, tracks and categorises events in relation to water and conflict. This project differs between conflicts in which water is the root of the tensions, a category which they term 'control of water resources', and in which water is a military tool, a political tool, the target or tool of terrorist actions of non-state actors, or the military tool of state actors, and lastly in which water is a source of dispute in relation to economic and social development (Pacific Institute, 2017). It is recognised that events can fall into more than one category and that the definitions above are 'imprecise' (ibid.). This chapter will give an overview of how different kinds of conflicts have been addressed in the academic literature but will also, in the latter half, provide a critical view on the specific kinds of conflicts that global policy tends to emphasise.

'Scarcity' is likewise not a straightforward concept but can rather be used to describe a number of different situations and causes for the lack of water. One common way of expressing the difference between different forms of scarcities is to distinguish between physical, economic and institutional water scarcity. *Physical scarcity* is when water is limited in quantity or quality. In contrast, *economic scarcity* depicts a situation where lack of funding and/or infrastructure is the reason that water does not reach the users, and, lastly, *institutional scarcity* describes a situation where the lack of capacity and institutional framework is the reason that reliable access to water cannot be ensured (see for example FAO, 2016).

There are also several different ways of assessing physical water scarcity. One way has been to divide countries into those that are water-stressed (when the annual water supply drops below 1,700 m^3 per person), water scarce (when the annual water supply drops below 1,000 m^3 per person) and suffering from absolute scarcity (when the annual water supply drops below 500 m^3 per person). Such a way of measuring scarcity fails, however, to take into account the differences between countries in terms of their specific patterns of water usage (FAO, 2012, referenced in WWDR, 2016). In order to come to terms with this, another measure has been proposed that instead focuses on the human pressure on water resources in a specific country. This is the way of measuring water scarcity that has been adopted in the Millennium Development Goals (MDGs) as well as the Sustainable Development Goals (SDGs) (WWDR, 2016).[1] There are, however, limitations of such measures as well as the fact that these do not take into account distributional issues within or between different countries. Basin analysis of water scarcity is, in turn, a way of dealing with such shortcomings (WWDR, 2016). For the argument of this chapter, the differences between such definitions and situations of water scarcity is of utmost importance as water scarcity is not viewed solely as a natural phenomenon but rather as connected to institutional factors as well as economic, cultural and social customs and practices.

A third central concept of this chapter is *power*. Power has multiple understandings (see for example Lukes, 2005) but in the context of this chapter it is understood as relational and productive and in a sustainable development context, particularly focused on the governing of populations. Such a view of power is indebted to the way that Foucault has theorised power (see Foucault, 1977; 1998; 2003[2]). That power is relational means that power is viewed as something that is exercised in social networks and relations in which actors acquire different positions. These different positions are not naturally given. They are to be viewed as the consequence of the productive aspect of power, which assigns different roles and structural positions to actors and the way these actors understand themselves through assemblages of knowledge/power. These assemblages, in turn, are productive of particular ways of seeing and understanding the world. Thus, power is productive of our realities, particular subjectivities, but it is also, especially in a sustainable development regime, productive of particular notions of populations and their relationships to resource use and environmental effects.

The relationship between scarcity and conflict

The role of resource scarcity (not only regarding water) in relation to conflict is a much-debated topic. In global policy, the case has, for some time now, been made that shortages of natural resources can trigger conflicts, social unrest and even civil wars (see for example UN, 2009, cited in Mildner et al., 2011).

The ways in which the links between scarcity and conflict are understood are part of a long trajectory. Ultimately, this debate dates back to the stipulations of Thomas Malthus' population thesis which put forward that population growth increases faster than its means of subsistence but is 'kept equal to the means of subsistence, by misery and vice' (Malthus, 1798). What is central along this way of reasoning is that if populations do not consider the future in their present consumption their actions will be destructive and population growth will eventually decline. Important to note here is also that in the original

Malthusian theories, it was *certain* populations that were seen as unable to instil a sense of futurity: the poor and the 'underdeveloped' populations of the colonies (Tellmann, 2013; see also Hellberg, 2018 for a development of this argument in specific relation to water governance).

In environmental discourse, the focus of neo-Malthusian perspectives has not been so much on the effects of population trends but on the effects of increasing populations and their resource use in relation to effects on the environment. Such problematisations have drawn attention to the question of 'overpopulation', as the root of environmental problems, one of the central figures in this debate being Paul Erhlich (see Ehrlich, 1968). Working within such frames of reasoning, the scarcity of resources following population growth has been argued to have a positive relationship to (violent) conflict since the increase in populations grow faster than the increase in the supplies of the means of existence.

Thomas Homer-Dixon argued at the beginning of the 1990s (see for example Homer-Dixon, 1994) that environmental scarcity causes violent conflicts and that such conflicts tends to be 'persistent, diffuse, and sub-national' (ibid., p. 36). Homer-Dixon also stipulated that the frequency of such conflicts will increase sharply in the coming decades because that scarcity (of such resources such as cropland, water, forests and fish) was projected to worsen in many parts of the world (ibid.).

Such stipulations have long been questioned by researchers who focus instead on the role of innovation in overcoming resource scarcity, such as Boserup (1973) and those who focus on the role of institutions and questions of inequality (for an overview of this debate see Mildner et al., 2011). Recently there has been a wealth of research which has argued that governance and distributional issues affect whether conflicts around resources escalate or not (see for example Benjaminsen and Ba, 2009; Moyo, 2005; Saad-Filho and Weeks, 2013). This means that the neo-Malthusian thesis has been strongly questioned in terms of the direct links between resource scarcity and conflict that such a perspective stipulates. One aspect is particularly central to the argument of this chapter. Mildner makes this explicit; she writes that '[c]ase studies that include institutions and power relations in their analysis paint different pictures of resource scarcity' (Mildner, 2011, p. 162).

The water context: different types of conflicts and perspectives on conflict and cooperation

In the specific context of water, the issue of water scarcity and the relationship to conflict was a hot topic in the 1990s. It was then that the hypothesis around the increasing risk for so-called water wars emerged in both policy and academic debates. At this period of time, such suppositions revolved around the conflicts between sovereign states, that is 'water wars' (see Starr, 1991). Subsequently, that water is the new 'oil' that we will go to war for in the future became an often-repeated mantra in media as well as in policy circles.

In academia, this debate has now matured. At present, there is a recognition that water, rather than being a cause of conflict, much more often is a catalyst for cooperation (see Wolf et al., 2003; Yoffe et al., 2003; Yoffe et al., 2004). The case has also been made that conflict and cooperation often co-exist and that there is a need for problematising the common view that all conflicts are inherently 'bad' and conversely that all cooperation is 'good' (Zeitoun and Mirumachi, 2008; Mirumachi and van Wyk, 2010). A critical perspective on cooperation, these authors argue, is needed because of the power imbalances between the parties in water agreements (ibid.). These dynamics have first and foremost been identified in transboundary settings. While this strand of research has remained central to the debate on water conflicts, a larger emphasis is now placed on internal and local conflicts instead of international ones. It is this type of conflict that this chapter will focus on in its remaining parts.

Research on this type of conflict has placed focus on relationships between actors such as communities and commercial farmers and the forestry and biofuel industries (see for example Funder et al., 2012; Gillet et al., 2014; Mutopo and Chiweshe, 2014). Another, albeit less explored, theme is intra-community dynamics in relation to water conflicts and how class, gender and ethnicity affect the evolvement and nature of such conflicts, which, for example can revolve around irrigation and infrastructure projects (ibid.).

Funder et al. provide important lessons to be learned about dynamics of conflict and cooperation in terms of intra-community dynamics. As is the case in many transboundary settings, the relationship between the different actors (in this case households) is characterised by asymmetrical power and dependency relations. Funder et al. find that the poorest in these contexts engage in colla-borative activities but also apply risk avoidance strategies in order to avoid sanctions from more wealthy households to which they are dependent, for example in terms of work opportunities. Because of this dependency, poorer households abstain from confronting more powerful actors in water conflicts, which in turn might end up sustaining inequalities (Funder et al., 2012).

This, Funder et al. argue, should in no way be seen as that the poor do not have agency in relation to navigating their own interest but rather that their way of acting in relation to water conflicts has the character of risk minimising. This, in turn, means that they might turn to 'alternative, less desirable sources of water rather than engaging in any direct confrontation with more powerful actors' (ibid., p. 32). Because of these dynamics that Funder et al. have identi-fied, the authors place focus on the problem of engaging grass-roots organisa-tions in water decision making as a way of accommodating community interests as these organisations might become biased towards the interests of the more well-off rather than working solely in the interests of the poorest.

Funder et al. suggest that a broad approach is needed in order to address the position of the poorest in water conflicts. Such an approach includes expanding the range of options available in institutional and socio-economic terms such as providing alternative organisational space where the poor can articulate their grievances. Examples that Funder et al. provide in relation to this matter are customary conflict resolution mechanisms, other community organisations, local government structures, NGOs or informal trusted parties (such as teachers and health workers). Another critical area that is identified by Funder et al. is that firm rights and water-sharing agreements need to be developed and, most importantly, monitored and maintained.

However, as will be argued in this chapter, for the grievances expressed through such alternative space to be taken seriously there is a need for a change in the attitudes of how we view different populations and their relationships to resource use and access. We must therefore go beyond creating better institutional frameworks in order to address the situation of the poorest. This since the frameworks put in place for participation in water governance are constructed within the very space which makes a separation between poor and rich communities in terms of their ability to act sustainably. Furthermore, they premiere the current political economy and its economic growth paradigm. Hence, without such a change, the interests of private companies and wealthier populations will continue to override the interests of the poor in mainstream water governance efforts.[3]

The water context: risk and water (in)security

The cumulative result of the research that has looked into dynamics of conflicts, both in transboundary and in national and local contexts, has involved a greater awareness of the different factors that potentially could lead to future water conflicts. Such aspects include shifts in water resource availability because of factors related to climate change, population growth, irrigation and dam construction as well as the lack of institutional capacity (Petersen-Perlman et al., 2017). Some have also placed special focus on the ways in which inequality affects (the risk of) conflict (see for example Funder et al., 2012; Gunasekara et al., 2014). This awareness, together with the acknowledgement of the complex relationships between these different factors, has placed the concept of *risk* at the centre of the water and conflict debate. At present, identifying, assessing and addressing risks for future hydro-political conflicts is thus one of the central tasks for policy and academia. One central concept within water governance in general, as well as in relation to risks, threats and vulnerabilities in particular, is the concept of *water security*, which has become one of the most influential in global water policy discussions during the last decade, especially in the context of climate change.

In the process of moving focus from *inter*national water conflicts to *intra*national, there has been a subsequent change in focus in terms of the subjects of (in)security. This change has involved a move from the focus on the relationships between *sovereign states* to that of internal conflicts between *actors within them*. Specifically, this has involved an increasing focus on the water security of individuals, as a part of *human security*. In tandem with this development, most notions of water security lean towards focusing on the individual level and have had little reference to military security and so-called water wars. There is, however, no single definition of the water security term as academics as well as policy institutions and organisations apply different definitions.

While the early definitions of water security were human centred (Srinivasan et al., 2017), typically focusing on access to sufficient and affordable water to satisfy human needs, most contemporary approaches embrace a broad understanding of water security focusing on *both* human and ecosystem needs (ibid.; Cook and Bakker, 2012). One example of such a broad definition, which is based on UNESCO's International Hydraulic Programme, is proposed in UN Water's analytical brief:

> Water security is defined here as the capacity of a population to safeguard sustainable access to adequate quantities of acceptable quality water for sustaining livelihoods, human well-being, and socio-economic development, for ensuring protection against water-borne pollution and water-related disasters, and for preserving ecosystems in a climate of peace and political stability. (United Nations University, 2013, p. 1)

Other definitions have been proposed. Global Water Partnership (GWP) presents the following definition:

> Water security, at any level from the household to the global, means that every person has access to enough safe water at affordable cost to lead a clean, healthy and productive life, while ensuring that the natural environment is protected and enhanced. (GWP, 2000 p. 1)

The 2015 WWDR builds on Grey and Sadoff's (2007) definition:

> Water security: The availability of an acceptable quantity and quality of water for health, livelihoods, ecosystems and production, coupled with an acceptable level of water-related risks to people, environment and economies. (Grey and Sadoff, 2007, cited in WWDR, 2015, p. 86)

I will come back to the concept of water security in the last section of the chapter. In particular, I will return to the definition proposed in UN Water's analytical brief as this definition places focus on the level of the *population*, which is central to the argument of this chapter. First, I will, however, introduce the concept of social sustainability within the larger frame of sustainable development and also outline how it relates to conflicts, especially in terms of how inequality might play a role.

Water, sustainable development and social sustainability

Sustainable development is a key concept in water governance. The overarching framework of global water governance, Integrated Water Resources Management (IWRM) embraces three basic criteria for water management systems that are closely connected to the mainstream definition of sustainable development in terms of its three pillars (social, economic and environmental).

These IWRM criteria are: social equity (ensuring access for all users to an adequate quantity and quality of water), economic efficiency (bringing the greatest benefit to the greatest number of users possible with the available financial and water resources), and ecological sustainability (ensuring the functioning of ecosystems) (see, for example, Lenton and Muller, 2009). It is recognised, however, that a relatively strong emphasis has been placed on economic efficiency and that there is a need for placing more weight on social equity and environmental sustainability. The 2015 WWDR states that 'the social equity goal is often given less priority when water allocation decisions are made' (WWDR, 2015, p. 21).

That the social dimension is not given due attention as compared to the other pillars of sustainable development has also been recognised in relation to the embracing of sustainability in general (see Holden, 2012, p. 528). Also in the academic water literature, an explicit focus on social sustainability is rare (for this argument see also Hellberg, 2017). This, despite all indicators pointing to the important role of social relationships and institutions regarding conflicts over water, as argued above.

Overall, social sustainability is the one pillar of sustainable development that is the least defined and understood and there is, in the academic literature, a large disagreement about the objectives of social sustainability (Omann and Spangenberg, 2002; Littig and Grießler, 2005; Dempsey et al., 2011; Holden, 2012). There is no common definition of the concepts but it commonly includes indicators and themes such as quality of life, equity, inclusion, access, a future focus and participatory process (Holden, 2012, based on Partridge, 2005). Such mentioned indicators involve a focus on *betterment of conditions of an individual*. However, in many understandings of social sustainability there is also a focus on the idea that to create social sustainability there is a need for social integration and a reduction of social and spatial fragmentation (see, for example, Stren and Polèse, 2000; Dempsey et al., 2011) and which hence focus not solely on the individual level but on the *relationship between individuals and populations in a given society*. It is on the last-mentioned factors that the subsequent part of the chapter places its focus because of the relational nature of water conflicts.

Sustainable development, different populations and conflict

Tying back to the beginning of this chapter, where Malthus stipulations around the population-resource nexus was presented, it was acknowledged how different populations were understood in relation to their ability to turn abundance into future sustainability or whether they would instead immediately make use of all existing resources and thereby stimulate population growth which, in turn, would need to be 'checked' by 'misery and vice' (Malthus, 1798). Such notions of different populations have persisted in environmental policy discourse especially through the way that poverty has been seen in relation to resource use and environmental effects.

The discourse of sustainable development has portrayed the relationship between poverty and environmental effects as a 'downward spiral.' According to this spiral the poor put pressure on resources and the environmental degradation that follows these pressures in turn leads to increasing poverty (Scherr, 2000, p. 481). The Brundland report used strong language to describe the poverty–environment relationships, arguing that 'the poor and hungry will often destroy the immediate environment in order to survive' (WCED, 1987, chapter 1, paragraph 8) and that poverty thereby is a major global scourge which will make the world 'prone to ecological and other catastrophes' (WCED, 1987, From One Earth to One World, paragraph 27). In economic terms these dynamics are described in terms of the poor 'operat[ing] with a higher rate of time preference' (Moseley, 2001) compared to wealthier individuals, which means that it is assumed that the poor are preoccupied with surviving the present rather than saving for the future and because of this exploit the environment, while the wealthier are assumed to be able to invest in the environment. In such descriptions the poor lack agency to act differently due to the lack of alternatives.

Even though research has shown that these assumptions are far from what happens in real life and that the poor do take measures to guard against future scarcities (Moseley, 2001; see also Scherr, 2000; Templeton and Scherr, 1999), these ideas still remain in global policy documents. In the water context, for example, the WWDR 2015 stipulated that:

> The relation between water and poverty is a two-way street. Poverty itself can have negative effects on the management of water resources and services. *The desperation and limitations arising from poverty can be a driver of pollution and unsustainable use of water resources*. Poverty can also render existing investments in water less efficient, since households and communities often find it difficult to finance, operate and maintain infrastructure such as rural water pumps. This poses a serious threat to long-term development and poverty reduction. (WWDR, 2015, p. 20, my italics).

The report further states that: 'As populations increase and ecosystem services decline, the risk of resource conflicts rises especially where tensions already exist along ethnic or socio-economic lines [...] Ecosystem degradation and climate change have significant potential to increase these tensions.' (ibid.).

The way that environmental discourse has framed conflicts in relation to resource use and the environment makes us see particular forms of conflicts as in this quote, in relation to populations who rely on local resources for their livelihood. In the quote, an imbalance between resources (for example services) and the population is stipulated in a local/regional context, which relates directly to a (neo-) Malthusian view of the relationship between populations and resources.

In effect, this has meant that different populations are viewed and governed differently within the frames of sustainable development. This naturalises differences in resource access between different communities and is in this way productive of a distinction between local and global populations. In turn, such a way of describing conflicts: that they are the results of water problems (scarcity, pollution, etc.) and subsequent negative effects on ecosystem services masks other types of conflicts. Such conflicts include those related to the global production system, which allocate different structural positions to different sectors and actors. It also masks conflicts regarding the distribution between different households.

Addressing the social sustainability of water management systems: a factor in creating water security

In order to understand water conflicts, both those which escalate into violent ones and those which remain silent but which nevertheless deserve attention, we need to address the social sustainability of water management systems. What this means is that we need to scrutinise the way that populations and their relationship to resources are constructed, hence what is deemed 'adequate quantities' for different populations. We, furthermore, need to understand that the way that different communities and individuals understand their situation is relative to others. We, therefore, also need to look into the *relationships* between different actors, sectors and populations in terms of their resource use and access.

In terms of social sustainability, this means that an approach that focuses solely on the betterment of individual life conditions is not enough to address (social) sustainability. Rather, addressing the social sustainability of water management systems and thereby the conflicts involved in water allocation requires that we, to a larger extent, focus on asymmetries in resource distribution and access to decision-making processes both in history and the present, and what the implications are of current decisions in water allocation for the relationship between different areas, populations and individuals.

Applying this way of reasoning also to the concept of water security, it means that in order to create preconditions for a 'climate of peace and political stability' (see definition of water security in United Nations University, 2013, p. 1), we need to place focus not only on 'the capacity of a population to safeguard sustainable access to adequate quantities of acceptable quality water' (ibid.) but also on the effects on the *relationships* between different populations as regards to their access and use as well as the unevenness of which these populations face risks in relation to water quantity and quality.

This means that we need to take seriously that water scarcity, rather than being merely a natural phenomenon, should be viewed as a result of the political economy and the subsequent decisions taken in the allocation of water. Or to put it in Loftus' words:

> Evacuating the politics from the distribution of water can quickly slip into environmental determinism leading to poverty and water insecurity being

viewed as a result of fate of one's birthplace rather than the outcome of a set of social relations that can be transformed (Loftus, 2015, p. 354).

Thus, the water scarcities and the conflicts experienced today are highly connected to economic and political structures which place different actors at different structural positions through which some actors can pursue their interest and some cannot. As these conflicts are highly asymmetrical these conflicts are often silent and will to a large extent go under the radar in policy understandings of what a resource conflict is.

Conclusion

The chapter has argued that within a sustainable development discourse, different populations are viewed and governed differently in relation to their resource use. The way that this discourse portrays poor populations as unable to live sustainably while wealthier populations are seen as able to invest in the future. This way of viewing different populations within the frames of sustainable development discourse, in turn, has the effect that inequalities in water use and access are neutralised and masks conflicts that are created by various economic interests and inequalities in water access.

Learning from research that has placed emphasis on power relationships and inequitable distribution of water, this chapter has therefore argued that in order to address water conflicts there is a need to broaden the view of the water disputes that is recognised in global water policy. In order to do so we need to place focus on *power* regarding resource distribution and the *relationships* between different actors and users in terms of water use and access as well as the political economy of *water scarcities*. In contrast to the way that global policy often depicts the risks of resource conflicts as related to increasing pressures on local resources because of an imbalance between resources and populations, such a broadened view opens up for seeing structural inequalities between different sectors' actors and uses as a central factor in relation to water conflicts.

In order to better capture the dynamics in relation to the competition between different water users and actors, a focus on *social sustainability* which takes into account the relationship between different populations in a given society has been proposed. In terms of *water security*, a central concept in relation to water governance in general, and that of water conflicts in particular, such an approach involves an additional focus being placed on the relationship between populations – as well as between different actors – and on the unevenness of how different populations are experiencing risks in relation to water.

Notes

1 The SDG indicator 6.4.2: 'Level of water stress: freshwater withdrawal as a proportion of available freshwater resources' builds on the MDG indicator 7.5 measure, but also takes into account, apart from measuring the pressure on water resources from

agriculture, municipalities and industries, environmental water requirements (UNSD, 2016, p. 19). These environmental water requirements 'are established in order to protect the basic environmental services of freshwater ecosystems' (ibid.). In the meta-data for the SDGs, it is, however, acknowledged that there are no universally accepted thresholds for assessing sustainability of water withdrawals (ibid., p. 21).

2   The specific form of power exercised at the level of the population Foucault terms *biopower*.
3   Funder et al. also argue that in order to address the situation of the poorest in terms of water, there is also a need to put efforts into reducing inequalities and supporting the livelihoods of the poor beyond issues that are directly related to water as it is inequalities and structural dependencies that limit space for action for the poorest.

References

Benjaminsen, T.A. and Ba, B. (2009) 'Farmer-herder conflicts, pastoral marginalisation, and corruption: A case study from the inland Niger delta of Mali', *Geographical Journal*, 175(1), 71–81

Boserup, E. (1973) *Jordbruksutveckling och befolkningstillväxt*, Gleerup, Lund

Cook, C. and Bakker, K. (2012) 'Water security: Debating an emerging paradigm', *Global Environmental Change*, 22(1), 94–102

Dempsey, N., Bramley, G., Power, S. and Brown, C. (2011) 'The social dimension of sustainable development: Defining urban social sustainability', *Sustainable Development* 19(5), 289–300

Ehrlich, P. (1968) *The population bomb*, Ballantine Books, New York

FAO (2016) *Coping with water scarcity in agriculture: A global framework for action in a changing climate*http://www.fao.org/3/a-i6459e.pdf

Foucault, M. (1977) [1975], *Discipline and punish: The birth of the prison*, Penguin Books, Harmondsworth

Foucault, M. (1998) [1976], *The will to knowledge: The history of sexuality*, I, Penguin Books, Harmondsworth

Foucault, M. (2003) *'Society must be defended': Lectures at the Collège de France 1975–1976*, Picador, New York

Funder, M., Bustamante, R., Cossio, V., Huong, P.T.M., van Koppen, B., Mweemba, C., Nyambe, I., Phuong, L.T.T. and Skielboe, T. (2012) 'Strategies of the poorest in local water conflict and cooperation – Evidence from Vietnam, Bolivia and Zambia', *Water Alternatives* 5(1), 20–36

Gillet, V., McKay, J. and Keremane, G. (2014) 'Moving from local to State water governance to resolve a local conflict between irrigated agriculture and commercial forestry in South Australia', *Journal of Hydrology*, 519, 2456–2467

Grey, D. and Sadoff, C.W. (2007) 'Sink or swim? Water security for growth and development', *Water Policy*, 9, 545–571

Gunasekara, N.K., Kazama, S., Yamazaki, D. and Oki, T. (2014) 'Water conflict risk due to water resource availability and unequal distribution', *Water Resources Management* 28, 169–184

GWP (Global Water Partnership) (2000) *Towards water security: A framework for action*-Global Water Partnership, Stockholm, Sweden

Hellberg, S. (2017) 'Water for survival, water for pleasure – A biopolitical perspective on the social sustainability of the basic water agenda', *Water Alternatives*, 10(1), 65–80

Hellberg, S. (2018) *The biopolitics of water, governance, scarcity and populations*, Routledge, London and New York

Holden, M. (2012) 'Urban policy engagement with social sustainability in Metro Vancouver', *Urban Studies* 49(3), 527–542

Homer-Dixon, T. (1994) 'Environmental scarcities and violent conflict: Evidence from cases', *International Security*, 19(1), 5–40

Lenton, R. and Muller, M. (2009) *Integrated water resources management in practice: Better water management for development*, Earthscan, London

Littig, B. and Grießler, E. (2005) 'Social sustainability: A catchword between political pragmatism and social theory', *International Journal for Sustainable Development* 8(1–2), 65–79

Loftus, A. (2015) 'Water (in)security: Securing the right to water', *The Geographical Journal*, 181(4), 350–356

Lukes, S. (2005) *Power: A radical view*, 2nd edition, Palgrave Macmillan, Hampshire and New York

Malthus, T. (1798) *An essay on the principle of population*, Dents and Sons, London

Mildner, S.-A., Lauster, G. and Wodni, W. (2011) 'Scarcity and abundance revisited', *International Journal of Conflict and Violence*, 5(1), 155–172

Mirumachi, N. and van Wyk, E. (2010) 'Cooperation at different scales: Challenges for local and international water resource governance in South Africa', *Geographical Journal* 176(1), 25–38

Moseley, W. (2001) 'African evidence on the relation of poverty, time preference and the environment', *Ecological Economics*, 38, 317–326

Moyo, S. (2005) 'Land and natural resource redistribution in Zimbabwe: Access, equity and conflict', *African and Asian Studies*, 4(1–2), 187–223

Mutopo, P. and Chiweshe, M.K. (2014) 'Water resources and biofuel production after the fast-track land reform in Zimbabwe', *African Identities*, 12(1), 124–138

Omann, I. and Spangenberg, J.H. (2002) *Assessing social sustainability: The social dimension of sustainability in a socio-economic scenario*, Paper presented at the 7th Biennial Conference of the International Society for Ecological Economics, 6–9 March 2002, Tunisia

Pacific Institute (2017) http://worldwater.org/water-conflict/

Partridge, E. (2005) *'Social sustainability': A useful theoretical framework?* Paper presented at the Australian Political Science Association Annual Conference, Dunedin, New Zealand, 28–30 September 2005

Petersen-Perlman, J.D., Veilleux, J.C. and Wolf, A.T. (2017) 'International water conflict and cooperation: Challenges and opportunities', *Water International* 42(2), 105–120

Saad-Filho, A. and Weeks, J. (2013) 'Curses, diseases and other resource confusions', *Third World Quarterly*, 34(1), 1–21

Scherr, S.J. (2000) 'A downward spiral? Research evidence on the relationship between poverty and natural resource degradation', *Food Policy*, 25, 479–498

Srinivasan, V., Konar, M. and Sivapalan, M. (2017) 'A dynamic framework for water security', *Water Security*http://dx.doi.org/10.1016/j.wasec.2017.03.001

Starr, J. (1991) 'Water wars', *Foreign Policy*, 82, 17–36

Stren, R. and Polèse, M. (2000) 'Understanding the new sociocultural dynamics of cities: Comparative urban policy in a global context', in Polèse, M. and Stren, R. (eds), *The social sustainability of cities*, 3–38, University of Toronto Press, Toronto

Tellmann, U. (2013) 'Catastrophic populations and the fear of the future: Malthus and the genealogy of liberal economy', *Theory, culture and society*, 30(2), 135–155

Templeton, S. and Scherr, S.J. (1999) 'Effects of demographic and related microeconomic change on land quality in hills and mountains of developing countries', *World Development*, 27(6), 903–918

UN (United Nations) (2009) *A more secure world: Our shared responsibility – Report of the Secretary General's high-level panel on threats, challenges and change*http://www.un.org/en/peacebuilding/pdf/historical/hlp_more_secure_world.pdf

UNSD (United Nations Statistics Division) (2016) *Metadata for Goal 6*, https://unstats.un.org/sdgs/files/metadata-compilation/Metadata-Goal-6.pdf

UNU (United Nations University) (2013) *Water security and the global water agenda: A UN water analytical brief*http://www.unwater.org/publications/water-security-global-water-agenda/

WCED (World Commission on Environment and Development) (1987) *Our common future*, Oxford University Press, Oxford

Wolf, A.T., Yoffe, S.B. and Giordano, M. (2003) 'International waters: Identifying basins at risk', *Water Policy*, 5, 29–60

WWDR (World Water Development Report) (2015) *Water for a sustainable world*, UNESCOhttp://unesdoc.unesco.org/images/0023/002318/231823E.pdf (Accessed: 8 October 2017)

WWDR (World Water Development Report) (2016) *Water and jobs*, UNESCO, http://unesdoc.unesco.org/images/0024/002439/243938e.pdf

Yoffe, S.B., Wolf, A.T., and Giordano, M. (2003) 'Conflict and cooperation over international freshwater resources: Indicators of basins at risk', *Journal of the American Water Resources Association*, 39(5), 1109–1126

Yoffe, S.B., Fiske, G., Giordano, M., Giordano, M.A., Larson, K., Stahl, K. and Wolf, A.T. (2004) 'Geography of international water conflict and cooperation: Data sets and applications', *Water Resources Research*, 40(5), 1–12

Zeitoun, M. and Mirumachi, N. (2008) 'Transboundary water interaction: Reconsidering conflict and cooperation', *International Environmental Agreements* 8(4), 297–316

4 Forest-related community–outsider conflicts through the lens of property rights, access and power

Josefin Gooch

Introduction

Forests cover nearly 30% of the Earth's land area (Keenan et al., 2015), constituting complex ecosystems where trees play a crucial role. Although trees are the most visible and prominent component of a forest, forests are much more than just trees. They give rise to exceptionally rich biodiversity around the world, especially in the tropics. They contain 80% of the world's terrestrial biomass, and over half of the world's known terrestrial (land-living) plant and animal species are found in forests (Aerts and Honnay, 2011). This rich biodiversity in turn fosters a strong human connection to and reliance on forests, where forests provide food, shelter, spiritual well-being and other different services and goods vital for our survival. The extent of forest dependency varies around the world. However, estimations suggest that approximately 300–350 million people depend on forests directly for their survival and that forests are particularly important for around 60 million people belonging to indigenous and tribal groups, who are virtually exclusively dependent on forests (MEA, 2005). Nonetheless, all people (including urban dwellers) are directly or indirectly dependent on forests to some extent, at least for products such as timber and paper. More importantly, forests and trees constitute a crucial part in the protection of soil, offering important vegetative protection against erosion from rain, wind and coastal waves and they are consequently important in the struggle to prevent decertification and salinisation (FAO, 2013; Miura et al., 2015, p. 36). Forests furthermore play a vital role in the world's water cycle, influencing the available amount of water, regulating ground and surface flows and maintaining high water quality (Miura et al., 2015, p. 36). Deforestation of upstream catchments often disrupts these systems, causing floods and drought (Myers, 1997, p. 216). Moreover, forests play a crucial part in stabilising global climate, and are increasingly recognised as important sinks for greenhouse gasses.

All of these positive aspects of forests are included in the term 'ecosystem services' – benefits that different ecosystems and ecosystem processes provide humans. The concept of ecosystem services provides a method to highlight the value of ecosystems for humans in a way that can influence policy and management decision making (Laitos, 2012, p. 109).

Commonly recognised ecosystem services provided by forest ecosystems include:

- goods such as timber, fuel and food, as well as non-timber forest products,
- ecological services such as storage of carbon, nutrient cycling, water and air purification, soil preservation, and maintenance of wildlife habitat
- social and cultural benefits such as recreation, refuges, traditional resource uses and spirituality

Forests are thus multi-functional landscapes that can provide components of critical ecosystems important for the planet, serve as sources of culturally significant livelihoods, or can be a resource to be extracted and consumed (Conca, 2006). Because different stakeholders view forests in very different ways, forest governance is often a deeply contentious process (Beevers, 2016, p. 326). Largely as a result of conflicting views on forests' multiple and often competing capacities for commercial, subsistence and cultural uses, conflicts over the use of forest resources are common all over the world (FAO, 2000, p. 2).

Common causes of conflict are disputes over rights to land and resources, conservation priorities, forest degradation and access to benefits from the forests (FAO, 2000, p. 2; Eckerberg and Sandström, 2013). As a complicating factor, conflicts over forests are often also intertwined with other conflicts such as ethnic differences between protagonists, historical resentments and personal enmities (Brown and Keating, 2015, p. 12), making forest conflicts very complex.

The intensity of conflicts over forests and forest resources can range from locally delimited disputes, which can be resolved within the local society itself, to serious acts of violence on a larger scale. Although in some cases disputes trigger violence and destruction, especially in states that portray high levels of corruption, weak governance and existing ethnic and political division most disagreements are nonetheless resolved peacefully by national authorities and local communities. Such disputes can sometimes even be seen as an essential part of progress and development (Coser, 1956; Brown and Keating, 2015, p. 5). Thus the outcome of conflicts need not always be negative – conflicts may actually be constructive as well as destructive. The term 'constructive' conflict is used to describe a conflict that has more benefits than costs. It may be through pulling people together and/or strengthening and improving their relationship. Such conflicts lead to positive change for all of the parties involved. Conflicts over the use of forests can help define the issues, encourage creative solutions to problems and ensure the inclusion of different interests (Coser, 1956) as well as lead to the development of new, more effective institutional structures (Conca, 2006). Destructive conflicts, on the other hand, have mainly negative results. They push people apart, destroy relationships and lead to negative changes, including escalating violence, terror and mistrust (Engel and Korf, 2005, p. 10).

The actors that are involved in forest-related conflicts will invariably depend on the specific circumstances of the particular case. Nonetheless and as a rule, the local community or communities are usually involved or affected to some extent, either as actors in the conflict or/and as victims of it. Among the most frequent forest-related conflicts are those that occur between local communities and external actors (UNFT, 2012, p. 21). Such conflicts are known as *community–outsider conflicts*. On the one side of the conflict is the community – e.g. local residents in and around the forest and indigenous peoples. On the other side are the 'outsiders' – external actors (Yasmi et al., 2013, p. 22). The identity of the 'outsiders' varies depending on the specific circumstances of the situation. They can be private subjects such as legal or illegal loggers, or plantation and mining companies. They can also be representatives of the state in the form of government agencies coming into the area to extract resources or to prescribe conservation efforts. The common determinant is that the local community feels threatened by their action and that a conflict arises as a result.

A word of caution is necessary here; while grouping people together as a 'community' can have a conceptual value for understanding conflicts, it is important to bear in mind that 'the community' is not a homogenous and clearly defined group – as noted by Agrawal and Gibson (1999). Members of the community can in fact have vastly different interests in the conflict. Neither can the state as an external actor be assumed to be homogenous and acting as a single part. As pointed out by Ribot (2004) and further discussed below, a state on the contrary often includes a variety of actors with different and sometimes conflicting interests and mandates. Thus bearing in mind that 'the community' is composed of individuals with different ideas and interests, the community–outsider theory holds value as a way of understanding forest conflict and will be used in this chapter. The approach taken in this chapter is furthermore to conceptualise forest conflicts through the lens of property – i.e. ownership, rights, tenure and access rights – to land and natural resources. The chapter will proceed by providing a conceptual framework for analysing forest-related conflicts using the community–outsider theory to understand the actors involved and the function of property and power to understand the object of the conflict and the relationships affecting it. The chapter then moves on to view two common situations of forest-related conflicts. The first situation is conflicts between local communities and plantation owners and the second is between communities and conservation efforts – typically prescribed by the state. The first situation concerns community conflict with private actors and the second concerns community conflict with state actors. The chapter thereafter presents and discusses global responses to try to prevent and mitigate such conflicts through the incorporation of increased community involvement in management of forests. The chapter ends with a short summary and conclusions.

Tenure, ownership, access and power

The issue at stake in community–outsider conflicts is frequently related to rights and access to the forest, combined with increasing pressure on forest resources. Forest *tenure* is a broad concept that incorporates ownership, tenancy and other arrangements for the use of forests. Tenure systems describe who owns and who can use what resources for how long, and under what conditions (FAO, 2002, p. 7). Tenure is consequently a way to describe who has access to a resource and the benefits from it. *Access* in this sense may be defined as 'the ability to benefit from things', such as the forest (Ribot and Peluso, 2003, p. 153).

All societies have a system for governing property rights. Commonly, property rights are either private or public. Private tenure is rights to property held by an individual, a corporate body, or a group of people etc., while state tenure means that the right to the forest is held by the state. Forests can also be communally owned or not owned by anyone – so-called open access forests. Communal tenure is a right of commons. An example is the independent right of members of a community to use a forest for household use. A forest under open access is a right for everyone to use a resource. An example of open access is the High Seas (FAO, 2002, p. 7).

In a global perspective, most forests (76% of the forested area in 2010) are publicly owned (Whiteman et al., 2015, p. 101). While high- and middle-income countries show a rather large percentage of privately owned forests, state ownership dominates in low-income states (MacDicken et al., 2015, p. 49). However, state-owned forests in developing countries are often *de facto* open access resources, generally because of lack of capacity to regulate the use of them or to enforce existing regulations (Bluffstone and Robinson, 2014).

An important factor in conflicts over rights and access to land is conflicting legal systems. Especially in developing countries conflicts commonly arise between the largely separate systems of statutory tenure (written rules applied by governments and codified in state law) on the one hand and customary tenure on the other (often based on traditional, unwritten rules determined at the local level) (Sunderlin et al., 2008). In many situations, there are multiple and overlapping legal systems, a condition commonly referred to as legal pluralism (Davies, 2010). This means that a forest and the use of it may be subject to contradicting statutory and customary rules, a situation that may lead to conflict between rights holders under the respective legal system.

Adding to the complexity of forest tenure is that different individuals or groups of people can hold different, overlapping rights to the same forest. Five different levels of tenure rights have been identified (Schlager and Ostrom, 1992) regarding natural resources such as forests, grasslands, the ocean etc.: right of access; right of withdrawal; management; exclusion; and alienation. A 'right of access' and a 'right of withdrawal' are the two 'lowest level' property rights. A person, or group of people, who has a right of access has a right to enter into the forest while a right of withdrawal describes a right to obtain certain forest products, e.g. to collect firewood. The next levels are management and exclusion rights. Individuals who possess access and withdrawal rights may or may not have these higher-level rights. An exclusion right is defined as a right to restrict access and withdrawal for others, and a management right is a right to decide how forestland or trees are used. The highest property level right is the right of alienation, which is a right to sell or lease forestland. Schlager and Ostrom (1992) see the distinction between the first two lower-level rights and the three upper-level rights as crucial as it defines the difference between exercising a right and participating in the definition of future rights to be exercised.

Based on the different rights to property, Schlager and Ostrom (1992) see four categories of rights holders: 'owners'; 'proprietors'; 'claimants'; and 'authorised users' (see Table 4.1). The rights progressively increase from an authorised user, through claimant and proprietor, to an owner. The owner holds the full range of rights over the property. Seen from the perspective of forest, an authorised user has a right to enter the forest and withdraw certain resources such as firewood from it. A claimant additionally has a right to manage the forest, which means a right to decide when and how the forest is harvested and to transform the forest by making improvements. To the rights of a proprietor is added the right of exclusion – a right to determine who else has a right of access to the forest, and how this right may be transferred. Lastly, an owner has a right of alienation on top of the other rights. This means that the owner has a right to sell or lease part or all of the other rights to another individual or group.

Table 4.1 Respective rights of categories of rights holders

	Types of rights holders			
	Authorised users	**Claimants**	**Proprietors**	**Owners**
Types of rights	Right to enter the forest Right to withdraw certain resources from it	Right to enter the forest Right to withdraw certain resources from it	Right to enter the forest Right to withdraw certain resources from it	Right to enter the forest Right to withdraw certain resources from it
		Right to manage the forest	Right to manage the forest	Right to manage the forest
			Right of exclusion	Right of exclusion
				Right of alienation

Ownership of a property thus generally includes all five levels of rights. However, even ownership may be curtailed in different ways. Depending on the political ideology and the strength of the state, private or communal ownership may be limited to a larger or lesser degree to make room also for other interests such as environmental concerns, conservation of species and the interests of other people. Restrictions can include limits to hunting or the felling of trees for environmental and conservation purposes, as well as demands to allow rights of general access for others to travel across it, to graze it, to pick wild berries or to collect firewood. For the same plot of forest, different persons or groups can consequently hold different rights. This has given rise to the concept of 'a bundle of rights' (Maine, 1917), which is a way to describe the complexity of land tenure. A common analogy is to refer to the bundle of rights as a bundle of sticks in which each stick represents an individual right (FAO, 2002, p. 9). Sometimes these rights are clearly defined and enforceable in formal legal courts or through customary structures in a community. In other cases the rights are relatively poorly stated and include ambiguities, making them open to exploitation (FAO, 2002, p. 7), or they overlap with other rights. Secure land tenure is often regarded to be of paramount importance for combatting poverty (as shown in SDG goal 1.4, United Nations, 2012). It is regularly also the basis for social identity, personal security and cultural survival of indigenous peoples and ethnic minorities and a strong determining factor regarding who benefits and who loses in the competition for economic goods and environmental services provided by forest ecosystems (Sunderlin et al., 2008, p. 3). Poorly defined, overlapping and instable tenure, on the other hand, may lead to conflicts, environmental degradation and the exclusion of vulnerable groups, such as women, indigenous people and the poor.

The bundle of rights theory has been further expanded by the inclusion of power relations. As pointed out by Ribot and Peluso (2003), property rights cannot fully explain who gains control and maintains access to natural resources such as forests. In addition to legally required rights to the forest and its resources, access can also be gained through illicit action such as illegal logging as well as through 'ideological and discursive manipulations' and 'relations of production and exchange'. They propose a focus on ability and power to broaden the range of social relationships constraining or enabling people to benefit from resources. Power can be gained through access to technology, capital, markets, labour, knowledge, authority, identity and social relations, for example. In the view of Ribot and Peluso (2003), power relations are a stronger denominator of who can access the benefits derived from the resource than is the right to it. Consequently, they see 'bundles of powers' as a more adequate description than 'bundle of rights'. However, in my view, both secure legal rights to the forest and the power to access these rights are necessary components for local communities to have secure access to the forest. In a situation of conflicting claims to the forest, legal rights provide the foundation for communities' entitlements to it, and the stronger the legal system is, the more important a legal right becomes.

Conflicts between local communities and plantation owners

The first example of forest-related conflicts is between local communities and plantation owners. Plantations can include a variety of plant species, but this chapter focuses on plantations of tree species. Plantations for industrial production of tree for wood, palm oil and rubber production constitute one of the fastest growing monocultures globally (Gerber, 2011). Especially in the tropics and subtropics, large-scale plantations regularly clash with the interests of local communities. Plantation owners are often 'outsiders' entering the area and when they enter, the natural-growth forest is typically cleared and replanted with other, economically valuable tree species. Large areas are affected, as plantations need to be of a significant size to be economically viable (Charnley, 2005, p. 37). In Indonesia for example, the optimal size of an industrial tree plantation is estimated to be 30,000 to 50,000 hectares (Hall, 2003). The pure size of such plantations means that they have a large effect on local communities, not least on the populations dependent on the forests that were removed to make room for the plantations.

The effect on the local populations of large-scale plantations varies depending on the tenure that they hold to the land. In Southeast Asia, plantations are mainly established on state lands that were previously inhabited by local communities with customary claims to land and the resources there (Hall, 2003). Charnley (2005) sees these state-owned lands that community residents depend on as de facto constituting common lands. When the land and forest is made available to timber companies for plantation, this dramatically alters customary rights. Transferring land to plantation concessions regularly means that these communities are evicted by the state, in some cases using military force. As a result of large-scale plantations, members of local communities around the world are often displaced and migrate. To protect the plantations the forestry companies then often enclose them, which causes local people to lose access to both land and other natural resources (Charnley, 2005, p. 44). Even if the members of the local community are not evicted from the land but are allowed to stay, they may face problems. As the tree plantations are monocultures, they don't provide the range of non-tree-forest products upon which many of the rural and poor depend for their livelihood. Also this is a cause of conflicts between local communities and industry (Charnley, 2005).

When access to the forest by members of local communities is based on ownership, it may be expected that their right to it is comparatively strong, as ownership is the strongest right to the forest. However, even in such situations, local communities have sometimes been threatened and made to give up land in exchange for unfair payments (Renner, 2002, p. 30–40), illustrating unequal power relations between buyer and seller. Even if they are not forced to sell, evidence has shown that small-scale landowners often do not benefit from these sales as they frequently migrate to cities after the sale and there have difficulties finding employment (Charnley, 2005, p. 44).

Again, it is, however, important to note that the 'community' is not a homogenous entity and that although many members of the local community are opposed to plantations, other members of the group may benefit from them through employment for example.

Conflicts around biodiversity conservation

The description above shows an example of conflicts between local communities and private external actors. The strength of tenure held by the community influences how secure their access to the land is. As noted above, governments usually retain certain rights to change the uses of land, also on privately owned land. A common right retained by the state is to restrict the use of land to safeguard important common values, such as environmental protection and conservation. However, environmental protection, which is a good thing on the one hand, often creates conflict with people living in the forest because it regularly restricts their access to the forest, often without giving them the opportunity to negotiate. As a result, conflicts regularly occur between conservation objectives stipulated by state actors and local people's livelihood strategies (see article on Van Gujjar pastoralists in this volume).

One of the primary strategies towards protecting biodiversity is designating the area as a protected area (Morales-Hidalgo, 2015, p. 69). A protected area is defined as 'an area of land and/or sea especially dedicated to the protection and maintenance of biological diversity, and of natural and associated cultural resources, and managed through legal or other effective means' (Dudley, 2008). Within this broad scope, protected areas can be designated for different purposes: mainly for science; for wilderness protection; for recreation; for conservation through management intervention; for landscape conservation; or for sustainable use of natural ecosystems (Dudley, 2008). The aim of protecting the forest will largely decide how the forest is managed, but a common constituent for all uses is that access to the forest is restricted, to a higher or lower degree. In some cases local people may still have a right to use forest products such as plants and fire wood within protected areas for household use, while in other cases all human uses and even entry may be prohibited. As pointed out by Charnley (2005), protected areas, just like plantations, are often sited in places that are already inhabited and/or used by local communities. The effect of the designation of protected areas may range from limited or denied access and use of resources, loss of land rights, threatened livelihoods, forced relocation, and even the breakdown of indigenous knowledge and traditional resource use and management systems (Charnley 2005). The more restrictions are imposed on these people on the use and access to the forest, the more likely it is that conflicts will occur between local communities and authorities.

Although the aim of assigning protected areas is to conserve the forest habitat and species from further degradation, research has shown that in many cases the effectiveness of protection has been unclear or contested. Critics maintain that apart from often leading to poverty for forest-dependent people (Fischer and

Hirsch, 2008), it risks depriving them of their means to livelihood. Others have claimed it to lead to progressive degradation of surrounding forests (Moorman et al., 2013) as demands for food and firewood still need to be met. People may respond to the restrictions of the protected area by trespassing, poaching, illegal logging and by destroying the natural resources and biodiversity that the reserves were designed to protect (Charnley, 2005).

Conflicts between biodiversity protection and protecting livelihoods are rooted at the very core of sustainable development and come about as a result of different weight being placed on different parts of the concept of sustainable development. The same type of conflict is occurring between the goals of combatting climate change and protecting livelihoods. Forests are increasingly being recognised for their critical role in regulating the climate of the world (Romijn et al., 2015, p. 110), as approximately 45% of the world's terrestrial carbon is stored in the wood, leaves, roots and soils of forests. The ability to store carbon is especially high in tropical forests, which on average can store 50% more carbon compared to other types of forests (Bonan, 2008; Romijn et al., 2015, p. 110). As a result, plantations are currently being promoted as carbon sinks and producers of sustainable energy (Gerber, 2011). There is a risk that many of these plantations will also deprive communities of their land rights and livelihood needs.

Tenure reforms

The conflicts outlined above indicate that if user groups are excluded from participating in the management of natural resources there is risk of conflict (FAO 2000, p. 2). Recalling the bundle of rights theory above, management is one of three upper-level property rights (the other two being exclusion and alienation). In an attempt to resolve, mitigate and prevent conflicts over forests, researchers and practitioners are increasingly relying on participatory methods to involve local communities (Elias et al., 2017, p. 2). This frequently requires changes to forest policies and laws, which in the past have often been formulated without the active and sustained participation of communities and local resource users (see e.g. FAO, 2000, p. 7). A wave of forest sector decentralisation reforms in developing countries has been occurring in an effort to create more participation. Barry et al., (2010) identify a demand for recognition of indigenous peoples right to their identity and ancestral lands and a global drive for biodiversity conservation as large international trends that have led to this wave of reforms to the forest sector. Decentralised forest management has been advocated as a policy initiative to increase the decision-making power and influence of local communities, households and individuals (Engel and Korf, 2005, p. 25), to better allow for local natural resources rights and practices (FAO, 2000, p. 7), to alleviate poverty and improve the socio-economic well-being of rural people in developing countries while also improving forest resource conservation (Agrawal et al., 2008; Kumar et al., 2015) as well as to reduce conflicts between the state and local communities over forest use (Kotru and Pradhan, 2012). Under the right circumstances, such reforms can lead to improvements on local communities' livelihoods and conservation efforts (Wright et al., 2016). As the conflicts studied in this chapter largely result from 'outsiders' encroaching on the livelihood potentials of local communities, forest reforms that improve secure livelihood also have the potential to reduce conflicts.

These reforms, however, largely recognise the customary tenure rights of communities already residing in officially state-owned forests, granting collective rights to the communities but maintaining the state as a principal rights holder. The reforms thus seldom afford local communities the full range of rights to the forest. The rights to sell the property (alienation rights) are generally not handed to communities (Larson et al., 2010). The state often also retains part of the management rights, specifically related to forest conservation. The claimed rationale for this is generally that forests are a common good and that conservation is best managed by the state (Barry et al., 2010). The result of forest reform is thus often a situation of co-ownership and co-management between the community and the state (Barry et al., 2010), where members of the community have a right of access, withdrawal and exclusion, but only partly of managing the forest and no right to sell or lease it. This limit to tenure is important; as long as the state retains important rights to the forest such as the right to sell or lease it, local communities cannot be considered to have secure tenure. However, even when there is secure tenure, local communities often face obstacles related to unequal power relations. Lack of knowledge or technical and organisational capacities as well as administrative restrictions imposed by the state may restrict local communities' ability to benefit from the forest and gain entrance to markets to sell products from the forest (Barrow et al., 2016).

Tenure reforms as a means to mitigate conflicts between local communities and plantation owners differ from those described above, which largely pertain to the conflict between local communities and conservation efforts. Plantations are generally monocultures where the biodiversity within the area and consequently the range of ecosystem services are severely reduced. There is limited room for the type of co-management sometimes found between communities and conservation efforts. Some efforts have, however, been made to include local communities in different stages of the production chain such as tree planting agreements and arrangements of benefit-sharing from industrial logging (Larson, 2011). Such measures go somewhere towards including the communities in the management, although they are not tenure reform.

Summary and conclusion

Because of conflicting views on the priority of the many and often competing functions of forests, conflicts of varying intensity over the use of forests are common all over the world. Common causes of conflict are disputes over rights to the forest and its resources. In most conflicts, the local communities living in or around the forest are directly involved or affected. This is especially true for the poor and marginalised who largely depend on the forest for their livelihood. Using the community–outsider theory to understand the actors involved, two conflict situations have been studied: conflicts between local communities and large-scale plantation owners, and conflicts between local communities and conservation efforts typically prescribed by the state. In both these conflict situations outsiders restrict the rights of communities to the forest and consequently limit their livelihood from it – a situation that leads to conflicts. The conflicts have been conceptualised through the lens of property, tenure and the bundle of rights theory.

The bundle of rights theory includes different rights to a property such as forests, ranging from a right to enter it (right of access) to full ownership where the owner has the right to use, manage and sell or lease the forest. The security to the forest and the livelihood derived from it for local communities largely depends on how many rights are included in their bundle of rights. The more rights to the forest they have, the more secure their being in the forest generally is. However, even when local communities have a strong right to the forest, they seldom hold the full range of rights to it as parts of the rights are usually retained by the state. Thus the state can limit rights to the forest, e.g. in the name of environmental protection.

Another factor that may limit local communities' ability to benefit from the forest is unequal power relations. A lack of knowledge or of technical and organisational capacities as well as administrative restrictions imposed by the state may limit their ability to benefit from the forest and gain entrance to markets to sell products from the forest. This implies that not only secure tenure but also capacity building and administrative capabilities are important for local communities to secure forest-dependent livelihood. Secure livelihood is a vital factor for reducing the type of conflicts over forests outlined in this chapter.

References

Aerts, R. and Honnay, O. (2011) 'Forest restoration, biodiversity and ecosystem functioning', *BMC Ecol* 11(29)

Agrawal, A. and Gibson, C. (1999) 'Enchantment and disenchantment: The role of community in natural resource conservation', *World Development* 27, 629–649

Agrawal, A., Chhatre, A., Hardin, R. (2008) 'Changing governance of the world's forests', *Science* 320, 1460–1462

Barrow, E., Kamugisha-Ruhombe, J., Nhantumbo, I., Oyono, R. and Savadogo, M. (2016) 'Who owns Africa's forests? Exploring the impacts of forest tenure reform on forest ecosystems and livelihoods', *Forests, trees and livelihoods* 25, 132–156

Barry, D., Larson, A.M. and Colfer, C.J.P. (2010) 'Forest tenure reform: An orphan with only uncles' in Larson, A.M., Barry, D., Dahal, G.R. and Colfer, C.J.P. (eds) *Forests for people: Community rights and forest tenure reform*, Earthscan, London

Beevers, M.D. (2016) 'Forest governance and post-conflict peace in Liberia: Emerging contestation and opportunities for change?', *The Extractive Industries and Society* 3, 320–328

Bluffstone, R. and Robinson, E.J.C. (2014) *Forest tenure reform in Asia and Africa: Local control for improved livelihoods, forest management, and carbon sequestration*, Routledge RFF Press

Bonan, G.B. (2008) 'Forests and climate change: Forcings, feedbacks, and the climate benefits of forests', *Science* 320, 1444–1449

Brown, O. and Keating, M., (2015) *Addressing natural resource conflicts: Working towards more effective resolution of national and sub-national resource disputes – Energy, Environment and Resources*, Chatham House

Charnley, S. (2005) 'Industrial plantation forestry', *Journal of Sustainable Forestry*, 21, 35–57

Conca, K. (2006) *Governing water*, MIT Press, Cambridge, MA

Coser, L. (1956) *The functions of social conflict*, The Free Press, New York

Davies, M. (2010) 'Legal pluralism', in Cane, P. and Kritzer, H.M. (eds), *The Oxford handbook of empirical legal research*, Oxford University Press

Dudley, N. (ed.) (2008) *Guidelines for applying protected area management categories*, IUCN, Gland, Switzerland, https://portals.iucn.org/library/sites/library/files/documents/PAG-021.pdf

Eckerberg, K. and Sandström, C. (2013) 'Forest conflicts: A growing research field', *Forest Policy and Economics*, 33, 3–7

Elias, M., Jalonen, R., Fernandez, M. and Grosse, A. (2017) 'Gender-responsive participatory research for social learning and sustainable forest management', *Forests, Trees and Livelihoods*, 26, 1–12

Engel, A. and Korf, B. (2005) *Negotiation and mediation techniques for natural resource management*, FAO, Rome

FAO (2000) *Conflict and natural resource management*, FAO, Rome

FAO (2002) *Land tenure and rural development* (FAO land tenure studies 3), FAO, Rome

FAO (2013) *Forests and water – International momentum and action*, FAO, Rome

Fischer, R. and Hirsch, P. (2008) 'Poverty and agrarian-forest interactions in Thailand', *Geographical Research*, 1, 74–84

Gerber, J-F. (2011) 'Conflicts over industrial tree plantations in the South: Who, how and why?' *Global Environmental Change*, 1, 165–176

Hall, D. (2003) 'The international political ecology of industrial shrimp aquaculture and industrial plantation forestry in Southeast Asia', *Journal of Southeast Asian Studies*, 34, 251–264

Keenan, R., Reams, G., Achard, F., de Freitas, J., Grainger, A., Lindquist, E. (2015) 'Dynamics of global forest area: Results from the FAO Global Forest Resources Assessment 2015', *Forest Ecology and Management*, 352, 9–20

Kotru, R. and Pradhan, N. (2012) 'Conflict management and sustainable forest management in the Himalayas', in Broekhoven, G., Savenije, H. and von Scheliha, S. (eds), *Moving forward with forest governance*, Tropenbos International, Wageningen, The Netherlands

Kumar, K., Singh, N.M. and Kerr, J.M. (2015) 'Decentralisation and democratic forest reforms in India: Moving to a rights-based approach', *Forest Policy and Economics*, 51, 1–8

Laitos, J.G. (2012) *The right of nonuse*, Oxford University Press

Larson, A.M., Barry, D. and Dahal, G.R. (2010) 'New rights for forest-based communities? Understanding processes of forest tenure reform', *The International Forestry Review*, 12, 78–96

Larson, A.M. (2011) 'Forest tenure reform in the age of climate change: Lessons for REDD+' *Global Environmental Change*, 21, 540–549

MacDicken, K.G., Sola, P., Hall, J.E., Sabogal, C., Tadoum, M. and de Wasseige, C. (2015) 'Global progress toward sustainable forest management', *Forest Ecology and Management*, 352, 47–56

Maine, H., (1917) *Ancient Law*, Dutton, Dent, New York

MEA (Millennium Ecosystem Assessment) (2005) *Ecosystems and human well-being: Synthesis*, Island Press, Washington, DC

Miura, S., Amacher, M., Hofer, T., San Miguel, S., Ernawati and Thackway, R. (2015) 'Protective functions and ecosystem services of global forests in the past quarter-century', *Forest Ecology Management*, 352, 35–46

Moorman, M., Donoso, P.J., Moore, S.E., Sink, S. and Frederick, D. (2013) 'Sustainable protected area management: The case of Llancahue, a highly valued periurban forest in Chile', *Journal of Sustainable Forestry*, 32, 783–805

Morales-Hidalgo, D., Oswalt, S.N., Somanathan, E., (2015) 'Status and trends in global primary forest, protected areas, and areas designated for conservation of biodiversity from the Global Forest Resources Assessment 2015', *Forest Ecology and Management*, 352, 68–77

Myers, N. (1997) 'The world's forests and their ecosystem services', in Daily, G. (ed), *Nature's services: Societal dependence on natural ecosystems*, Island Press

Renner, M. (2002) *The anatomy of resource wars*, Worldwatch Institute, Washington, DC

Ribot, J.C. and Peluso, N.L. (2003) 'A theory of access', *Rural Sociology*, 68, 153–181

Ribot, J. (2004) *Waiting for democracy: The politics of choice in natural resource decentralisation*, World Resources Institute, Washington DC

Romijn, E., Lantican, C.B., Herold, M., Lindquist, E., Ochieng, R., Wijaya, A., Murdiyarso, D. and Verchot, L. (2015) 'Assessing change in national forest monitoring capacities of 99 tropical countries', *Forest Ecology and Management*, 352, 109–123

Schlager, E. and Ostrom, E. (1992) 'Property-right regimes and natural resources: A conceptual analysis', *Land Economics*, 68, 249–262

Sunderlin, W.D., Hatcher, J. and Liddle, M. (2008) *From exclusion to ownership? Challenges and opportunities in advancing forest tenure reform*, Rights and Resources Initiative, Washington DC

UNFT (United Nations Interagency Framework Team for Preventive Action) (2012) *Toolkit and guidance for preventing and managing land and natural resources conflict: Renewable resources and conflict*, UNFT, New York

United Nations (2012) *The Millennium Development Goals Report 2012*

Whiteman, A., Wickramasinghe, A. and Piña, L. (2015) 'Global trends in forest ownership, public income and expenditure on forestry and forestry employment', *Forest Ecology and Management*, 352, 99–108

Wright, G.D., Andersson, K.P., GibsonC.C. and Evans, T.P. (2016) 'Decentralization can help reduce deforestation when user groups engage with local government', *Proceedings of the National Academy of Sciences of the United States of America*, 113, 14958–14963

Yasmi, Y., Kelley, L.C., Enters, T., (2013) 'Community–outsider conflicts over forests: Perspectives from Southeast Asia', *Forest Policy and Economics*, 33, 21–27

5 Conflicts in the management of fisheries

The change in roles and perception of the Swedish fishing industry

Staffan Larsson

Introduction

During the last decades, few sectors have experienced so many changes as the fisheries sector. Fish resources were for a long time considered to be inexhaustible and sustainability was not an issue. The public administrations dealing with fisheries, if they existed, were focused on encouraging the fishermen to fish more. Now, through experience gained, we know that fish resources are not endless, and that fishing has to be managed. For most countries, the modern form of fisheries management has evolved since the 1970s. To manage a common resource such as fish is complicated and involves many interests with various and sometimes diverse opinions. The establishment and structuring of this management has been a dynamic process – and it is a process that is still going on.

The development of the Swedish fisheries sector holds a rather particular historic feature: the establishment of the Swedish fishermen's organisations and the development of a voluntary self-management scheme that started in the 1930s.

Today the complex interplay between the fisheries sector, fisheries research and administration in general and the environmental NGOs in particular, could be well illustrated by two areas that manifest the conflicts and perceptions of management of marine natural resources: the seal issue and the Baltic cod issue.

This chapter will clarify the developmental trajectories of the Swedish fishery, the changes in dialogue and cooperation between the main agents: fishermen's organisations, fisheries administration and fisheries scientists. There has also been a shift in the perception of the fishing sector, from being respected food providers to being considered an environmental threat. The latter perception is at least how the fishing sector experiences the attacks from environmental NGOs.

General aspects of the governance of fisheries

Globally, marine fish resources were for a long time considered to be inexhaustible. In 1609 Hugo Grotius formulated *Mare Liberum* or The Freedom of the Seas, that the High Seas are common and cannot be placed under the sovereignty of any state and that marine living resources are inexhaustible (Juda, 1996). For centuries these ideas were the beacon for the general perception of the high seas and the fisheries resources. Fishing was not seen as a threat. Is was not until the end of the 1960s and 1970s, with emerging fish stock problems and the awareness of over-fishing, that the need for fisheries management became clear.

In 'The tragedy of the commons' Garrett Hardin presented a theory where he also refers to fishing. He says, 'Professing to believe in the inexhaustible resources of the oceans, they bring species after species of fish and whales closer to extinction' (Hardin, 1968). The theory describes a situation in a shared-resource system where individual users are acting independently and according to their own self-interest. This is contrary to the common good of all users and leads to the depletion of the common resources. This theory describes in essence the need for management. Fishing on a common renewable resource, in a large system, needs to be regulated in order for it to be sustainably harvested.

However, limiting the access to fish resources that had previously been free could easily lead to conflicts of interests between fishermen or between nations. The cod war in 1972 between the UK and Iceland is an example of such an international conflict. Iceland wanted to protect its cod fishery by proclaiming a 50 nautical miles fishing zone around the island. The conflict led to dramatic clashes and triggered the process which ultimately led to the UN Convention on the Law of the Sea (UNCLOS) in 1982. This opened up for coastal nations to extend their territorial waters to an Exclusive Economic Zone (EEZ) up to 200 nautical miles from land. In waters where the economic zones coincided in the North Sea and the Baltic, centrelines have been applied. This implied that most fishing waters came under coastal state jurisdiction which created the legal foundation for imposing fisheries measures.

For most countries this was the starting point for the modern management of fisheries. Various organisational models, structures and responsibilities have been tried out and changed over time, also within the EU Common Fisheries policy as described below. Moreover, in recent decades, outside the formal fisheries management structure, environmental NGOs have become involved as new stakeholders and act as a kind of public guardian of the fish resources.

The Swedish government's role – the encouragement to increase fishing

In the past, the role of the Swedish authorities was to apply a commercial approach towards the fisheries with a focus on supporting and promoting the development of the sector (Westerberg and Ask, 2011). Fishing was important for the national supply of food, as well as for the national economy and employment, especially from a local and regional perspective. At an early stage, Swedish fisheries research was oriented towards improving the fishery and making it more efficient. Bottom trawling was introduced by government fishery officers in the late 19th century.

During the Second World War the fishing became particularly important as a domestic food supply. A special government agency was established to cater for all domestic food supply. Fishing was encouraged by offering fixed prices on most of the important fish species. Fishing became lucrative, but with high costs in terms of loss of boats and human lives. Fishing in the Baltic was safer, so fishing boats from the west coast were encouraged to move their fishing there.

In the same spirit of important national interest, the construction of fishing harbours was considered an important basic infrastructure and was therefore supported by the government. A governmental agency, the Swedish Board of Fisheries, was established in 1948 to coordinate and implement the very few governmental regulations that then existed and to support the sector at national level.

Establishment of fisheries organisations and voluntary self-management

The current organisational structure of the Swedish fishermen originates from the Swedish West Coast Fishermen's Federation (SVC), established in 1930. It was followed by similar organisations for fisheries on the south and east coasts. These organisations formed a national federation in 1948 (Hasslöf, 1949).

By this time market issues were the main concern for the fishermen. Natural fluctuations in the abundance of fish led often to surpluses with declining fish prices and sometimes unsold fish. The economic recession in the 1930s exacerbated the situation. The SVC gradually introduced a number of *voluntary regulations* for their members:

Minimum prices – With public financial support, a scheme for minimum prices was introduced for some of the main fish species. This became the start of a program to guarantee a minimum price level that lasted until Sweden joined the EU in 1995.

Minimum landing size – In dialogue with fisheries scientists and the administration as well as fish traders, the fishermen agreed within their organisations not to land fish below certain sizes (length of fish). This was initially an instrument to limit the supply to the market, but it also led to improved quality which in turn gave higher prices. This instrument also coincided with the aim to protect the fish stocks.

Minimum mesh size – SVC proposed a minimum mesh size of the trawls and Danish seines, matching the minimum landing size, which led to a public regulation in 1936. This later became part of the development of the common gear regulations through the North Sea Convention which was created in 1954.

Limiting fishing effort – The fishing week was limited to six days, fishing on Sundays was banned. No boat was allowed to leave the port to fish before Monday 5 am. A compulsory summer break for the vacation was also introduced later. These limitations remained in force until the 1970s.

Quotas – Landing quotas were based on a quantity allowed to be landed per crew member per week. Other time periods such as monthly and annual quotas were also used.

Control – The Swedish West Coast Federation had their own control and inspection system which included fines for infringements. Inspectors were employed by the organisation stationed on the Swedish west coast and the main landing ports in Northern Denmark and later also temporarily in UK ports.

Fishing effort limitations and quotas are still practised by the EU Common Fisheries Policy today. Regardless of whether these were primarily designed for market purposes or, as today, for stock management purposes, they have a restrictive impact on the fish stocks.

The development of the SVC self-management scheme was related to the instruments described above, but also to the expansion of the organisation. The quota landing system was first applied by the fishermen around Gothenburg. As it soon became evident that this system resulted in higher and more stable prices, more fishermen joined the organisation and after some years all fishermen along the west coast were members. In most aspects, the development of a voluntary system did follow the *Ostrom's 8 principles for managing common resources (CPR)* (Ostrom, 1990). She reported on a successful self-management of common resources-provided the existence of certain prerequisites such as 'The CPR has clearly-defined boundaries (effective exclusion of external unentitled parties)' and 'Rules are enforced through effective monitoring by monitors who are part of or accountable to the appropriators' (ibid.). There was a common understanding among the fishermen in the SVC of the benefits and a sound form of peer control among the members.

Further development of the Swedish fishery and fisheries management

Post war–1970s – modernisation and expansion and depletion of the herring fishery

There was no need for fishing quotas during the Second World War (see above), but the quota system was resumed after the war. New technology such as eco-sounder, synthetic net materials and navigational instruments boosted the development of the fisheries. Fishing expanded up to a peak in 1964. Landings of herring dominated the fisheries, both in terms of quantity and value. Landings were mainly carried out in the Danish ports in Northern Jutland. The fishermen were doing well, the quota system was solid and there was good compliance. Catches in the last haul beyond the set quotas could be landed, but the payment from this surplus was then donated to the Seaman's Church.

In the latter part of the 1960s a growing concern for the sustainability of the herring stocks emerged amongst many fishermen. There was a clear decline in catches, but leading scientists within ICES (International Council for the Exploration of the Sea) could not agree on whether this was due to natural fluctuation or overfishing (Ask et al., 2015). Between 1968 and 1970 a large part of the Swedish herring fleet on the west coast was sold. The decline in the Swedish fishery coincided with an expansion in industrial production in Sweden with good work opportunities for former fishermen.

The quota system for herring imploded in the 1970s as some larger fishing vessels left the organisation and the quota system. They found the quotas too small and the system too limiting. This undermined the credibility and the foundation of the system.

The 1970s – establishment of modern fisheries management

During the 1970s the conditions for fishing and fisheries management changed fundamentally. With the drastic decline in the North Sea herring stock a quota (TAC, Total Allowable Catch) was for the first time introduced in 1974 by NEAFC (North-East Atlantic Fisheries Commission) which was established in 1959. This was the first time there were public restrictions on landed quantities. The fishermen's organisations, such as SVC, were trusted to allocate individual quotas for their members.

For the Baltic, the International Baltic Sea Fishery Commission (IBSFC) was established in 1974 and quotas (TAC) for the Baltic were introduced for herring and sprat in 1977.

Through the creation of exclusive economic fishing zones (EEZ) Sweden was excluded from traditional fishing grounds in the North Sea, but it gained exclusive rights to considerable parts of the Baltic Sea.

To support the restructuring of the Swedish fishing industry, the Swedish Board of Fisheries provided funds in 1976–1980 for research projects to investigate fishing on alternative species to herring, such as tobis. These research projects were carried out by the Institute of Marine Research of the Swedish Board of Fisheries in cooperation with fishermen's organisations using mostly fishing vessels for the trials. There was a close and open dialogue and cooperation between fishermen, scientists and the fishery administration.

In 1977 the herring fishery in the North Sea was closed. This opened the market for the Baltic herring which compensated for the loss of North Sea herring. The Board of Fishery was active in supporting the west coast fleet to start fishing herring in the Baltic sea. This also gave a boost to the east coast fleet.

The 1980s – the Baltic cod boom

With more nutrients in the Baltic, the stocks of cod, herring and sprat had increased substantially between the 1950s and the 1970s. Moreover, during several years with favourable conditions for cod reproduction, due mainly to strong inflows of water from the western waters, the Baltic yielded exceptionally large cod populations between 1976 and 1982. These formed the basis for the considerable growth in the Baltic cod fishery between 1980 and 1985. For decades the cod fishery had traditionally been dominated by trawlers, but later in the 1970s the number of gillnet fishing boats expanded. There were extensive fisheries carried out by all the Baltic States.

The first international quotas (TAC) for the Baltic cod came as late as 1989. However, prior to that, the Swedish fishery organisations applied voluntary landing quotas in order to balance the fishing with market demand.[1]

The dialogue between fishermen's organisations and the Board of Fisheries gradually involved more conflicts concerning the management. In the early 1980s a licencing system was introduced to limit fleet capacity but on the other hand the Boards of Fisheries was active in supporting the modernisation of the fleet.

1990s – a chaotic cod fishery, Swedish accession to the EU and the Common Fisheries Policy

During the 1990s the Baltic still played an important role for the Swedish fishing industry as the cod fishery was reduced but the pelagic (herring and sprat) fishery expanded. In the cod fishery most of the Soviet (and the later independent Baltic states and Poland) cod fleets were converted to large-scale gillnetters at the end of 1980s. Unfortunately, this gillnet fishery initially targeted the larger-sized cod. This had a severe impact on the cod population and a negative impact for the reproduction of cod.

The fall of the 'iron curtain' in 1989 meant a drastic shift for the Baltic states within the former USSR and Poland, from a centralised production system where production and management were integrated within the same organisational structure, into a new structure with independent production units and a separate independent fisheries management structure. This restructuring took time and the fisheries administration was for some periods non-existent:

> ... intensity of the fishery increased further with the introduction of a gillnet fishery at the end of the 1980s and beginning of the 1990s. The reported landings in 1992–1995 are known to be incorrect due to incomplete reporting. The extent of unreported landings in 1992–1995 reflects a chaotic situation in the fishery and problems in enforcing regulations at that time (ICES Advice, 1999).

Sweden joined the EU in 1995 and thereby adopted the management package of the EU Common Fisheries Policy consisting of three main policy areas: fisheries management; market and trade; structural adjustment of the sector, (the latter a comprehensive subsidy program). This resulted in support for a modernisation of the fishing industry which on the one hand enhanced capacity of the fleet, but on the other hand was negative for the management of the resource.

The resource management became more centralised and uniform in structure and this distanced and weakened stakeholder involvement and created a sense of alienation. However, the fishery could bypass the system by directly approaching the national governmental representatives involved in the EU work in order to present their views.

EU reform in 2002

The shortcomings of the Common Fisheries Policy and the fisheries management were expressed in the Green Paper published by the Commission of the European Communities (2001), followed by the reform of the Common Fisheries Policy in 2002. A more coherent fisheries management system was introduced, combining traditional fisheries management tools (catch limits, gear restrictions, etc.) with a more effective fleet policy in order to ensure a balance between fishing effort and resource availability. Subsidies were reduced, and the fisheries management moved towards a more long-term management perspective and a wider ecosystem approach. Moreover, in order to establish a more open dialogue and to involve more stakeholders, from the fishing industry and environmental NGOs and other interests, Regional Advisory Councils (RACs) were introduced. Their roles were to advise EU Commission and Member States on fisheries management for specific regional areas.

EU Common Fisheries Policy reform 2013

Later, it turned out that the 2002 reform was not enough. The EU Commission analysed the situation in its Green Paper from 2009, and identified five structural failings:

> ... fleet overcapacity; imprecise policy objectives resulting in insufficient guidance for decisions and implementation; a decision-making system that encourages a short-term focus; a framework that does not give sufficient responsibility to the industry; and lack of political will to ensure compliance and poor compliance by the industry. Further documenting, deciding, implementing and controlling the vast and diverse European fisheries through such micromanagement is increasingly complex, difficult to understand and very costly to manage and control ... (Commission of the European Communities, 2009).

The Common Fisheries Policy reform from 2013 was in many aspects more radical. The resource management structure acquired multispecies multiannual plans focused on Maximum Sustainable Yield (MSY). It reinforced the role of science and improved the collection of data and sharing of information (EU, 2013). A landing obligation (discard ban) was introduced which completely shifted the focus from, as in the past, when the fishermen were forced by the EU to throw back into the sea all fish unintentionally caught outside allocated quotas, to instead land all the fish caught. It also introduced a decentralised regional governance, bringing some of the policy formulations and decision processes closer to the fishing sector. It aimed to simplify the technical measures regulation whereby EU legislators should define the general framework while the Member States at regional level should cooperate and develop the implementing measures. The advisory councils (ACs) with the stakeholders involved were anticipated to play an active advisory role in this process.

The current EU management system is considered complex and costly for the member states. In an international comparison Sweden has one of the most expensive fisheries administrations in relation to the landed value of the catches (OECD 2015).

Changed roles for the Swedish fisheries management

The cooperation and interaction between the fisheries sector, research bodies and the fisheries administration have changed over the last decades. For Sweden, as an EU member, the route has to a great extent been defined by the recurrent reform processes within the EU.

The modern elements of fisheries management that began in the 1970s starts with the assessment of a stock through ICES, resulting in advice on the total allowable catch (TAC) and possible advice on technical measures. The formal Swedish management structure consists of: the Swedish University of Agricultural Sciences (SLU) with the Department of Aquatic Resources as part of the ICES community; the Swedish Agency for Marine and Water Management (SWAM) as the government agency; and finally, the Ministry of Enterprise and Innovation at government level.

The process of finally agreeing on a TAC, for example in the Baltic, involves all the EU member states around the Baltic Sea. This process has been influenced by the fishing industry in the Baltic nations defending the interest of the sector and which in some cases has ultimately led to the EU agreeing on higher quotas (TAC) than were originally advised by ICES.

In Sweden before the 1980s, conflicts between the fishing industry, the research bodies and fisheries administration were scarce, simply because there were few official restrictions and there was an open dialogue. Gradually, as regulations such as quotas or technical restrictions were introduced, causes of conflicts emerged. The extent to which a proposed management action would be considered justified by the sector could depend on the level of prior dialogue between the fishing industry and the administration.

The former EU Common Fisheries Policy management was complicated and based on a top-down paternalistic approach which assumed that the fishery could be regulated by decree and by means of a comprehensive control system. The system had a uniform design focusing on adhering to and complying to in some cases rigid rules, rather than focusing on the ultimate result. For instance, the TACs only regulate the fish landed, whereas it would have been more relevant to regulate the total fish mortality caused by fishing by including discarded by-catch. Since the early 1980s, the Common Fisheries Policy has over the years accumulated up to 90 different technical regulations for the fishery to comply to. Unfortunately, some are redundant, or even worse, counter-productive (DG MARE, 2014).

In the latest revision to the Green Paper, the Commission of the European Communities (2009) advocated the introduction of individual transferable fishing rights as an instrument to reduce overcapacity of the fishing fleet and to improve the economic performance of the fleet. Fishing rights were also considered to support the notion of ownership and thereby a responsible fishery. Individual fishing quotas have also been considered to be a necessary instrument for the successful introduction of the landing obligation, particularly in mixed fisheries.

The new Common Fisheries Policy from 2013 (EU, 2013) open possibilities for more regional adaptation of the fisheries management. It still remains a formal public management system, but it includes mechanisms for a proper dialogue in order to develop an appropriate regional management structure.

The former Swedish voluntary scheme in today's context

Today it would hardly be possible to create a similar system as to the former Swedish fishermen's voluntary scheme, because the situation and the conditions are no longer at hand. But the logic and driving forces behind it could, using a results-based management approach, be used to develop relevant measures which focus on how to reach a common desired result. A more relevant process should be to focus on:

- *creating a common understanding of the problem*
- *agreeing on the relevant action to address the problem through dialogue and cooperation between fishermen, fisheries scientists and fisheries managers*

Such a process will give the system legitimacy and a common understanding of the importance of compliance and fairness in implementation

This will further create a climate of compliance and the need for an official fisheries control system reinforced by a peer control system. It is easier to cheat an official control system than your fellow fishermen. (Source: Staffan Larsson)

Box 5.1 The conflict between the small-scale coastal fisheries and seals

The conflict between the small-scale coastal fisheries and seals illustrates perhaps more than anything else the divergent and conflicting interests and perceptions of interest groups which in the end are leading to devastating consequences for the fishermen.

Seals – the lack of management

During the last decades, the grey seal (*Halichoerus grypus*) population in the Baltic has recovered from a low level at threat status to a level of continuous expansion, resulting in a serious threat to the coastal small-scale fisheries.

Since the 1990s the Swedish Board of Fisheries has been running a research program for the development of fishing gear to limit the impact of seals and has been giving advice and information to the public about this conflict (Königson, 2011).

In spite of this program the conflict has got worse as summarised here:

- Direct competition between seals and the fishery for the available cod and other species
- Direct predation by seals of fish in the nets as well as destroyed fishing gear (Figure 5.1)
- Seals caused parasite infection of the cod population, seal worm found in the muscle of fish. This reduces the value of the landed catch for the fishermen.
- The effect of the seal parasites (mainly liver worms) is assumed to have a negative impact on the growth and mortality of the Baltic cod.

The different positions in this conflict are illustrative:

In 2013, a representative of a major and influential NGO reacted to the proposal of hunting seals by the Swedish Environmental Protection Agency on public radio (SVR 25 June 2013), by claiming that the seal population has not yet reached its full potential and as the fishermen are causing overfishing, they do not deserve aid or support schemes.

Another NGO has been using the seals in campaigns to raise funds by using pictures of cute seal cubs to present the image of seals as victims in a vulnerable nature. For the fishermen the same picture symbolises one of their major problems and the lack of management of natural resources.

During the last decades, the small-scale fisheries have been more or less eradicated, mainly because of the increased seal population. The situation calls for a seal management program.

Figure 5.1 Cod damaged by seals (Photo: Sven Gunnar Lunneryd)

Box 5.2 The development of the Baltic cod issue

The development of the Baltic cod has more than anything else symbolised the conflict between the Swedish fishery and the environmental NGOs.

The Baltic cod – Swedish symbol of fisheries management

Over the past decades, the Baltic cod has become the major symbol for the Swedish fishery, and within EU fisheries management it even has a special Swedish emphasis.

The TV film 'The last cod' broadcast in 2001 (Lövgren 2001), rightfully criticised the EU fisheries policy, but at the same time made the Swedish fishermen the scapegoats. This was followed by a condition set by the Swedish Green Party to support the Social Democratic government, which was to unilaterally stop the Swedish cod fishing for Baltic cod. The Swedish fishermen organised a drastic and visible protest by sailing an armada of 28 fishing boats from the southern part of Sweden to the capital Stockholm to protest directly to the ministers concerned and the Green Party (Figure 5.2). The Swedish fishermen, fishing inside given quotas, were pictured as the problem. In reality there was considerable illegal fishing by non-EU members. However, at the time it was not politically correct to criticise countries that had just been liberated from the Eastern Block on their illegal fishing. This increased the frustration for the Swedish fishermen. The Swedish Board of Fisheries questioned the relevance of a unilateral cod stop.

There is no doubt that the cod had been overexploited until the mid-2000s. In 2004, Poland and the three Baltic states became EU members and subject to the EU fisheries control system. In 2008 Poland was punished for its previous overfishing of Baltic cod. Later ICES could establish that from the mid-2000s there was a rapid decline in fishing mortality for the Eastern Baltic cod. This together with good recruitment resulted in a considerable stock increase.

However, amid this positive development came another blow, with the book entitled *Quiet Sea* (Lövin, 2007) which criticised the EU fisheries policy but also further denigrated the Swedish fishery. On top of this came a red listing of the Baltic cod by World Wildlife Fund, (WWF). The Swedish market for Baltic cod more or less disappeared; the price fell by 24% from 2008 to 2009. This happened during a period when the fishermen experienced good catches. In 2010 discussions started on eco-labelling the Eastern Baltic cod. Certified in 2011, the cod went from red listed to eco-labelled in three years.

For some years ICES recommended increased quotas (TAC) for the Eastern Baltic cod but this was questioned by the fishermen. Since 2012 the Swedish fishermen have not been fully utilising their annual cod quotas. Poor fishing and low market prices are the main reasons for this. Since 2015 ICES has applied a precautionary approach due to problems associated with carrying out a proper fish stock assessment.

The Baltic Sea is a brackish inland sea with complicated environmental conditions, pushing the Eastern Baltic cod to its limits in an ecosystem that could even be considered 'cod hostile'. Earlier there were three functional breeding grounds; now only the Bornholm depth remains due to the severe environmental conditions. The situation for the Western Baltic cod, west of Bornholm, is more positive.

The NGOs are concerned and offer simple solutions. They have been running a campaign using well-known media profiles who refer to the abundance of cod stock during the 1980s compared to the present situation and advocate a ban on bottom trawling. Another organisation argues that cod fishing should only be allowed in coastal areas by fishing boats using passive gears.

This is contrast to the MSC eco-label for cod created in 2011 and where only cod caught by trawl, long lines and traps were eligible for the label. The gill net, which is the second most common method of fishing cod, did not meet the MSC standard (MSC Certificate of Conformity 2011 and 2015).

For most fishermen these NGOs' positions are unrealistic. The gill-net fishing in coastal areas is most affected by the seals. Trawling on the high seas is at the moment the only fishing method using equipment that is out of reach of the seals, to catch cod less infested by seal worm.

There are currently (2018) various problems facing the Eastern Baltic cod. Water salinity and oxygen concentrations are fundamental environmental factors for the success of cod reproduction and distribution. There were no major inflows of fresh salt water into the Baltic between 2003 and 2015. The impact of the inflow in 2015 was insufficient (Köster et al., 2016).

Figure 5.2 Fishing boats protesting in Stockholm (Photo: Kent Hult)

Balance conflicts and cooperation for future fisheries management

Implementing the new EU Common Fishery Policy is a challenge which calls for new forms of cooperation between the parties involved. In line with the centralised EU fisheries policy in the past, the dialogue between the fishing sector and fisheries scientists were strained. ICES was in the past a closed organisation but has now become more open and transparent.

The Swedish fishing industry is in general experiencing an open and structured dialogue with both fisheries science and fisheries administration. There have been a number of joint projects between Swedish fishermen and scientists at SLU (Swedish Agriculture University), the main scientific body involved in fisheries management research. One concrete challenge has been to adapt the fishing gear towards improved selectivity so as to be more suitable to meet the obligation to land all fish caught. A program was implemented and included a clear division of labour – the fishing industry would develop the fishing gear and SLU would provide the scientific evaluation of the proposed gear. A number of new products have been developed. For Baltic Sea cod fishing, Swedish fishermen have developed fishing equipment which has much better selectivity than the gear the fishermen have previously been obliged to use. It is anticipated that this will lead to a considerable reduction in the fishing mortality. The equipment has been approved by the EU (EU, 2018).

Unfortunately, there is a greater divergence between the fisheries sector and the environmental NGOs. At the regional level the BSAC provides an important forum for developing common advice for relevant actions and for a regional adaption of the fisheries management. Most fisheries organisations and a large number of environmental NGOs from around the Baltic are members. Since its start in 2006 the BSAC has been able to provide advice in most areas, even though diverging positions sometimes had to be presented to the European Commission and Member States.

In essence it is a conflict based on different perceptions of nature. What should be the appropriate guidance for fisheries management, a sustainable balanced harvesting or the preservation of nature? Some organisations are dogmatic and campaign oriented and would rather see commercial fishing phased out, whereas others have a more pragmatic approach and are open for a dialogue and reaching compromises.

The Baltic Sea has a well-established management structure for fisheries with ICES as a coordinating scientific body and the EU as the fisheries management body, with a regional structure in BALTFISH where the eight Member State fisheries administrations cooperate and compromise despite sometimes holding differing positions.

Sweden in particular has a broad spectrum of environmental NGOs, other researchers and interest groups which run campaigns in the media with their views on, in particular, the management of Baltic cod. From the Swedish fishing industry perspective, they consider them to be more hostile towards the fishing industry compared to the situation in neighbouring Member States. There might be a risk that campaigns by NGOs and other research bodies undermine the credibility of the existing management system and influence the adoption of irrational management actions.

This conflict exists elsewhere, for example in the USA, as Ray Hilborn, a world-famous fishery scientist, concluded in a recent (2018) report:

> Effective lobbying by anti-fishing NGOs leading to public concern about the environmental impacts of fishing, are leading to increasing restrictions on commercial fishing far beyond any regulation needed to assure the sustainability of the fishery. Commercial fishing as a livelihood and economic activity is under threat in much of the world (Hilborn, 2018).

Conclusion

This chapter demonstrates the complexity of managing a common shared resource such as fish in general and in the Baltic Sea, as an inland sea with complicated and challenging environmental status and shared between nine nations, in particular. The historical background and later development form the foundation for the actual situation as it is today. There have been problems and shortcomings in the fishing sector, the fisheries administration as well as the fisheries science in the past. Any desired development must start with a process of defining the problem in relation to a formulated target.

The development of the EU Common Fisheries Policy gives guidance on the broad targets. Fishing shall be sustainable long term, consistent with the objectives of achieving environmental, economic, social and employment benefits and sustainable food supply. All fish resources should reach maximal sustainable yield (MSY) level by 2020 at the latest. The latter is a harvesting target for long-term fishing with an ecosystem-based and regional approach. Fulfilling those targets the Common Fisheries Policy will be on the right track to deliver appropriate regional adapted management. But as demonstrated with the Swedish fisheries, the present situation is full of diverse and contradictory interpretations and perceptions, of which some are based on preconceived ideas. The way forward is a dialogue with mutual respect and trust as prerequisites for a process that could be very successful.

Note

1   Author interview with fishermen's representative Reine Johansson, 2018

Acknowledgements

I am grateful for comments and critique from the editors of the book and a number of anonymous reviewers who helped to improve the text. I also wish to thank the following fishermen's representatives who were interviewed for this project: Björn Beckman, Fredrik Lindberg, Anton Paulrud and Peter Olsson.

References

Ask, L., Gustavsson, T. and Westerberg, H. (2015) 'Varför har fiskeriförvaltningen inte varit lyckosam?' (Eng. Why has Swedish fisheries management not been successful?), *SLU Aqua reports 2015*, 14

Commission of the European Communities (2001) '*Green Paper on the future of the Common Fisheries Policy*' COM (2001) 135 final https://eur-lex.europa.eu/legal-content/EN/TXT/PDF/?uri=CELEX:52001DC0135&from=EN

Commission of the European Communities (2009) '*Green Paper: Reform of the Common Fisheries Policy*' COM (2009) 163 final https://eur-lex.europa.eu/LexUriServ/LexUriServ.do?uri= COM:2009:0163:FIN:EN:PDF

DG MARE (2014) *A study in support of the development of a new technical conservation measures framework within a reformed Common Fisheries Policy*, MRAGhttps://ec.europa.eu/fisheries/sites/fisheries/files/technical-conservation-measures-final-report_en.pdf

EU (2013) *Regulation (EU) No 1380/2013 of the European Parliament and of the Council of 11 December 2013 on the Common Fisheries Policy*https://eur-lex.europa.eu/legal-content/EN/TXT/?uri=celex%3A32013R1380

EU (2018) *Commission delegated regulation (EU) 2018/47 of 30 October 2017 authorising the use of alternative T90 trawls in Baltic Sea fisheries*https://eur-lex.europa.eu/legal-content/EN/TXT

Hardin, G. (1968) 'Tragedy of the commons', *Science*, 162, 1243–1248

Hasslöf, O. (1949) *Svenska Västkustfiskarna. Studier i en yrkesgrupps näringsliv och sociala kultur*, Esselte, Stockholm

Hilborn, R. (2018) *Losing grounds: Self-report or report by force*, National Fishermen, Portland, USA

ICES Advice (1999) *Cod in subdivisions 25–32*www.ices.dk/publications/library/

Juda, L. (1996) *International law and ocean use management: The evolution of ocean governance*, Routledge, London

Königson, S. (2011) 'Seals and fisheries, A study of the conflict and some possible solutions', PhD thesis, University of Gothenburg

Köster, F., Huwer, B., Hinrichsen, H.H., Neumann, V., Makarchouk, A., Eero, M., Dewitz, B., Hüssy, K., Tomkiewicz, J., Margonski, P., Temming, A., Hermann, J-P., Oesterwind, D., Dierking, J., Kotterba, P. and Plikshs, M. (2016) 'Eastern Baltic cod recruitment revisited—dynamics and impacting factors', *ICES Journal of Marine Science*, 74(1), 3–19

Lövgren, P. (2001) 'Den sista torsken' (Eng. The last cod), in *Dokument Inifrån*, Broadcast on Swedish Television 8 November 2001

Lövin, I. (2007) *Tyst hav* (Eng. Quiet Sea), Ordfront, Stockholm

OECD (2015) 'Fisheries support estimate'http://www.oecd.org/agriculture/fisheries/fse.htm

Ostrom, E. (1990) '*Governing the commons: The evolution of institutions for collective action*', Cambridge University Press, Cambridge, UK

Swedish Radio (2013) 'Dagens Eko' Tuesday 25 June 2013 5.47 pmhttps://sverigesradio.se/sida/artikel.aspx?programid=83&artikel=5574894

Westerberg, H. and Ask, L. (2011) '*Staten och fisket – nedslag i fiskeriförvaltningens historia*' (Eng. Development of the fishery governance in Sweden) Fiskeriverket, Gothenburg

Part II
Case Studies

6 The raptor and the lamb

Reintroduction of carnivores in agricultural landscapes in Ireland

Eileen O'Rourke

Introduction

Conflict between people and wildlife is today among the most critical threats to both the conservation and reintroduction of many species worldwide (Madden, 2004; Woodroffe et al., 2005; Dickman, 2010; Redpath et al., 2013; Manfredo, 2015). Conflict is an inevitable outcome of human interaction, but as stated by Lederach (1997) it is the consequences of the conflict that determine whether it is constructive or injurious. Madden (2004, p. 248) defines human–wildlife conflict (HWC) as situations where 'the needs and behaviour of wildlife impact negatively on the goals of humans or where the goals of humans negatively impact on the needs of wildlife'. It is increasingly recognised that behind the overt HWC is nearly always underlying human–human social conflict; driven by fundamental differences in values, goals, identity, lifestyle, power imbalance and distrust, often in combination with historic wounds. Conflict involves people and as stated by Madden (2004 p. 248–249) HWC can become 'not only conflict between humans and wildlife, but also between humans about wildlife'. Conservation and wildlife management has its roots in the natural sciences and it has traditionally promoted a biological and technical managerial approach to conflict mitigation, with possible financial compensation as a resolution strategy. The failure of many wildlife conservation projects has resulted from this misrepresentation and over-simplification of a purely scientific and legalistic approach to HWC (Redpath et al., 2013; Madden and McQuinn, 2014, Jacobsen and Linnell, 2016) For example, Jacobsen and Linnell (2016), reporting on HWC surrounding large carnivores in Norway, found that recognition justice in the form of acknowledging a group's identity, lifestyle, knowledge, mutual respect and the extent to which they regarded the management system as being just and fair was far more important to them than compensation for livestock predation losses endured by farmers and herders. Naughton-Treves et al., (2003) also found that compensation for livestock losses had no influence on tolerance levels for wolf predation in Wisconsin, USA; rather deep-rooted social identity and occupation was a far more powerful predictor of tolerance level.

Long-term conservation success requires conservationists to understand and address the underlying social and psychological factors embedded in nearly all HWC. However, conservation biologists rarely have the training or skills to address these wider societal issues (Redpath et al., 2013; Bennett et al., 2017). Best practice today calls for the adoption of a holistic inter-disciplinary approach, along with an acknowledgement of the key role of stakeholders in human–wildlife conflict mitigation (Woodroffe et al., 2005; Reed, 2008; Madden and McQuinn, 2014). Public participation and acceptance can be as important a determination of the success of wildlife projects as the underlying biology. We also know that many species rein-troductions fail not because of biological / ecological reasons, but due to accidental or human induced mortality (Kellert et al., 1996). However, given the frequent differences in value systems and incompatible goals, meaningful stakeholder participation can be very difficult. Similarly what passes for 'participation' can range from manipulation and passive dis-semination of information to active engagement and empowering stake-holders in decision making (Arnstein, 1969). But, there is evidence that effective participation, including sustained dialogue and relationship build-ing, increases trust and reduces conflict (Wilson, 2004; Reed, 2008 Redpath et al., 2013). We must also acknowledge that stakeholder participation is not a panacea and needs to be handled carefully. Expected results may not be achieved, and key stakeholders may refuse to take part in the participa-tory process (Gerner et al., 2011). Redpath et al., (2013) warns against the assumption that participatory approaches lead to idealised 'win-win' solu-tions, rather than recognising the merits of the arguments in a conflict. Evidence suggests that long-term human–wildlife conflict resolution is rare, even where appropriate strategies have been implemented and negotiated trade-off may be the only acceptable outcome (Dickman, 2010). Often the most one can hope for is to render the conflict manageable. Increased par-ticipation may not always improve HWC, but as argued by Jacobsen and Linnell (2016, p. 204), it is necessary in order to 'ensure that the political choices are made through means that are regarded as legitimate by the sta-keholders'. Participation is intrinsic to democratic processes and is increas-ingly recognised in international policy, such as the UN Aarhus Convention (1998), which aims to improve information access, justice and public parti-cipation in decision making in environmental matters.

Each conflict situation brings with it its unique combination of geography, history, social, cultural, economic, political and biological complexities. This realisation mitigates against the use of a generic 'tool kit' approach for both stakeholder engagement and conflict mitigation. Madden and McQuinn (2014) propose a Conservation Conflict Transformation (CCT) model that is not just an approach and set of techniques but a way of thinking about, understanding and relating to conflict. The model recognises the deep-rooted historic and identity-based conflict that often exists between stakeholders, along with the relationship building and equity and transparency of the decision-making process necessary to transform conservation conflict. Ultimately it calls for a change in orientation in HWC studies away from the current narrow focus on the 'dispute' to a broader and more holistic approach that can position the conflict within its underpinning social context. The two-step conceptual model – 'Levels of Conflict Model' and the 'Conflict Intervention Triangle' (see Figs 6.1 and 6.2) that are the main components of Madden and McQuinn's (2014) CCT approach – is used in the below case study research to help analyse the conflict surrounding the reintroduction of the white-tailed sea eagle to Ireland. The major obstacle to the success of the project ultimately proved to be human induced mortality of the birds.

Methods

This case study research is based on over thirty in-depth interviews with the various stakeholders involved in the sea eagle reintroduction project, including conservationists (Golden Eagle Trust, the National Parks and Wildlife Service personnel who were directly involved in the project), hill sheep farmers in the eagle release area, the Irish Farmers Association (IFA – the main farmers union) and tourism interests, including hoteliers and members of the Killarney Chamber of Tourism and Commerce. These in-depth interviews, along with attendance at stakeholder public meetings and site-visits, were conducted between 2011 and 2012, and were subsequently qualitatively analysed. The research also involved following the media coverage of the project in the local and national press, on television and on the internet from the start of the project in 2006 up to the present. A lot of background reading of technical reports on the eagle reintroduction project in both Ireland and Scotland was also undertaken.

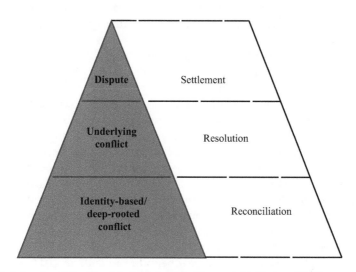

Figure 6.1 Levels of Conflict Model (after Madden and McQuinn, 2014)

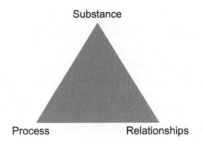

Figure 6.2 Conflict Intervention Triangle (after Madden and McQuinn, 2014)

White-tailed sea eagle

The white-tailed sea eagle (*Haliaeetus albicilla*) is a large raptor, with a distinctive white wedge-shaped tail, dark brown plumage and a large yellow bill. Sea eagles are widely distributed over northern Eurasia, with the largest European population of an estimated 3,000 pairs found along the Norwegian coast (Halley et al., 2006). They have a varied diet of fish and sea birds and they also scavenge on carrion. They are not on the IUCNs Red List of endangered species, but they are protected under European Law and are listed on Annex 1 of the EUs Birds Directive (2009/147/EC) and in Appendix II of the Bern Convention. The sea eagle became extinct in Britain in 1918 and in Ireland in the late 19th century, with the last sited recording in County Kerry in 1898 (D'Arcy, 1999; Love, 1983). They suffered heavy predation at the hands of gamekeepers, egg collectors, sportsmen and landowners. Sea eagles were reintroduced from Norway to Scotland between 1975 and 2012, and today the Scottish population is securely established with over a hundred breeding pairs (O'Toole et al., 2002; RSPB, 2017).

A collaborative project between the Golden Eagle Trust (GET) (an Irish non-government organisation) and the state-run Irish National Parks and Wildlife Service (NPWS), to reintroduce the white-tailed sea eagle to Ireland, began in 2006 with the majority of the funding (70%) coming from the NPWS. The aim of the project was 'to re-establish a viable, self-sustaining breeding population of sea eagles in south-west Ireland after an absence of 110 years' (Mee, 2009). The proposed re-introduction site for the sea eagles was within Killarney National Park, at the eastern end of the mountainous Iveragh peninsula in County Kerry. The peninsula is surrounded by the Atlantic Ocean on three sides, and the park's pre-release site was about 20 km from the coast (see Fig. 6.3). The donor eagle population, as in the Scottish reintroduction project, came from Norway. In collaboration with the Norwegian Institute for Nature Research (NINA), a hundred juvenile sea eagles were introduced to Killarney National Park over a five-year period from 2007 to 2011, at an estimated cost of over €1.5 million.

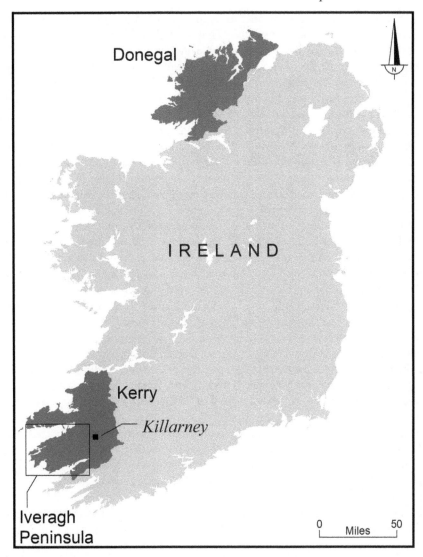

Figure 6.3 Location map, showing the reintroduction site of the white-tailed sea eagles in Killarney, Co. Kerry and that of the golden eagle in Donegal.

(Map produced by Mike Murphy, Cartographer in the Geography Department, University College Cork.)

Species reintroduction – sea eagles

Species reintroduction is defined by the International Union for the Conservation of Nature (IUCN, 1998 p. 6) as, 'an attempt to establish a species in an area which was once part of its historical range, but from which it has been extirpated or become extinct'. Apart from biological and ecological criteria, the

IUCN guidelines make distinct reference to local consultation and social acceptance of re-introduced species. They state that, 'A thorough assessment of attitudes of local people to the proposed project is necessary to ensure the long-term protection of the re-introduced population, especially if the cause of species' decline was due to human factors' (IUCN, 1998, p. 9; IUCN/SSC, 2013). In compliance with international regulations a pre-release feasibility study, under the auspices of the IUCN Species Reintroduction Guidelines, was undertaken by the NPWS and GET. The project's steering group, which initially consisted of only natural scientists (ornithologists and conservationists), acknowledged that the outcome of the project would largely depend on the local community's attitude to the project (O'Toole, 2006). They also stated that a well-planned media campaign and an agreed clear message needed to be adopted before the first project press release (O'Toole, 2006). Burke et al. (2015) remind us that mass media – newspapers, TV, internet – is often the public's primary source of scientific knowledge and the media played a key communications role in the sea eagle project. The sea eagle's economic benefit to the area was also seen as an important aspect of the reintroduction project. The eco or wildlife tourism potential for watching white-tailed eagles visiting winter food dumps around the Lakes of Killarney is, according to O'Toole (2006), 'enormous'. It is estimated that sea eagle tourism on the island of Mull in Scotland generates over £5 million annually and supports over 100 full-time equivalent jobs (Molloy, 2011). County Kerry, and in particular the Lakes of Killarney, is one of Ireland's major tourist destinations, with over 2 million tourists visiting the area annually. The tourism sector, concentrated around the hotel owners and the town's Chamber of Tourism and Commerce, was quick to see the potential economic benefits of the sea eagle's reintroduction and strongly supported the project. The sea eagle along with the native red deer (*Cervus elaphus*) of Killarney is seen to imbue the area with prestigious eco-tourism attractiveness (O'Rourke, 2000). A tourism representative joined the project's Steering Committee when invited to do so in March 2007, prior to the arrival of the first eagle chicks in June that year. However, the project's relationship with the farming community got off to a bad start; not only did they refuse the initial invitation in March 2007 onto the Steering Committee, but over a hundred farmers demonstrated at Kerry Airport when the plane from Trondheim carrying the first batch of sea eagles touched down on 18 June 2007 (Lucey, 2007a).

Of the 15 birds initially released in 2007, a quarter died in the first year, the majority due to ingesting poisoned meat bate in the spring lambing season (O'Rourke, 2014). 24 of the original hundred birds released were recovered dead by the end of 2012, and 32 confirmed dead by the end of 2016 (www. goldeneagletrust.info). Of the 32 deaths, 14 birds were confirmed to have died from poisoning, three from wind turbine collisions, one from colliding with overhead power lines, two from shooting, one from natural causes and the rest from reasons unknown, with suspected poisoning being the main culprit (www.goldeneagletrust.info). The majority of mortalities were human induced.

Thirgood and Redpath (2008, p. 1553) argued that given that humans have been at the root of most species' extinction, central to successful reintroduction projects and conflict mitigation is an understanding of 'what is – and conversely what is not – acceptable to stakeholders'.

Hill Sheep farmers and conservationists

The main land use on the Iveragh peninsula is hill-sheep farming, and sheep farmers are the people who come into direct contact with the eagles (O'Rourke and Kramm, 2009). They are also the group who were suspected of either intentionally or accidentally poisoning them. The principal problem the sheep farmers and their union, the Hill Sheep Branch of the powerful Irish Farmers Association (IFA), had with the eagles was that they were 'imposed' on them. There had been no serious pre-release consultation, with many farmers learning about the project only after the eagles had arrived[1] (Lucey, 2006; O'Rourke, 2014). This was the reason the IFA gave for initially not joining the project's steering committee when invited to do so, three months before the birds arrived. They rightly pointed out that they had no say in the initial decision to reintroduce the sea eagles, and inviting them on board at the implementation stage of the project was just a 'tick box' exercise for what was to pass for stakeholder consultation and participation. It is generally accepted that a crucial aspect of any participatory process is the identification and consultation of stakeholders at an early stage, prior to any formal management plan being put in place (Reed, 2008; Madden and McQuinn 2014).

The IFA's stated opposition to the project was centred on livelihood issues. They feared the eagles would take young lambs around spring lambing time, that they might introduce disease to their flocks, and they were unhappy with the lack of compensation for livestock loses (Interview data; Lucey, 2007b). The Golden Eagle Trust (GET) assured the farmers that sea eagles do not take lambs: of the 3,000 breeding pairs in Norway they stated that there had not been a single incident of sea eagles praying on live lambs, but they were useful for cleaning up carrion, including dead sheep and lambs on the hill (Halley et al., 2006; Mee, 2007). However, a different story was emerging from the Island of Mull in Scotland, where some sea eagles were openly taking lambs. This was confirmed by research commissioned by Scottish Natural Heritage. The research concluded that the proportion of lambs killed was insignificant compared with overall annual mortality and financial impacts would be negligible at broad spatial scales (Marquiss et al., 2003; Simms et al., 2010). Their findings did not preclude the fact that losses could be significant for individual farmers, with one farmer on Mull claiming to have lost 30 lambs to eagle predation in one season. The Irish white-tailed sea eagle project manager, Dr Alan Mee, admitted that in exceptional cases 'rogue eagles' who had not been properly introduced may take non-viable lambs. Still the project manager assured the Irish farmers that the overall number of lambs taken was very small – 1–2% of annual lamb mortality (Mee, 2007, 2009, 2010). This confused and contradictory message along with poor overall communications and information exchange did not engender trust from the farming community. Redpath et al. (2013: 103) argue that 'distrust is one of the main barriers to collaboration and processes that help build trust, such as transparency, are likely to encourage engagement'.

Apart from the stated livelihood issues, there was a lot more going on under the surface of the Irish 'raptor–lamb' conflict. The farmers' greatest fear was not lamb predation but landscape designations such as a Special Protection Area (SPA) – from the EU Birds Directive, which could restrict planning and land use (Creedon, 2007). The farmers were particularly concerned about opposition to lucrative wind turbine projects that were already in the planning process. The GET promised no designations for 20 years until breeding populations were established and territories created (www.goldeneagletrust. info). To date at least three eagles have been killed by wind turbine blades from an existing wind farm on the Kerry/Cork border. In 2016 the NPWS objected to the development of another 38 turbine farms, again along the Kerry/Cork border. The NPWS argued that the sea eagle was particularly susceptible to collision with turbine blades, stating that 39 eagles had died in Norway at one large wind farm between 2005 and 2010 (Lucey, 2016a; 2016b). The NPWS's objection was not upheld and planning permission was granted but the incident proved that the farmers' initial fears in relation to conflict with wind farm developments were not unfounded. Overall the farming lobby resented the 'imposition' of the project that threatened not only their economic livelihoods but also their social legitimacy as the managers and custodians of the country-side. The IFA tried but failed to negotiate trade-offs with the NPWS, such as the removal of SAC designations from riverine areas, or a top-up to their agri-environment payments (Interview data).

A history of unresolved disputes

There was a history of conflict in the eagle reintroduction site between the farming community and the National Parks and Wildlife Service (NPWS), whom the farmers saw as their natural enemies. There was an ongoing conflict between the two parties surrounding the management (and over-population) of the protected red deer of Killarney National Park, who frequently break fences and graze the surrounding reclaimed agricultural land. There are annual conflicts over the burning of upland heather and gorse, which theoretically requires a permit from the NPWS and is restricted to certain times of the year. But this regulation is rarely respected and nearly impossible to implement, as one has to be caught in the act of setting the fire. There was an ongoing heated battle between the NPWS and the IFA in relation to Special Protection Area (SPA) designations for the hen harrier (*Circus cyaneus*) in North Kerry. In North Kerry the IFA backed a campaign not to allow NPWS personnel onto farmland (Lane, 2003). It is often difficult to differentiate between the rhetoric and the reality. Publically the IFA stated that all these environmental designations are sterilising the countryside and reducing the price of land, while privately some farmers admitted that they were very happy with the extra (agri-environment) payments associated with having land in an SAC/SPA (Interview data). One sheep farmer with land adjoining Killarney National Park summarised the conflictual relationship between the farmers and the NPWS, when he stated: 'There is no point in complaining, we just have to "play ball" with them' (Interview data). 'Playing ball' often involves taking matters into their own hands. Another farmer stated: 'The former landlords were down on the peasantry, now the eagles and new found environmental lobby are down on the peasantry' (Interview data). Nowadays the victims and villains are not so easily identified. The ongoing and historic social conflict between the NPWS and the farming lobby made meaningful stakeholder engagement in relation to the sea eagle project very difficult. The NPWS was aware of its reputation among the farming community, which is why it wanted the sea eagle reintroduction project to be fronted by the Golden Eagle Trust (GET). But the farmers quickly saw through that; they were all the same as far as they were concerned: they shared the same values, had the same mind-set and were ultimately their enemies. Perhaps it was also this history of conflict that forewarned the Golden Eagle Trust and NPWS that prior consultation with their old enemies would not work and the better option might be to 'impose' the eagles and then defend the project, which is essentially what they did.

Sea eagle poisoning

In County Kerry, and throughout much of Ireland, there is a tradition of setting poisoned meat bate around lambing time to control foxes and corvids, which all sheep farmers recognised as the main threat to new born lambs. This indiscriminate poisoning also affects non-target species, including dogs, pine martens and other animals protected under the Irish Wildlife Act 1976 (Amendment 2000). Being carrion eaters, the eagle reintroduction team always knew that poisoning posed the greatest threat to the birds. The Golden Eagle Trust had been calling for legislative change for some years prior to the commencement of the sea eagle reintroduction project (Irish Raptor Study Group, 2012). But when it was not forthcoming they still proceeded with the project. Neither had they addressed the traditional practice of sheep farmers setting poison bait around lambing time. Once it was quickly established that poisoning was the main cause of mortality for the reintroduced birds, the GET again set about changing the legislation. The public outcry at the sight of poisoned eagle carcases in the media brought political pressure to bear on this long-running issue. In 2009 the Golden Eagle Trust submitted a formal complaint to the European Commission, on the basis of a breach of the Birds Directive. This eventually led to an amendment to the Irish Wildlife Act in October 2010, which rendered all forms of poisoned bate illegal in the Irish countryside (O'Rourke, 2014; Burke et al., 2015).

Legislation in relation to poisoning is one thing, but policing and implementing it is quite another. Thirgood and Redpath, (2008) remind us that law enforcement has been ineffective in reducing persecution of the hen harrier in the Scottish Highlands and has contributed to the alienation of the hunting stakeholders. In 2010 the Irish Department of Agriculture, in collaboration with the GET, distributed an advice leaflet on the control of foxes and crows to sheep farmers in South Kerry and West Cork, clearly stating that it is now illegal to poison foxes and crows (Department of Agriculture, Fisheries and Food, 2009; 2011). They proposed shooting as the safest means of controlling foxes (along with use of low electric fences and bright lights around lambing paddocks), and Larsen traps for crows. However, the problem on the ground did not go away, and the sea eagles continued to be either intentionally or accidentally poisoned. Poisons remained widely available in the form of herbicides (e.g. carbofuran) or liver fluke products such as Trodax (which contains the active compound nitroxinil), or alphachloralose, which is still approved for the control of mice and rats. These freely available compounds continued to be the most commonly found poisons in the dead eagle carcases.

A farmer whose sheep still lamb on the hill mocked the suggestion of erecting an electric fence as a fox deterrent around his mountain – 'they think they will educate us' (Interview data). He went on to complain about the lack of prior consultation, the fact that the eagles were 'imposed' on them, along with more 'rules and regulations'. He sees himself as the shepherd of his flock and his job is to protect his sheep and lambs. There is a general dislike of officialdom and outsiders telling them what to do. They hold what could be described as a 'resistance' mentality, expressed in their ability to endure despite the tough physical and socio-economic environment they find themselves in. All the farmers interviewed had a deep-rooted attachment to their sheep and their mountain, and the majority of them had no time for a 'nuisance' of a bird, with nothing to offer them. 'The eagles may be a nice attraction for the tourists, they just want something to look at, but it is a threat and a nuisance to the farming community' (Interview data).

Highly mediatised dead eagles giving out the wrong message

In the media the farmers who continued to set poisoned bait for foxes and thus accidentally or intentionally continued to target the eagles, were presented as 'mavericks' and anti-social bachelors with mental health issues. The IFA also distanced themselves from such illegal practices. The mediatisation of the dead eagles, the stark images of the project manager holding up dead birds in the countryside, along with images of dead eagles undergoing autopsies in sterile toxicology laboratories, enraged the general public, especially the urban population of Dublin, reflected in letters to several national newspapers. The eagle project became a surrogate for wider urban–rural, 'local populist' versus external science-based 'general interest' tensions (Skogen and Krange, 2003). Wilson's (2004) observation that attitudes to reintroductions tended to be favourable among an increasingly environmentally aware and urbanised general public, but negative among those likely to be adversely affected, rings true.

The poisoning of the eagles also enraged the donor country Norway, and the Norwegian ambassador to Ireland frequently expressed his concern and was quoted as saying: 'We in Norway are deeply concerned about the situation and hope that all can be done to make such poisoning illegal' (cited in Burke et al., 2015). The bad press was also affecting Ireland's substantial agricultural exports, who sell the image of Ireland's lush green pastures and almost 'organic' wholesome products. The Irish food board, 'An Bord Bia', had recently launched its 'Origin Green' international marketing strategy (www.bordbia.is). This in turn enraged the farming community – the 'nuisance' of a bird had gone too far. The polarisation of views and adversarial politics, the pitting of conservationists and farmers, rural and urban populations against each other and all widely covered in the media was ultimately serving nobody's agenda. Even if the conservationists had the general public on their side, they knew the fate of the vulnerable eagles rested in the farmers' hands, who were quick to point out that they 'can take out the birds at anytime' (Interview data). Ultimately the two sides needed to co-operate, and belatedly they came to recognise they had a shared problem!

In April 2010 Teagasc (The Irish farm advisory and research service) called what they claim to be the first public meeting on the eagles in a community hall, outside Killarney. It was attended by over 200 people, including the NPWS and the Golden Eagle Trust. It was a very heated meeting and much anger was expressed towards what the IFA claimed was the project manager's addiction to publicity and the mediatisation of eagle deaths. Ultimately this meeting led to the establishment of the 'Kerry Sustainable Rural Environment Group', a multi-agency group whose aim was to try to retrospectively manage the situation. They tried to promote dialogue between the stakeholders and to negotiate acceptable solutions. They held 'Farm Walk and Talk' events, where they demonstrated alternative predator management methods, other than that of poisoning, to sheep farmers. Most importantly, in agreement with the GET, they set about keeping the project out of the media limelight and to stop mediatising eagle mortalities. The media focus subsequently became less intense and shifted from its negative focus on dead eagles to a more positive message, such as the fact that over 13 Irish-born chicks have successfully fledged their nests (Lucey, 2016c).

Discussion and conclusion

The cultural, political and practical barriers to species' reintroductions cannot be underestimated (Wilson, 2004; Manning et al., 2009). As we move from exclusive protection areas to community-based conservation, there is no doubt 'the human dimension is an inextricable element of 21st century conservation' (Macdonald, 2009, p. 425). Given the increased public knowledge and interest in environmental issues, along with a postmodern scepticism about science, stakeholder participation in environmental decision making is increasingly regarded as a democratic right. It is also critical to the success of wildlife management and conflict mitigation.

Among the principal shortcomings of the Irish sea eagle reintroduction project was the initial lack of consultation with stakeholders on the ground, especially the farming community that had legitimate livelihood concerns. Neither is this situation unique, rather historically it was the norm where natural scientists tended to be the sole or primary source to guide conservation action (Bennett et al., 2017). The imposition of policy through institutionalised power has been a repeated feature of the Irish Government's *modus operandi* (Flynn, 2007). Research shows that people are far more likely to accept risks undertaken voluntarily, as opposed to risks imposed externally (Dickman, 2010). The evidence also suggests that conservation outcomes will be less durable when conservationists assert their interests to the detriment of others (Redpath et al., 2013). The project was designed and implemented solely by natural scientists with no training or skills in communication, education and stakeholder facilitation. It lacked an interdisciplinary approach, which the management team argue was due to tight budgets (Interview data). When budgets are tight the first casualties are what are perceived to be non-essentials, such as education and stakeholder facilitation, both of which subsequently proved to be the project's major stumbling block. The reintroduction project quickly assumed an adversarial approach. There was also a history of conflict in the eagle reintroduction site between the NPWS and the farming sector. The intractability of the conflict between the conservationists and farmers meant that they only cooperated, or rather tolerated each other, in the end because they had to, due to the bad press surrounding the poisoning of the birds.

Returning to Madden and Mcquinn's (2014) two-part Conservation Conflict Transformation (CCT) model we can see that the application of Part 1 – Levels of Conflict Model – did help with a deeper understanding of the current dispute. The 'Dispute' was the outward manifestation of unresolved deeper historic and identity-based conflict between the farming community and the conservationists. However, it is in the application of the second part of the CCT model (see Fig. 6.2) – 'The Conflict Intervention Triangle' – that it becomes apparent that attempts to move beyond the 'Substance' of the dispute to actually transform the conflict in a positive way, were hindered by structural weaknesses in the design and implementation of the sea eagle reintroduction project. It is in the 'Relationship' and 'Process' (decision-making design) aspects of the model that the eagle project falters. The eagles were introduced with the necessary backing of a Government agency, NPWS, without sufficient prior attention to communication and relationship building among the various stakeholders who stood to be impacted both positively and negatively by the project. All of which would have required time, finance and institutional capacity building. This in turn mitigated against the quality and durability of the decision-making process. As remarked by Madden and McQuinn (2014, p. 102), Governments and Government Agencies show a marked reluctance to cede any decision-making power, because they 'associate it with a lack of control' (see also Flynn, 2007). This political culture inevitably framed the conflict in a hierarchical power struggle. Conservation and species reintroductions are scientifically, technically, politically and socially complex. Decisions need to be made not just on the best science, but they also have to incorporate a better understanding of the human dimension, so that the outcomes are more democratic, legitimate and ultimately more sustainable in the long term.

Note

1   There had been some media coverage on local radio and in the press along with negotiations with the local IFA. However, it was more information dissemination rather than consultation with the local community. The IFA held a large public meeting in Killarney in February 2007, where the participants unanimously voted to oppose the project.

Acknowledgements

I wish to thank all the interviewees who participated in this project, and also those who provided me with follow-up documentation and project technical reports.

References

Arnstein, A. (1969) 'A ladder of citizenship participation', *Journal of the American Institute of Planners*, 26, 216–233

Bennett, N.J., Roth, R., Klain, S.C., Chan, K., Christie, P., Clark, D.A., Cullman, G., Curran, D., Durbin, T.J., Epstein, G., Greenberg, A., Nelson, M.P., Sandlos, J., Stedman, R., Teel, T.L., Thomas, R., Verissimo, D. and Wyborn, C. (2017) 'Conservation and social science: Understanding and integrating human dimensions to improve conservation', *Biological Conservation*, 205, 93–108

Burke, B.J., Finn, A., Flanagan, D.T., Fogarty, D.M., Foran, M., O'Sullivan, J.D., Smith, S.A., Linnell, J.D.C. and McMahon, B.J. (2015) 'Reintroduction of white-tailed eagles to the Republic of Ireland: A case study of media coverage', *Irish Geography*, 47, 95–115

Creedon, T. (2007) 'Designations pushing Irish farmers out of existence', interview with John Stack, Kerry IFA President, *The Kerryman*, 17 January 2007, 17

D'Arcy, D. (1999) *Ireland's lost birds*, Four Courts Press, Dublin

Department of Agriculture, Fisheries and Food (2009/2011) *Advice leaflet on control of foxes and crows*. Dublin, April 2009 and January 2011, 6

Dickman, A.J. (2010) 'Complexities of conflict: The importance of considering social factors for effectively resolving human–wildlife conflict', *Animal Conservation*, 13, 458–466

Flynn, B. (2007) *The blame game: Rethinking Ireland's sustainable development and environmental performance*, Irish Academic Press, Dublin

Gerner, J., Heurich, M., Günther, S. and SchramlU. (2011) 'Red deer at a crossroads—An analysis of communication strategies concerning wildlife management in the 'Bayerischer Wald' National Park, Germany', *Journal of Nature Conservation*, 19, 319–326

Golden Eagle Trust http://www.goldeneagletrust.info/

Halley, D.J., Nygård, T. and Folkestad, A.O. (2006) 'An evaluation of the proposed sea eagle *Haliaeetus albicilla* reintroduction area in Ireland', Norwegian Institute for Nature Research, Trondheim, Norway

Irish Raptor Study Group (2012) *Irish Raptor Study Group 2011 annual raptor round-up report*, Irish Raptor Study Group, Ireland

IUCN (International Union for the Conservation of Nature) (1998) 'Guidelines for re-introductions', IUCN SSC Re-introduction Specialist Group, Gland, Switzerland and Cambridge, UK. 10 pp http://www.iucnsscrsg.org/

IUCN/SSC (2013) *Guidelines for reintroductions and other conservation translocations*, Version 1.0, IUCN Species Survival Commission, Gland, Switzerlandhttp://www.iucnsscrsg.org/

Jacobsen, K.S. and Linnell, J.D.C. (2016) 'Perceptions of environmental justice and the conflict surrounding large carnivore management in Norway – Implications for conflict management', *Biological Conservation*, 203, 179–206

Kellert, S.R., Black, M., Rush, C.R. and Bath, A.J. (1996) 'Human culture and large carnivore conservation in North America', *Conservation Biology*, 10(4), 977–990

Lane, E. (2003) 'Farmers urged not to allow Dúchas officials on to their lands', *The Kerryman*, 6 March 2003, 43

Lederach, J.P. (1997) *Building peace: Sustainable reconciliation in divided societies*, United States Institute for Peace Press, Washington, DC

Love, J.A. (1983) *The return of the sea eagle*, Cambridge University Press, Cambridge, UK

Lucey, A. (2006) 'IFA oppose reintroducing eagles', *The Irish Times*, 24 August 2006

Lucey, A. (2007a) 'White-tailed eagle back in Kerry after 100-year absence', *The Irish Times*, 19 May 2007

Lucey, A. (2007b) 'IFA fears birds will take lambs and salmon', *The Irish Times*, 26 January 2007

Lucey, A. (2016a) 'Wind turbines killed eagles in Kerry-Cork, says parks service', *The Irish Times*, 31 July 2016

Lucey, A. (2016b) 'Wind turbines blamed for death of three sea eagles', *The Irish Times*, 2 September 2016

Lucey, A. (2016c) 'Six Irish-born white-tailed eagles fly nests in 2016', *The Irish Times*, 9 September 2016

Macdonald, D.W. (2009) 'Lessons learnt and plans laid: Seven awkward questions for the future of reintroductions', in Hayward, M.W. and Somers, M.J. (eds), *Reintroduction of top-order predators*, Wiley-Blackwell, Chichester, UK, 411–448

Madden, F. (2004) 'Creating coexistence between humans and wildlife: Global perspectives on local efforts to address human–wildlife conflict', *Human Dimensions of Wildlife*, 9, 247–257

Madden, F. and McQuinn, B. (2014) 'Conservation's blind spot: The case for conflict transformation in wildlife conservation', *Biological Conservation*, 178, 97–106

Manfredo, M.J. (2015) 'Essays on human–wildlife conflict 10 years after the Durban World Parks Congress: An introduction', *Human Dimensions of Wildlife*, 20, 285–288

Manning, A.D., Gordon, I.J., Ripple, W.J. (2009) 'Restoring landscapes of fear with wolves in the Scottish Highlands', *Biological Conservation*, 142, 2314–2321

Marquiss, M., Madders, M., Irvine, J. and Carss, D.N. (2003), 'The impact of white-tailed eagles on sheep farming on Mull: Final report', (Contract number: ITE/004/99), 47 pp

Mee, A. (2007) 'Minutes of Kerry County Council Meeting convened to discuss the introduction of the white-tailed eagle to Killarney National Park', Tralee, 16 April 2007

Mee, A. (2009) 'Irish white-tailed sea eagle reintroduction programme 2007–2008', Report to the Directorate for Nature Management, The Golden Eagle Trust, Trondheim, Norway

Mee, A. (2010) 'Safe lambing in sheep country', *Irish Farmers Journal*, 3 April 2010

Molloy, D. (2011) *Wildlife at work: The economic impact of white-tailed eagles on the Isle of Mull*, The RSPB, Sandy, UK

Naughton-Treves, L., Grossberg, R. and Treves, A. (2003) 'Paying for tolerance: Rural citizens' attitudes towards wolf depredation and compensation', *Conservation Biology*, 17(6), 1500–1511

O'Rourke, E. (2000) 'The reintroduction and reinterpretation of the wild', *Journal of Agriculture and Environmental Ethics*, 13, 145–165

O'Rourke, E. and Kramm, N. (2009) 'Changes in the management of the Irish Uplands: A case study from the Iveragh peninsula', *European Countryside*, 1(1), 53–59

O'Rourke, E. (2014) 'The reintroduction of the white-tailed sea eagle to Ireland: People and wildlife', *Land Use Policy*, 38, 129–137

O'Toole, L., Fielding, A.H. and Haworth, P.F. (2002) 'Re-introduction of the golden eagle into the Republic of Ireland', *Biological Conservation*, 103, 303–312

O'Toole, L. (2006) 'A proposal to reintroduce white-tailed eagles to Ireland', *Golden Eagle Trust Internal Report*, January 2006, p.12

Redpath, S.M., Young, J., Evely, A., Adams, W.M., Sutherland, W.J., Whitehouse, A., Amar, A., Lambert, R.A., Linnell, J.D.C., Watt, A. and Gutiérrez, R.J. (2013), 'Understanding and managing conservation conflicts', *Trends in Ecology & Evolution*, 28(2), 100–109

Reed, M.S. (2008) 'Stakeholder participation for environmental management: A literature review', *Biological Conservation*, 141, 2417–2431

RSPB (2017) 'East Scotland white-tailed sea eagles' http://www.rspb.org.uk/ community/ourwork/b/eastscotlandeagles/default.aspx (Accessed: 1 June 2017)

Simms, I.C., Ormston, C.M., Somerwill, K.E., Cairns, C.L., Tobin, F.R., Judge, J. and Tomlinson, A. (2010) *A pilot study into sea eagle predation on lambs in the Gairloch Area: Final report*, Scottish Natural Heritage Commissioned Report No. 370

Skogen, K. and Krange, O. (2003) 'A wolf at the gate: The anti-carnivore alliance and the symbolic construction of community', *Sociologia Ruralis*, 43(3), 309–325

Thirgood, S. and Redpath, S. (2008) 'Hen harriers and red grouse: Science, politics and human–wildlife conflict', *Journal of Applied Ecology*, 45, 1550–1554

Wilson, C.J. (2004) 'Could we live with reintroduced large carnivores in the UK?', *Mammal Review*, 34, 211–232

Woodroffe, R., Thirgood, S., Rabinowitz, A. (eds) (2005) *People and wildlife: Conflict or coexistence?*Cambridge University Press, Cambridge, UK

7 From dystopia to utopia – and back again

The case of the Van Gujjar forest pastoralists in the Indian Himalayas

Pernille Gooch

Introduction

In August of 2018 history appeared to repeat itself. Flashed on Indian media were messages such as 'No country for pastoralists' (the Wire); 'Van Gujjars are constant threat to wildlife' (Indian Express); 'encroachers on forest land' (Times of India). The Indian environmental magazine *Down to Earth* wrote about 'A repeat of historical injustice' (Asher, 2018). The background to this sudden media interest in the Van Gujjars was an order, issued on 6 August by the High Court of Uttarakhand for the removal of *Van* (forest) Gujjar pastoralists from the Corbett and Rajaji tiger reserves, part of their traditional winter grazing grounds. What especially caused *Down to Earth* to react was the High Court's labelling of the Van Gujjars as 'illegal occupants' and 'encroacher upon forest land' in forests where they have lived for centuries (ibid.). After an intervention by forest rights activists the Supreme Court of India later issued a stay order, resulting in the maintenance of *status quo* (Santoshi, 2018). Status quo in this context means that the Van Gujjars are still in the forest with their animals while continuing to live under very insecure tenure rights, where the threat of eviction is never far away. The eviction order directly affected a couple of hundred pastoral families still dependent on the forest within the tiger reserves for their livelihood, but indirectly the threat of eviction and being labelled as 'illegal encroachers' affect all Van Gujjar families, still subsisting as pastoralists with their herds of milk buffaloes during winter in the state forest of the Shivalik Foothills in the Central Indian Himalayas.

As an anthropologist I have now followed the Van Gujjars for more than three decades, starting with a pilot study in 1987, and with the most intensive fieldwork period stretching from the late 1980s to the first parts of the 1990s, a period covered in this chapter where many things changed for the community (Gooch, 1992; 1998). Another longer study was conducted between 2008 and 2010 (Farooquee et al., 2011; Gooch and Kaushal, 2011). During fieldwork I have stayed with the Van Gujjars; they have shared their homes and food with me and discussed their situation and worries over the future. Most of the life of Van Gujjars centres on their buffaloes (see Fig. 7.1) as their needs direct the actions of their human caretakers and a large part of my fieldwork was spent with a stick in my hand following buffaloes along narrow forest paths. This

Figure 7.1 Buffaloes are seen as persons with intelligence and agency (Photo: P. Gooch).

means that my interpretation of the situation is to a large degree shaped by my position in the forest, being with the Van Gujjars. It was a position I found muted when I first arrived and which then needed representation (Gooch, 1999). There are, of course, countless other perspectives, other positions, from which the situation and the conflict around the environment and forests in the region may be understood, and I have looked at other perspectives by interviewing differently positioned people such as representatives of NGOs, forest officials, decision makers, academicians, environmental activists and journalists. Though the situation for the pastoral Van Gujjars in the forests of the Central Indian Himalayas is complex and unique, it is also in many ways representative of the situation of forest dwellers, not only in India, but also in other places of the world.

Headlines, such as those I am reading now in August 2018, take me back more than a quarter of a century to the summer of 1992. That year the Van Gujjar families, who had their winter camps in what was then the *proposed* Rajaji National Park, were likewise seen as 'encroachers' in the forest and denied entrance to the park area after returning from the summer pastures in the higher ranges of the Himalaya. This was the beginning of a conflict, which came to give the 'victims of conservation' a human face among the Indian public and which developed into a movement for forest rights and the sustainable management of the forest (Gooch, 1997). It was also the culmination of a conflict that was more than 150 years old, with its roots in colonial times, over the right to livelihood in the forest.

Going back to pre-colonial times we find that the rights to forests and forest produce between different users were regulated through local institutions. However, in the second half of the 19th century, India's forests were taken over by the British colonial administration as Crown land and scientific forest management was introduced (Gooch, 2012). Through the colonial conquest and control the local was drawn into global connections, changing the trees of the Himalayan forests from natural resources for local livelihood needs into produce for commodity chains, supplying material for the growth of the British Imperial power, based on one hand on industrialisation at home and on the other on capital accumulation from the colonies through extraction of raw material. It was also the start of a process of deforestation and change of forest ecosystems as indigenous trees, with multiple uses for local people as well as being important sources of fodder for wildlife were replaced by plantations of trees for commercial use (Stebbing, 1982). As pastoral nomads entirely dependent on access to large stretches of state forest for their livelihood, Van Gujjars were one of the communities hardest hit by colonial policies (Gooch, 2009).

After Independence in 1947 India chose a path of economic development based on modernisation of industry and agriculture advocated by Nehru, rather than the Gandhian way, which favours decentralisation and small-scale rural development (Gooch, 2012). The result was that the degradation of India's natural resources and the disruption of the relationship between nature and local communities accelerated in the decades after independence. Since the structural adjustment in the early 1990s, however, forest management in the Himalayas has undergone a new transformation from commercial forestry to the conservation of nature as more and more forests are now set aside as protected areas. This has brought increasingly more forest under government control on one hand while on the other local people have lost their traditional rights and access over the forest and its natural resources (Farooquee and Maikhuri, 2007). Such policies have led to new conflicts between local communities and government authorities. As their pasture land is increasingly turned into Protected Areas we find that again Van Gujjar pastoralists have been one of the communities hardest hit by government policies.

Pastoralism through Himalayan landscapes

The Van Gujjars have specialised and adjusted pastoral production, to the mountain ecosystem of the Central and Western Himalayas (Gooch, 1998). By means of their buffaloes they transform meadow grass, forest foliage and spring water into the commodities milk and butter through a livelihood practice finely attuned to the ecology of the landscape. One feature of the mountain environment to which they have had to adapt is the seasonal variation in climatic conditions and thereby in the growth of vegetation. As a result, migration is an ecological necessity. The transhumance of the Van Gujjars oscillates between two fixed points in their landscape of pastoral movement: the subtropical mixed forest in the foothills where they stay in winter (see Fig. 7.2), feeding their buffaloes on leaves cut from trees – so-called lopping; and the temperate or sub-alpine spruce and pine forests in the high range adjacent to the *bugiyals*, the alpine pastures, where they go for grazing during summer. In between the two are the migration routes, with their halting places. They have thus adapted their way of life to changes in the season and to the ecological zones at different attitudes of their forest and mountain environment, being at each time of the year in the zone that promises survival for them and their herds. As they rely on a wide variety of indigenous trees as fodder for buffaloes and return to the same places both in their summer and winter pastures they need a forest where biodiversity is maintained. As they are specialised pastoralists with buffalo herding as their sole profession the whole family from the youngest child to the oldest grandmother partake in the circle of transhumance and share work and responsibilities. That women are equally important in production to men has resulted in very strong positions for women within the community (Gooch, 1998).

Through their transhumance the Van Gujjars see themselves as partaking actively in the 'way of the land' and its cyclic changes, characterising themselves as the *aana-jaana-log*, the people coming and going by following the life of nature (*kudrat*) that alternatively provides green fodder in the foothills and in the *bugiyals* (Gooch, 2008). Contrary to many other forest dwellers, and, I think, to about all other pastoralists of the world, the Van Gujjars are mainly

Figure 7.2 Gujjar *dera* (camp) in the foothills of the Shivaliks (Photo: P. Gooch)

vegetarians and they do not see wild predators, such as tigers and leopards, as essentially antagonistic to them and their herds, and they do not seek vengeance when one of their animals is carried off. What they say is that tigers and leopards also belong in the natural order of the forest, and that they – just as the Gujjars and their buffaloes – are part of wildlife and have the right to be there. In order to survive as pastoralists and in order to use the land in a sustainable way, the Van Gujjars have to maintain access to a landscape that allows them to be flexible. However, the opportunities for nomadic pastoralism along the altitudes are rapidly decreasing and many options for flexibility are now either severely curtailed or completely lost.

An epic journey

I spent the summer of 1992 with a group of Van Gujjar families in their summer camp in the alpine pasture of Uttarakhand just below the treeline at about 3,400 meters. Here, I experienced at close range the results of more than 150 years of state forest policies for the community. During the summer I assisted in herding livestock in lush meadows with a rich biodiversity of grasses and herbs, against a stunning background of snow-clad mountains. At the end of the summer I walked back down with them. Prior to leaving the foothills, Gujjars staying in the Rajaji area had been forced by the Forest Department to put their thumb print on a piece of paper saying that they would not be allowed back into the forest when they returned in autumn. They were anxious and worried over an unknown future and what would be their destiny, when it was not the usual all-embracing forest that was waiting to receive them at the end of the track. Most of them were convinced that neither they nor their animals would be able to survive a removal out of the forest. Fakar, an old man, expressed the sentiments of his community thus, 'This [the forest] is my country and everything outside is like another country where I cannot live.' And he continued, 'This is my life and I do not want any other life.' Bibo, a woman who shared her camp with me, put all her hopelessness and despair into the exclamation:

> It would be better if the government just killed us all at once. We have no land [*zamin*] and now they are taking the forest [*jangal*] from us. We have nothing. Even the bear has a better life than we do. It has got somewhere to creep in for the night, but the Gujjars have nowhere. The villagers burn down our huts and the Forest Department [*janglat*] 'eat' money, *ghee* [clarified butter], milk, everything. The government might just as well shoot all of us, children and everybody, and throw us down over the edge of a cliff.[1]

She saw it as a case of complete injustice that in a forest for the bear there was no longer a place for her and her family. For the Van Gujjars the struggle was a question of survival for their culture and way of life, and as Sethi (1993) points out, conflicts dealing with questions of survival raise two sets of issues: those that concern the specific struggle in question, and those related to the nature of the discourse they give rise too. Both these aspects will be looked into here.

Destroyers or protectors

Two contradictory discourses have dominated discussions surrounding the Himalayan environment and the people subsisting on their natural resources (Gooch, 1998). One is the 'Theory of Himalayan Environmental Degradation' depicted as the prediction that the Himalayan region is inevitably drifting into a situation of environmental collapse caused by the alleged population explosion among the mountain people (Ives and Messerli, 1989). As more and more people (and their cattle) are utilising the same common resources of forests and pastures for survival as well as for individual gains, a 'tragedy of the commons' would seem inevitable. The only viable solution to such a scenario would be a strong centralised state controlling the natural environment and its use through state institutions such as the Forest Department. This Malthusian approach became very popular during the 1970s and 1980s and has its most memorable expression through Indira Gandhi's utterance at the Stockholm Conference for the environment in 1972: 'Poverty is the worst pollutant.'

It is the wealthy blaming the rural poor, not only for their own miserable condition, but also for the degrading hills, and ultimately for the environmental catastrophe perceived to be threatening the Gangetic plains below, one of the world's most densely populated regions. Supported by the local conservation lobby and officials of the Indian Forest Department those were the tales that completely dominated the discussion when I first started fieldwork among the pastoral Gujjars (Gooch, 1998). The other approach sees both nature *and* the mountain subsistence peasant as victimised by 'modern development' and supports decentralisation: that local people themselves take over the responsibility for protecting the environment for which they are dependent for survival. Martinez-Alier (2002) has referred to them as 'environmentalists of the poor'. This set of thoughts was supported by Indian social environmental activists, such as the Centre of Science and Environment (CSE) with headquarters in Delhi, and has further developed into a generalised concept through what we may call the assumption of the 'eco-system people'. According to this:

> Eco-system people should be given far greater access to and control over the natural resource base of their own localities. Ecosystem people should also be given an important role in a new, largely decentralised system of governance.... Thus the key Gandhian prescriptions that make perfect sense are that ecosystem people must be empowered (Gadgil and Guha, 1995 p. 118–119).

This pro-people discourse gained importance in the 1990s, and developed into what has been described as the *Standard Narrative* in the early 2000s (Scott, 2001). Both approaches presented above have developed their own imaginaries of *utopias* – or *dystopias*, which have been used as rallying points for political action surrounding the use of natural resources. In one 'people' are seen as external to the ecosystem and the harbingers of environmental *dystopia* while in the other 'people' have been included in the natural processes and are the providers of hope for a future *utopia*.

The arguments contained in those contradictory approaches may be discerned in a third dominant discourse that sees the Himalayan environment as a 'wilderness' to be conserved as parks and sanctuaries. Here, we find that agents – although agreeing on the importance of the endeavour – differ on how conservation may be best achieved. There are three main models for managing protected areas. The adherents of the first line of thought tend to see villagers and forest dwellers as a threat to nature and advocate 'pure conservation' for wildlife but without people in a forest managed scientifically by a state authority such as the Forest Department. This may be seen as the *managerial* discourse (Krishna, 1996). The second approach sees people as the stewards of nature – or even part of nature – and argues for the involvement of local people in the management of national parks and sanctuaries. This would then be the *popular* discourse (ibid.). A compromise between the two is the suggestion that forests should be managed in a joint venture between the Forest Department and local communities (cf. Saxena, 1995).

Dystopia

What I found during fieldwork in the early 1990s was a Van Gujjar community living with their herds on the fringe of Indian society and presented by local authorities within the neo-Malthusian narrative of Himalayan mountain populations as 'destroyers of nature', multiplying beyond the carrying capacity of their forest resource base. In order to illustrate how global mega-narratives have been used to define what is happening at the local level, I use a text by Ashok Kumar (1993), Indian representative of WWF at the time, in which the Van Gujjars were represented as a direct threat to their environment. This text was used politically at the start of the conflict over conservation and the message it delivered was very typical of how the Van Gujjars and their use of the forest was presented by state representatives and by the conservation lobby at the onset of the conflict. Here, the Van Gujjars are used to exemplify the *Theory of the Himalaya-Ganges Problem*. Or, if we see it from the other side, the theory is made to fit the Gujjar case in order to explain why they, by 'scientific necessity', have to leave the forest. It also shows how the conflict over the forest may be perceived from differently situated perspectives. What it describes is a total *dystopia*. Kumar writes:

> To an outsider it may look that Gujjars lead an idyllic life in harmony with their habitat. This is not so. ... the size of Gujjar families and their cattle continue to increase. The question is how long it will take before the Gujjars make their habitat inhospitable for themselves and in the process destroy the Park .... *What is at stake is not merely the nature reserve called the Rajaji National Park* – a wonderland of natural beauty which will be destroyed within a decade. *Also at stake is the way of life in villages and*

agricultural fields immediately to the south of the Shivalik foothills and possibly most of the Upper Gangetic plains. The destruction of the forest cover in the Shivalik hills will lead to severe land erosion, silting of rivers, floods followed by droughts …. *An exploding population* [the Gujjars] *cannot live in harmony with their environment.*

While Ashok Kumar singled out the Van Gujjars as the main threat to the park and the first to be removed, we find that the reality of Rajaji at the time was not quite *the wonderland of natural beauty* made out by him. Like other national parks in India, Rajaji had (and has) a large human population both within the park and in towns and villages on the periphery. As stated by D. Kumar, modern development has also made major encroachments on the park. Among the more significant are: a large army ammunition dump, an army shooting range close by, an electricity plant with an adjoining township, a chemical factory, a railway line, a railway station and several major roads. Apart from this the area has been part of forest development schemes where indigenous species, providing food for wild animals, have been cut down and replaced with plantations of commercially valuable trees (Kumar, 1995). As stated by the Van Gujjar leader Mustooq,

> Why start with us? We are the easiest to remove. But what use is it that we have been removed when the ammunition dump and the industrial plants are still there? Move them first and then you can think about the Gujjars.

Out of the woods

Returning to the caravans of Van Gujjars with the herds on the way down the Himalayas in the fall of 1992, following ancient migration trails now turned into highly trafficked mountain roads, they were anxious and unsure of what awaited them at the end of the trail. However, for them the situation was changing. It was now not just the officials of the Forest Department that were waiting to receive them upon their return. The forest officials – in accordance with a wildlife legislation that advocated nature conservation without people – had closed off all entrances to the Park large enough to let a buffalo slip through, but the predicament of the Gujjars had now also become known beyond the close circles of forest officials. While the Van Gujjars had continued their traditional life of transhumance in the upper Himalayas, the ground had been prepared for discussions highlighting their specific problems. This was the summer of the Rio Earth Summit 1992 where environmental issues were high on national and global agendas as well as in the media. The year 1992 was also the year when America celebrated Columbus' discovery, 500 years earlier, of the 'New World'. The celebration of the 'globalisation of European culture' also sharpened the critique of Western cultural hegemony and became a celebration of its antipodes: the non-western and local in the form of cultural diversity while saving nature, and right to land for indigenous people. This was being expressed through the emergence of strong indigenous movements all over the world and received official global recognition in the UN declaration that 1993 was the year of the indigenous peoples. Coming out of the forest with their herds at the end of the journey the Van Gujjars now stepped into the limelight. Through them the conservation debate – juxtaposing biodiversity and forest dwellers – got a human face in the Indian media.

The role of NGOs as agents of change

Being illiterate and living within the interior of the forest, the Van Gujjars did not have the means to mobilise on their own. Sharing their growing anxiety over an unsure future with me they sent me out of the forest with the message, 'We are jungle log', literally forest people or forest dwellers. 'We belong in the forest and we are not the ones that destroy forest. Tell this to the people outside'. By reacting to this plea my research project turned into 'engaged anthropology', where, for a while, I became an active participant in the 'Van Gujjar story'.

Another consequence of the 1992 Earth Summit was the increasing role of NGOs as representatives for civil society (Pianta, 2005). The one to come to the assistance of the Van Gujjars was Avdesh Kaushal, a well-known environmental and social activist. Kaushal is the chairperson of RLEK (Rural Litigation Kendra), a local NGO placed in Dehradun, the regional capital. Using my research results as inspiration he now turned out as an agent of change in the Van Gujjar conflict over conservation of the forest (RLEK, 1997). He had earlier been the main agent in a high profile local environmental conflict, the limestone case, for which the government had awarded him the prestigious Padam Sri award (Madsen, 1997). He had the necessary connections with key persons within media and local administration, politicians, national environmental NGOs, and also strong connections with decision makers and journalists in Delhi. He now turned out to be the person who could take the conflict to the next level of mobilisation, that is make it leave the interior of the forest and enter national and global scenes. While waiting for the arrival of the Van Gujjars on their way down the mountains he had contacted journalist friends from Delhi and now there were people interested in advocating the Gujjars' position in the conflict waiting for their return.

As a result of the emerging conflict around Rajaji National Park and the attention the Van Gujjar case gained through the media, they were not evicted from their forest in the autumn of 1992. What happened was that the voice of the Van Gujjars which up to then had been muted – never reaching further than the offices of the Forest Department – now emerged as one of the parts in the environmental debate. The message delivered was powerful: an indigenous voice expressing an alternative to existing policies of forestry and nature conservation (Gooch, 2006). The very first meeting of Van Gujjars after facing eviction from the Rajaji Park area was held in the small township of Mohand, on the Delhi/Dehradun Highway in October 1992. It took place under a large tree at the entrance to the proposed park. The forest that had been home to the Van Gujjars for centuries was so close but at that time the Van Gujjars were not allowed to enter it. They were homeless, confused and angry and the atmosphere was naturally agitated but they spoke with force and conviction to the assembled journalists about their age-old ties to the forest and its wildlife. Talib, one of the Van Gujjars threatened with eviction, pointed to the green mass of Rajaji forest behind us and said,

> look, here the Van Gujjars have lived for centuries and the forest is still green, but where other people have lived the forests have gone. How can you then say that it is the Van Gujjars who destroy the forest?

This was the first time the Van Gujjars met representatives from the media. It was also the beginning of the Van Gujjar movement for environmental justice and their right to stay in the forest with their animals. This also made the involvement of new sets of actors in the conflict necessary as NGOs with their social and environmental activists, politicians and the crucial media people joined in support on the Van Gujjars' side of the controversy. Through the movement the pastoral Gujjars also gained a new identity with a new name. Earlier they were just known as Gujjars or as the buffalo-people. Now they would say, 'we are not just Gujjars. We are *Van* (forest) Gujjars'. 'We are the ones who take care of the forest and its wildlife'. What the Van Gujjar movement did was to place an alternative image in the public mind: of a hill community 'traditionally living in harmony with the surrounding environment'. What might be discerned is in reality not just one movement but the grass-roots movement of the Van Gujjars, a very real struggle for their life-world of forest and mountain being drawn into national and global ideological debates on conservation, environmentalism and the rights of indigenous people. However, behind such a shift in perspective there was a fierce political struggle going on over the power over the forest and its natural resources.

One version of the history of the conflict between Van Gujjars and the Forest Department over the proposed Rajaji Park may be illustrated through the images flashed as headlines in national newspapers over a four-year period after the conflict came out in the open in October 1992:

> Gujjars up in arms against eviction (October 1992); 'No more bribes, Gujjars tell foresters' (November 1992); 'Tribal existence vs. a national park', 'Gujjars offer to run Rajaji park' (April 1993); 'Symbiotic relationship of Gujjars and forest should not be disturbed' (August 1993); 'People first, not parks, say NGOs', 'Forest land for forest dweller', 'Conservation by participation, not exclusion' (November 1993); 'Survival of forests and people go together', 'The barefoot botanists' (September 1994); 'Whose forests are they anyway?' (May 1996); 'Gujjars in peril' (November 1995); 'Will Rajaji be the first people's national park?' (January 1996).

These examples are just a small sample of the headlines affecting readers of the English media in India after the conflict over Rajaji. All are fetched from large national dailies, such as *The Times of India, Indian Express, The Observer, The Hindu, The Pioneer, The Statesman, The Telegraph, The Sun* or *The Hindustan Times*, and all of them sympathetic to the Van Gujjars and their case.

As the controversy surrounding Rajaji intensified and was flashed in the national media, a need for an alternative to the existent forest policies emerged. The state's policies – embodied in the Forest Department's management of India's forests – were criticised as anti-people and that made it necessary to come up with a counter-image that would embody a pro-people approach to forest management. In February 1996 – less than four years after the Van Gujjars had been threatened with eviction from their forest – I was invited to partake in a workshop in Dehradun, arranged by RLEK, presenting the *Van Gujjar management plan for Rajaji National Park* (RLEK, 1997).

Imagining a utopia in Himalayan forest

The workshop was held at the National Petroleum Institute and the inauguration ceremony took place in the large central hall with room for more than 400 people (Gooch, 1999). Around 11 0'clock the hall started filling up with people. But what one saw here were not just the usual conference attenders. The people who started pouring in were bearded men in *loongi* and *kurta* with rough blankets in soft red colours thrown over their shoulders and a smaller number of women also wrapped in homespun blankets. Several hundred Van Gujjars had come out of their forests and completely aware of their importance at this occasion they started filling the hall by occupying the front rows first. Quite obviously they had come with a sensation of hope and a new confidence.

As a *Community Forest Management Plan for Protected Areas*, CFM for short (RLEK, 1997), the plan challenged earlier concepts of forest management and has been seen as a *concrete* presentation *of a utopia* (voices at the workshop). According to the plan Van Gujjars should be allowed to actively participate in the management and conservation of the park area in order to secure the survival of their livelihood together with the sustainability of the forest ecosystem. As expressed by Mustooq, a Van Gujjar leader and spokesperson: 'Give the forest to us we will turn it into a diamond' (RLEK, 1997). This was how he presented his people at the conference:

> The Van Gujjars are my brothers and sisters. [Our] relationship with the forest is not a new one. It has been established over the centuries and it is characterised by looking after the trees and looking after the buffaloes. All Van Gujjars share this feeling that if one harms the forest we would want to fight with that enemy. This power is not with us; it is actually with the Forest Department. The Forest Department is making this forest into a

national park that includes the trees and the animals *but nobody thought of including the Van Gujjars*.

A very important part of the message was the establishing of a special Van Gujjar identity close to nature: 'there are many Gujjars in India but we are the Van Gujjars. The Gujjars who have looked after the forest ... have lived in harmony with it' (Mustooq). Or as expressed by Gulam Nabi, another Van Gujjar leader, 'As long as forests have existed the Van Gujjars have lived in them and when everybody else left the Van Gujjars stayed back and continued their work of taking care of the forest and the wild animals'. One of the main aims of the Van Gujjars, as expressed at the workshop and repeated during interactions with the media, was to demonstrate that they are an integral part of their environment, that they are the best guardians of the forests, and that they can protect and regenerate their habitat while using it. What was proposed in the Van Gujjars' movement for the right to stay in the forest was not just an essentialised and '*imagined*' identity but rather an innovative use of pre-existing forms of living within nature that came at the right time to fit into ongoing national and global discourses (Gooch, 2006).

Discussion

After the workshop the Van Gujjars had high hopes for finally obtaining rights to continue pastoralism in the forest. However, in the end what was presented as a *concrete* utopia at the workshop was a path not taken. While the Van Gujjars gained massive support from the media, from many politicians, social activists and even from forest officials, the case was never finally settled in their favour (Gooch, 2009). One reason was that the plan was ahead of its time and that it was not possible to realise it in practice within the regulation of 'The Wildlife (Protection) Act', which banned human activity within the park. A realisation of the plan was also seen as opening a Pandora's box that would give rise to similar demands from other groups threatened with eviction from Protected Areas. As a result, the participatory process of community forest management, demanded in the plan, never really started (see Gooch, 2006). However, all the publicity resulted in a stalemate between the Forest Department and the side supporting the Van Gujjars, with the result that the latter were not immediately evicted from the park area. However, during the last 25 years, most families, earlier staying in Rajaji National Park in winter, have gradually been settled in two colonies outside the park area. As a consequence of the earlier mobilisation in their case, they have not been downright evicted from the forest, rather they have been persuaded by forest officials to take the land offered. This they did as they were told that no other alternative really existed. Still, there are about 200 Van Gujjar families left in Rajaji National Park. These are the families, threatened with eviction, mentioned at the introduction of this chapter. To this come approximately 1,500 Van Gujjar families, still subsisting as pastoralists with their herds of milk buffaloes during winter in the state forest of the Shivalik Forest Division, outside of the park area. For them the tenure is highly insecure but there is no immediate threat of eviction.

In this chapter I have looked at the transformation of the situation for the Van Gujjars during the last quarter of a century. What I found at my first visits were a pastoral people still living within their living green world of forest, or as they said themselves, 'we live behind the veil of forest' (Gooch, 1992). During long periods of fieldwork I followed them during daily life and observed the care with which they treated other living creatures within that world. The Van Gujjars live directly from the natural resources of their forest. They see immediately if anything harms the forest and want to stop that harm (as they used to tell me). For them the conflict over the forest has been not only to protect their livelihood but also the environment surrounding them. Their struggle thus evolved into what Scheidel et al. (2018) have defined as an 'ecological distribution conflict'. During that conflict we saw how they changed from being 'Victims of conservation' to being 'Warriors of sustainability' as they fought for the right to participate in the sustainable management of the forest on which their whole life depends. Today their way of life is threatened (Benanav, 2015) and they are ready to settle down if land for resettlement is offered to them. This is a great loss not only for the Van Gujjars themselves, but also for all of us. Today more than ever we need people like that, people who do not use much of the world's resources, who use them directly, and handle them with great care and concern.

Note

1   All quotations by the Van Gujjars are translated from Hindi.

Acknowledgements

I am grateful to the Swedish Research Council for financial support for my research on pastoralists in Uttarakhand and to all Van Gujjars who shared their camps with me.

References

Asher, M. (2018) 'Van Gujjars a repeat of historical injustice' *Down Earth*, 17 September, www.downtoearth.org.in/blog/forests/van-gujjars-a-repeat-of-historica l-injustice-61655

Benanav, M. (2015) *Himalaya bound: An American's journey with nomads in North India*, Harper Collins, India

Farooquee, N. and Maikhuri, R.K. (2007) 'Role of the state on forests: Case of Uttarakhand', *Economic and Political Weekly*, 42(35), 3537–3540

Farooquee, N., Gooch, P., Maikhuri, R.K. and Agrawal, D.K. (eds) (2011) *Sustainable Pastoralism in the Himalayas*, Indus, New Delhi

Gadgil, M. and Guha, R. (1995) *Ecology and equity: The use and abuse of nature in contemporary India*, Routledge, London and New York

Gooch, P. (1992) 'Transhumant pastoralism in Northern India: The Gujjar case', *Nomadic Peoples* 30: 84–86

Gooch, P. (1997) 'Conservation for whom? Van Gujjar and the Rajaji National Park', in Lindberg, S. and Sverrisson, A. (eds), *Social movements in development*. Macmillan, London, 234–251

Gooch, P. (1998) *At the tail of the buffalo: Van Gujjar pastoralists between the forest and the world arena*, Lund Monograph in Social Anthropology, Lund

Gooch, P. (1999) 'A community management plan: The Van Gujjars and the Rajaji National Park', in Madsen, S.T. (ed.), *State, society and the environment in South Asia*, Curzon Press, Richmond, 79–112

Gooch, P. (2006) 'We are Van Gujjars', in Karlsson, B.G. and Subba, T.B. (eds), *Indigeneity In India*, Kegan Paul, London, New York, Bahrain, 98–116

Gooch, P. (2008) 'Feet following hooves', in Ingold, T. and VergunstJ. L. (eds), *Ways of walking: Ethnography and practice on foot*, Ashgate, London, 67–80

Gooch, P. (2009) 'Victims of conservation or rights as forest dwellers: Van Gujjar pastoralists between contesting codes of law', *Conservation and Society*, 7, 239–248

Gooch, P. and Kaushal, P. (2011) 'Trails towards the unknown', in Farooquee, N., Gooch, P., Maikhuri, R.K. and Agrawal, D.K. (eds), *Sustainable pastoralism in the Himalayas*, Indus, New Delhi, 102–119

Gooch, P. (2012) 'Trees: Conflicts between pastoralists, loggers and conservationists in the Himalayas' in Hornborg, A., Clark, B. and Hermele, K. (eds), *Ecology and power: Struggles over land and material resources in the past, present, and future*, Routledge, London, New York, 194–205Ives, J.D. and Messerli, B. (1989) *The Himalayan dilemma: Reconciling development and conservation*, Routledge, London and New York

Krishna, S. (1996) 'The environmental discourse in India: New directions in development', in Sathyamurthy, T.V., (ed.), *Class formation and political transformation*, Vol. 4, Oxford University Press, Delhi

Kumar, A. (1993) 'Gujjars eat away the heart of Rajaji', in *Indian Express*, 15 January 1993

Kumar, D. (1995) *Management plan of Rajaji National Park* Vols 1 and 2, Rajaji National Park, Dehradun

Madsen, S.T. (1997) 'Between people and the state: NGOs as troubleshooters and innovators', in LindbergS. and Sverrisson, A. (eds), *Social movements in development*, Macmillan, London, 252–273

Martinez-Alier, J. (2002) *The environmentalism of the poor: A study of ecological conflicts and valuation*, Edward Elgar Publishing, Cheltenham

Pianta, M. (2005) *UN world summits and civil society: The state of the art*, Civil Society and Social Movements Programme, Paper Number 18, United Nations Research Institute for Social Development, August 2005

RLEK (1997) *Community forest management in protected areas: Van Gujjar proposal for the Rajaji area*, Natraj Publishers, Dehradun

Santoshi, N., (2018), 'Supreme Court directs status quo on relocation of Van Gujjars', *Hindustan Times*, Nainitalwww.hindustantimes.com/dehradun/supreme-court-directs-status-quo-on-relocation-of-van-gujjars/story-jRe4EZIiRF5HYsS5CFLzTM.html

Saxena, N.C. (1995) *Forests, people and profit: New equations for sustainability*, Natraj Publishers, Dehradun

Scheidel, A., Tember, L., Demaria, F. and Martinez-Alier, J. (2018) 'Ecological distribution conflicts as forces for sustainability: An overview and conceptual framework', *Sustainability Science* 13, 585–598

Scott, J.C., 2001, 'Foreword', in Agrawal, A. and Sivaramakrishnan, K. (eds), *Social nature: Resources, representations and rule in India*, Oxford University Press, New Delhi, vii–viii

Sethi, H. (1993) 'Survival and democracy: Ecological struggles in India', in Wignaraja, P. (ed.), *New social struggles in the South: Empowering the people*, Vistaar Publication, New Delhi

Stebbing, E.P. (1982) [1922] *The forests of India*, Vol. 1, A.J. Reprints Agency, New Delhi

8 Undermining the resource ground

Extractive violence on Laevas and Adnyamathanha land

Kristina Sehlin MacNeil

Introduction

On my very first visit to Laevas reindeer herding Sami community I briefly met with the community's board and a few potential research participants. The conversation quickly turned to problems the community was facing, as their grazing lands were quickly diminishing due to intrusions by extractive industries, such as forestry and mining. One person turned to me and said: 'I cannot explain to you, in your language, why that particular piece of land is so important to me.' That sentence has stayed with me throughout the years as my understanding of extractivism, Indigenous connections to land and the conflicted and violent structures that frame it all, has evolved. The significance lies not in the issue of languages, but rather in differing worldviews, in different perspectives on what land is and how it should be treated. As I worked with the Adnyamathanha group these perspectives were clearly articulated and connections between language and land were also highlighted. Both the Laevas and Adnyamathanha research participants described, albeit in different ways, what Stammler and Ivanova (2016, p. 60) call partnership logic, where Indigenous peoples live in reciprocal relationships with land and resources. Both Laevas and Adnyamathanha research participants expressed that connection to land was paramount and permeated all aspects of life. Furthermore, this connection was also seemingly invisible to the extractive industries and various industrial proponents, including governments, that continued to threaten and sever Laevas and Adnyamathanha lands. As some Indigenous people are intrinsically linked to their lands, threatening or destroying land also means threatening or destroying health and well-being (Reid and Taylor, 2011). This chapter draws on two case studies to explore conflicts related to natural resource exploitation, experienced by Laevas reindeer herding Sami community in northern Sweden and Adnyamathanha Traditional Owners[1] in South Australia. The relationships between people and land, described by the groups of research participants, as well as the asymmetric power structures that enable extractivism to flourish in their areas, constitutes the foundation for the concept of *extractive violence* (Sehlin MacNeil, 2018; Sehlin MacNeil, 2017). This will be further explored in the following section.

Extractive violence on Indigenous country

The pressures placed on Indigenous peoples all over the world, in relation to resource extraction, has a long history. With large scale colonisation of the Americas, Africa and Asia, the idea of extracting goods from lands conquered and colonised, in order to ship the riches back to the motherland started over 500 years ago (Acosta, 2013; Loomba, 2015). In a world where extractivist and neoliberal ideologies have become the norm, resource exploitation is most often seen as the way forward or the progressive path (Howlett et al., 2011). Not only does this mean that other perspectives on land and resource management are often ignored, there is also an assumption that Indigenous peoples would be better off if they simply adhere to the dominant perspectives. Whereas it may be correct to argue that extractivism and neoliberalism, in some places, have created room for Indigenous groups to exercise agency and participate in resource development, this still does not necessarily mean participation on equal terms. On the contrary, it can require Indigenous groups to abandon their perspectives on land and heritage protection and to adopt the perspectives stemming from the very colonial practices that created the asymmetric power relations to begin with.

Bufacchi (2017) argues that colonialism *was* inherently violent as he lists brutal assaults perpetrated by colonisers on colonised peoples. Bufacchi's (2017, p. 203) definition of violence is

> when the integrity or unity of a subject (person or animal) or object (property) is being intentionally or unintentionally violated, as a result of an action or an omission. The violation may occur at the physical or psychological level, through physical or psychological means.

Although colonialism as international practice was rejected by the UN in 1960, the injustice it has caused is far from forgotten in international relations (Lu, 2011). In light of Bufacchi's view of violence I would argue that colonialism and the structures it built and left behind *is* still inherently violent. As Tuhiwai Smith (2012, p. 101) points out: to Indigenous peoples colonialism is not finished. The asymmetric power relations, described by Galtung (1969; Galtung and Fischer, 2013, p. 38) as structural violence, where the 'topdog' exploits the 'underdog', persist for Indigenous peoples. In asymmetric conflicts, where the problem lies in the relationship structure, rather than specific issues dividing the parties, it is never in the interest of the party with excess power to change the structure (Ramsbotham et al., 2011, p. 24). The party that holds the most power always wins and the party with less power always loses.

Galtung's (1996) model, known as the violence triangle, is useful for understanding how these structures affect Indigenous peoples in conflict with extractive industries. The violence triangle includes structural, cultural and direct violence, one at each tip. Direct violence is physical or psychological violence that affects the body. Structural violence is understood as unjust power structures where some have much and others have little; it shows up as discriminatory societal systems. Cultural violence is described as culture that justifies the structural and even direct violence and is demonstrated as discriminatory ideas and attitudes. (For more reading on the violence triangle see for example Galtung, 1969; 1990; 1996).

In both case studies included in this chapter structural and cultural violence were clearly present. However, direct violence, according to Galtung's definition was not. Yet, the many hours of interviews, where the participants shared their experiences and perspectives conveyed a sense of urgency when it came to the threat of and actual destruction of land. It seemed clear that the research participants experienced a form of direct violence directed at and felt in them, through the destruction of their lands. In order to explain this I modified Galtung's violence triangle to include the concept of *extractive violence,* which replaced direct violence at the third tip (see Fig. 8.1). My definition of extractive violence is 'A type of direct violence against nature and/or people and animals that is caused by extractivism and that primarily affects peoples closely connected to land.' (Sehlin MacNeil, 2017, p. 23; Sehlin MacNeil, 2018). In order to understand extractive violence, it is necessary to first explore Indigenous connection to Country. Here it should be mentioned that not all Indigenous people have or share connections to Country; however, the research participants of this particular study all discussed and described connection to land.

In Australia the connection between Aboriginal people and their land is commonly known as connection to Country. The term Country is explained by Kowal (2015, p. 194) as 'a wider term than "land" or "area", describing a living, creative entity with a deep ongoing relationship with the humans responsible for it, rather than the passive piece of territory typically part of Western imaginations of land.' When it comes to Adnyamathanha people the spiritual relationship or connection between people and Country is known as Muda (Marsh, 2010, p. 124). Although the Laevas participants did not discuss a particular word for this connection, Stoor (2017, p. 202) describes how yoik, Sami song, has a similar way of connecting people and land. Regarding the perception of land being more than just the ground one walks on, there were many similarities in the Laevas and Adnyamathanha participants' descriptions of

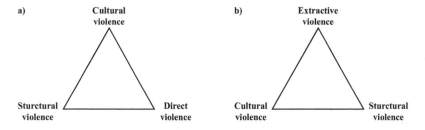

Figure 8.1 Galtung's (Galtung, 1990, p. 294) original model (a) and my modification where extractive violence replaces direct violence (b)

their connections to their lands. Therefore, in this chapter the term *connection to Country* will be used to describe both Adnyamathanha and Sami connections to land. Connection to Country as described by Indigenous scholars and writers, involves a deep understanding of the land, its resources and how people are indistinguishable from their lands (Arbon, 2008; Marsh, 2013; Liddle, 2015). This understanding of humanity's place in relation to land and the resources it harbours stands in stark contrast to extractivism where the sole purpose is to break the ground in order to extract resources and produce goods. Where Indigenous connections to Country, like Muda or Sami yoik, inform us that human beings are part of the system that is Earth and cannot rule over it, extractivist ideologies tell us the opposite. It is within this complicated and conflicted relationship, between Indigenous groups and extractive industries, that the following case studies are located.

Asymmetric power relations in Sweden and Australia

The two case studies, included in this chapter, were conducted with Adnyamathanha Traditional Owners in South Australia in 2014–2015 and with Laevas reindeer herding Sami community in northern Sweden in 2013–2014 (Sehlin MacNeil, 2015; 2016). The Adnyamathanha group consisted of seven research participants of varying ages, four women and three men. The Sami group consisted of six research participants at the onset of the project, four men and two women of varying ages. Both communities had extensive experiences of extractivism on their lands, which was the main reason for why they were approached and asked to participate in the project. The methodological framework was the same for both case studies and included data collection through a number of semi-structured interviews, conducted as yarning sessions (yarning is an interview method focused on relationship building, for further reading see for example Bessarab and Ng'andu, 2010; Dean, 2010; Fredericks et al., 2011). In analysing the data a thematic approach was used to identify main themes (Ehn and Löfgren, 2001). The themes were then analysed using concepts from Galtung's violence triangle with the inclusion of extractive violence. Ethical considerations were addressed not only through formal ethics applications completed at Swedish and Australian universities but also through agreed ethical protocols between researcher and research participants as well as my firm commitment to honouring the research participants' voices and perspectives. Through the inclusion of critical and Indigenous methodologies the research rests on three ethical cornerstones: Respect, Reciprocity and Relationships (Archibald, 2008; Reid and Taylor, 2011; Sehlin MacNeil and Marsh, 2015; Sehlin MacNeil, 2017; Wilson, 2001).

Nuclear waste on Adnyamathanha Country

Aboriginal and Torres Strait Islander peoples have lived in Australia for between 50,000 and 65,000 years. Theirs are the oldest living cultures in the world. Aboriginal Australians lived with the land, in ways that suited both Country and people. Rather than developing agricultural economies, which would have made them vulnerable to droughts and extreme climate conditions common to this particular continent, they developed foraging economies. It is believed that Aboriginal people in Australia spent as little as three hours per day gathering food, which left ample time for socialising and developing the spiritual connection with land that signify Aboriginal cultures, sometimes called Dreaming in English. This way a holistic and sustainable relationship between humans and Country was created (see for example Broome, 2010; Gammage, 2011; Marsh, 2010).

In 1788 the British claimed Australia, calling the continent 'waste and uninhabited' (Reynolds, 2003, p. 5). One of Australia's Indigenous peoples, Adnyamathanha are descendants of a number of dialect groups whose traditional land is in and around the South Australian Flinders Ranges (Marsh, 2013). For Adnyamathanha people it took many years until colonialism had any great impact on their communities. However, by the 1850s, settlers had moved onto Adnyamathanha Country, bringing sheep and cattle, thus pushing the natural fauna off the land and also cutting Adnyamathanha people off from their water supplies. When adapting to the new situation and hunting the new animals for food, Adnyamathanha people were often fired upon by settlers and police (Brock, 1993). The extensive knowledge held by Adnyamathanha people about their Country – and the fact that sacred sites often were connected to riches in the ground – was also exploited by settlers, who soon started to mine Aboriginal sites for minerals (Brock, 1993; Marsh, 2010).

In 1995 a number of Adnyamathanha persons initiated a Native Title process and since March 2009 Adnyamathanha have held non-exclusive native title rights, including rights to fish, hunt, camp and live in the area, protect heritage sites, conduct ceremonies and use natural resources, over parts of their land (Federal Court of Australia 2009). Australia's Native Title Act of 1993 (amended in 1997) recognises Indigenous rights to land but has been widely questioned and criticised for undermining Indigenous land rights rather than strengthening them (Cleary, 2014; Dodson, 2004; O'Faircheallaigh, 2016).

In 2015 Adnyamathanha people found themselves facing two parallel processes around proposed nuclear waste repositories in South Australia and on Adnyamathanha Country. Adnyamathanha land is already mined for uranium at the Beverly Uranium and the Beverly Four Mile mines, both heavily resisted by Adnyamathanha people whose cultural knowledge informs them about the dangers of the mineral (Marsh, 2010). The proposed nuclear waste repositories presented a new form of extractive activity where the ground would be broken and used to store dangerous waste for an almost unforeseeable future. While the Australian Government called for nominations for possible sites to host a national nuclear waste repository, the South Australian Government initiated the Nuclear Fuel Cycle Royal Commission (NFCRC) with the mission to investigate how South Australia could further benefit from the nuclear fuel cycle (Australian Government Department of Industry, Innovation and Service, 2017; NFCRC, 2016a). Part of the NFCRC investigation was the suggestion that South Australia become host to an international high-level nuclear waste repository where other countries could pay to store their nuclear waste

(NFCRC, 2016a). During 2015–2016 I worked with a group of Adnya-mathanha Traditional Owners in order to investigate their experiences of interactions with both the Australian and the South Australian Governments and government consultation processes around the nuclear waste dumps (Sehlin MacNeil, 2016).

In the narratives shared by the research participants three main themes could be identified as recurring and of particular importance: consultation and Free, Prior and Informed Consent; culture and power of language; and the right to Country.

Community consultation was a major issue brought up in the yarning ses-sions. The research participants pointed out that the two processes, run by the Australian (federal) and South Australian (state) Governments respectively, were difficult for community members to separate as they were conducted at the same time and the same consultant was employed to work with both processes. The confusion this created meant that some community members were not fully able to participate in consultations. Other breaches to Free, Prior and Informed Consent (FPIC) were highlighted by the research participants as lack of language services in consultations and lack of appropriate information about the consultation processes. When the Traditional Owners voiced their concerns to the government representatives they were ignored.

The second main theme explored was linked to culture and language. The research participants explained that their language, Yura Ngawarla, was central to the community's knowledge systems and thus there was a strong need to be able to have a say in Yura Ngawarla. Despite this and the fact that the NFCRC Tentative Findings clearly stated that language services should be provided for Aboriginal communities, there were no interpretation services available (NFCRC, 2016b, p. 22). Furthermore, there was no plain English information about the nuclear processes provided, rather the information was technical and not comprehensive to all, resulting in community members feeling alienated and not able to fully participate.

The third main theme, the right to Country, involved the research partici-pants' concerns about native title and heritage protection. As the group con-sisted of seven individuals, different views on land management were presented; however, the participants were remarkably consistent in stressing the impor-tance of protecting Adnyamathanha Country and their connection to it. When it came to native title several participants said that while native title had given the community some power, it was a framework prone to corruption and one that could be used by extractive industries or governments to divide and rule the community. For instance, government representatives had been known to approach individuals rather than the community.

Laevas and LKAB – cooperation or coercion?

Similar to Aboriginal and Torres Strait Islander peoples in Australia, Sami people are subjected to the effects of colonialism, passed and present. Sápmi, the Sami homeland, covers parts of Norway, Finland, Sweden and Russia where the Sami are ethnic minorities as well as an Indigenous people (Hansen and Olsen, 2006). Thus the borders drawn by nation states do not necessarily reflect Sami worldviews. In this chapter, when Sápmi is used, it refers to the part of Sápmi that exists within the borders of the Swedish nation state. Whereas no one would think of denying the colonisation of Australia, the official position in Sweden has been that Sápmi was not colonised (Fur, 2013; Johansson, 2008; Össbo, 2014). Rather a discussion about colonialism has been avoided by use of the Blue Water Thesis, which states that a coloniser must be geographically removed from the colony – hence, colonisation cannot happen within a country (Johansson, 2008). Therefore, the official position in Sweden has built on a view of coexistence between Sami and Swedes, rather than Swedes colonising Sami lands. In recent years this view has become increasingly challenged (see for example Bränn-lund, 2015, p.16; Lantto and Mörkenstam, 2015, p. 47; Reimerson, 2015, p. 23; Svonni, 2015, p. 902; Össbo, 2014, p. 53).

One of the colonial constructs that affect all Sami people in Sweden are the regulations of how, where and by whom reindeer husbandry can be carried out through the Reindeer Grazing Act (SOU, 2006, p. 14). It is estimated that there are 20,000–40,000 Sami people in Sweden. There are 51 reindeer grazing Sami communities and there are 4,677 Sami reindeer owners in Sweden (Sápmi, 2017). This means that a vast majority of Sami people in Sweden are involved in reindeer husbandry. Reindeer husbandry and the reindeer are closely connected to land, language, Sami knowledge, culture, society and history (Stoor, 2017). However, with the present regulations the reindeer herding communities are under massive pressure. Extractive industries and extractive activity disturbances often cut off the reindeer migratory routes. The animals move in herds and with the seasons, from forest lands in the winter to mountainous areas in the summer. When these migratory patterns are disturbed the animals can get agitated and confused which in turn can affect reproduction among other things (Skarin et al., 2015). It should be mentioned that there are many more disturbances affecting reindeer and reindeer husbandry including predators and climate change.

Laevas reindeer herding Sami community is, like all reindeer herding Sami communities in Sweden, both an economic association and a specific geographical area. The community annually elects a board and community members can engage in reindeer herding within the designated area (Löf, 2014, p. 45). Laevas reindeer grazing land in the north of Sweden stretches along the north side of the Kalix River and covers some of the Kiruna area. Kiruna is home to the world's largest underground iron ore mine, run by the Swedish government-owned mining company, LKAB. In 2016 LKAB reported revenue of more than 16 billion Swedish kronor and the company employed 4,200 people in 13 countries (LKAB, 2017). LKAB has a very strong standing in Kiruna as a large employer and Nilsson (2009, p. 9) describes how locals call the mine mother, aunty or the hand that feeds.

Similar to the situation experienced by Adnyamathanha people, the power relations between Laevas and LKAB were clearly asymmetric. While LKAB had been mining iron on Laevas grazing lands for over 100 years the Sami community had never received any compensation for destruction of land or loss of time due to consultations. In 2012–2013 Laevas made an effort to change this and achieve an agreement with LKAB, in order to receive some compensation. The agreement was finalised in the summer of 2013.

At the same time a conflict between mining protestors (some of them Sami) and a mining company had erupted further south in Gállok or Kallak, outside of Jokkmokk. The mining conflict in Gállok made headlines all over the world and the severe effects of mining on reindeer herding Sami communities in Sweden were made visible to the general public (Cocq, 2014; Sehlin MacNeil and Lawrence, 2017; Sjöstedt Landén, 2017). While mining on reindeer grazing land was debated in the media the Sami Parliament in Sweden released a statement declaring that it could not accept any more exploitation in Sápmi, as mining in Sápmi should be considered human rights offences (Sametinget, 2013). Shortly after the Sami Parliament published its statement, an article was published in the Swedish national tabloid, Aftonbladet. It was headlined: We have different interests but we can cooperate. The subheading stated: Mines can grow without threatening reindeer herding or tourism (Kuhmunen et al., 2013. Author's own translation). Among others the article was signed by the chair of Laevas reindeer herding Sami community and the CEO of LKAB, making it seem like Laevas was open to mining on its lands and actively contradicted the Sami Parliament.

The article was a product related to the agreement signed between Laevas and LKAB. Upon signing the agreement, LKAB presented a finished text to be published in Aftonbladet, in order to communicate to the public about the agreement. While the Laevas representatives did not object to communicating publicly about the agreement – for them it could possibly help reinforce the fact that they should receive compensation – they objected to some of the article's content, as they did not agree with the message it conveyed. The Laevas representative in charge decided not to sign it. Pressure was then applied by LKAB and in the end, after making some changes to the article, the Laevas board agreed to sign. However, they never saw the headlines, had limited insight into the final content and neither did they know that the chair of Laevas would be shown as one of the top signatures, indicating that he was a primary author.

The case study involving Laevas reindeer herding Sami community centres on the research participants' experiences of the process around the creation and publication of the Aftonbladet's article. Three main themes were identified in the interviews: power relations between Laevas and LKAB; the timing of the article; and divide and rule tactics used by the mining industry.

The power relations between LKAB and Laevas are extremely asymmetric and the research participants described how they often felt uncomfortable criticising LKAB as the company had such a strong standing in the region. They feared the conditions for reindeer herding would become even worse if they would 'go against' the mining company. Because of these unbalanced power relations the research participants felt a need for the interactions with the mining industry to be strategic. They discussed how it could be better not to protest a proposed mine that was going to be opened on an old mining site as that ground was already broken and it might give them a stronger case for resisting other proposed mines on unbroken ground.

The timing of the article was the second main theme. The pressure applied by LKAB to publish the article at once was described by one of the research participants as Laevas being 'steamrolled'. The research participants further discussed the timing of the article as crucial for LKAB and the Swedish state, as the mining protests in Gállok were calling attention to the effects of mining on reindeer herding. Pictures on television showed police forcibly removing elderly Sami, peacefully protesting the destruction of their traditional lands and livelihoods. The research participants believed the article was designed to stifle the mining debate and that was the reason for the rushed publication. The Laevas representative in charge explained how his only opportunity to edit the final version was to have it read to him over the phone while he was working in remote Norway.

The third and final theme explored involved divide and rule tactics used by the mining industry. Following the publication of the article in Aftonbladet, the Laevas board members were inundated by angry messages and phone calls from fellow reindeer herders. They found themselves in a situation where they had to spend time trying to rectify a situation of internal unrest, created for them by LKAB. For Laevas the incident caused great stress and discomfort as well as damaged relationships. The research participants discussed this as a way for a mining company to divide and rule.

Violence present in the system

The two case studies, involving two groups of Indigenous people on opposite sides of the world, share some similarities. Both the Adnyamathanha and Laevas groups found themselves caught in asymmetric structures with unbalanced power relations making their situations unfavourable. Galtung (1969, p. 175) suggests 'the general formula behind structural violence is inequality'. Thus both cases contain the general formula for structural violence. More specifically Galtung (1996, p. 199) describes structural violence as exploitation with *penetration* (where the party with excess power 'implants' their perspectives in the party with less power), *segmentation* (where the party with excess power keeps information from the party with less power), *marginalisation* (where the party with excess power keeps the party with less power 'on the outside') and *fragmentation* (where the party with excess power keeps the party with less power divided and apart) as components. Therefore, in the Adnyamathanha case study, structural violence was evidenced through lack of communication about the processes to the community; lack of comprehensive or Yura Ngawarla or plain English information to the community; lack of interpretation or language services; blurred boundaries between state and federal processes; and government representatives approaching individuals rather than the community. In the Laevas case structural violence was evidenced through lack of insight into the process around the creation and publishing of the article; the Laevas representative being forced to edit the text over the phone because of time constraints; and the damage that the article caused to relationships for Laevas.

According to Galtung (1990, p. 292) cultural violence is 'the way in which the act of direct violence and the fact of structural violence are legitimized and thus rendered acceptable in society.' In other words, cultural violence can be described as discriminatory and racist ideas and attitudes that underpin unjust societal structures and violent actions. In the Adnyamathanha case cultural violence was visible through Australian colonial attitudes to Indigenous land rights and Aboriginal connections to Country, exemplified in both the state and federal nuclear processes. Rigney (1999, p. 111) states 'racism in all forms is deeply entrenched in Australian society.' Supported by the findings of several official reports, Rigney (1999, p. 111) further states that Indigenous Australians experience racism in most aspects of their lives. Similarly, scholars have argued that present day discrimination of Sami in Sweden stems from racist and colonial attitudes constructed in the late 19th and early 20th centuries (see for example Lantto, 2012; Mörkenstam, 1999; Nordin, 2002; Åhrén, 2008). Cultural violence in the Laevas case was evidenced by the attitudes that the Sami community did not need opportunities for equal participation in the creation of the article or equal decision-making power when it came to editing the content and publishing the text.

These manifestations of cultural and structural violence, in both cases, underpin the extractive violence experienced by both groups. One of the Laevas research participants shared the effects of seeing the mining area every day: 'This mining project is like a wet hand weighing down on us the whole time ... It affects our hopes for the future and that affects my children very strongly.' On the other side of the world, the Adnyamathanha group shared their views on mining with one research participant saying: 'Mining companies will never understand us ... They understand what they want to do and what they want to get out of it. They don't care about us.' Extractive violence in the Adnyamathanha case was evidenced through the threat of destruction to sacred sites, would the proposed nuclear waste dumps go ahead. In the Laevas case extractive violence was demonstrated through the ongoing mining activities undertaken by LKAB that continue to interfere with reindeer herding. Through the modified violence triangle, where cultural, structural and extractive violence are at interplay with each other, we can see that these two groups, although from opposite sides of the world and with very different conditions, share certain experiences. Cultural violence, in both cases, is demonstrated by Indigenous perspectives not being regarded as important as extractivism. Indigenous perspectives on wanting to protect and maintain land the way that it is can instead be viewed as backwards or unreasonable, particularly when posed against arguments such as extractive industries creating jobs and saving remote towns. These attitudes underpin asymmetric power structures and structural violence, ensuring that Indigenous groups have less power than extractive industries, and in turn enabling the extractive violence as threats to or actual destruction of land due to extractive activities.

Conclusion

All over the world Indigenous peoples are calling attention to the detrimental effects of extractivism and natural resource exploitation on their countries and communities (Hilson, 2002; Lewis, 2016; Åhrén, 2016). Some conflicts between Indigenous groups and extractive industries have led to severe human rights abuses including murders and forced displacement (Acosta, 2013). While this type of direct physical violence does not necessarily occur in all situations, the violence committed to Country through extractive activities can have grave impacts on Indigenous people and communities. Investigating the relationships between Indigenous groups and extractivism through the remodelled violence triangle allows us to see the different dimensions of these conflicts and the asymmetric power relations experienced by Indigenous peoples. This unequal power distribution has historical roots and can be traced back to the start of colonialism.

This chapter builds on two single case studies performed with research participants from Laevas reindeer herding Sami community in northern Sweden and Adnyamathanha Traditional Owners in South Australia. The analysis shows that both groups were subjected to prejudice attitudes as well as discriminating societal structures that enabled a continuing threat of extractivism on their respective lands. These attitudes and structures were identified as cultural and structural violence. The threat or action of extractivism on Indigenous land was identified as extractive violence.

Subjecting Indigenous groups to cultural, structural and extractive violence, not only threatens cultures, traditions, histories and languages, but also extensive knowledge about how to manage our planet in sustainable ways. Both groups of research participants pointed out, albeit in different ways, that in their view people are part of the land and are thus responsible for protecting and sustaining it. Contrary to the message that LKAB wanted to convey in the Laevas case, new mines cannot grow without threatening reindeer herding. For Adnyamathanha people the proposed nuclear waste dumps threatened to sever land holding their story and song lines and destroying Muda (Booth, 2016). These are perspectives that should be included and heard by industries and decision-makers when proposing extractive activities on Indigenous lands. Any genuine efforts to achieve conflict transformation between extractive industries and Indigenous peoples would need to include interactions on equal terms. This means making changes to asymmetric power structures, promoting sustainable long-term relationships and abandoning the assumption that Indigenous peoples should adopt dominant perspectives and 'catch up' to their extractivist or Western opponents.

Note

1 Traditional Owners are Indigenous Australians who as members of descent groups have certain rights and responsibilities in relation to land or sea (see for example Marsh, 2013).

References

Acosta, A. (2013) 'Extractivism and neoextractivism: Two sides of the same curse', in LangM. and Mokrani, D. (eds), *Beyond development: Alternative visions from Latin America*, Transnational Institute/Rosa Luxemburg Foundation, Quito/Amsterdam, 61–86

Åhrén, C. (2008) *Am I a genuine Sami? An ethnological study of identity-work by young Sami*, PhD thesis, Umeå University

Åhrén, M. (2016) *Indigenous peoples' status in the International legal system*, Oxford University Press, Oxford, UK

Arbon, V. (2008) *Arlathirnda Ngurkarnda Ityirnda: Being – knowing – doing: De-colonising Indigenous tertiary education*, Post Pressed, Teneriffe, QLD, Australia

Archibald, J-A. (2008) *Indigenous storywork: Educating the heart, mind, body and spirit*, UBC Press, Vancouver

Australian Government Department of Industry, Innovation and Service (2017) http://www.radioactivewaste.gov.au

Bessarab, D. and Ng'andu, B. (2010) 'Yarning about yarning as a legitimate method in Indigenous research', *International Journal of Critical Indigenous Studies*, 3(1), 37–50

Booth, M. (2016) 'Fears nuclear dump will end their story' *The Australian*http://www.theaustralian.com.au/national-affairs/Indigenous/fears-nuclear-dump-will-end-their-story/news-story/0bf29b3b919547bad0c797ac1b9a4631

Brännlund, I. (2015) *Histories of reindeer husbandry resilience: Land use and social networks of reindeer husbandry in Swedish Sápmi 1740–1920*, PhD thesis, Umeå University

Brock, P. (1993) *Outback ghettos: Aborigines, institutionalisation and survival*, Cambridge University Press, Cambridge, UK

Broome, R. (2010) *Aboriginal Australians: A history since 1788*, 4th edition, Allen & Unwin, Crows Nest, Australia

Bufacchi, V. (2017) 'Colonialism, injustice, and arbitrariness', *Journal of Social Philosophy*, 48(2), 197–211

Cleary, P. (2014) 'Native title contestation in Western Australia's Pilbara region', *International Journal for Crime, Justice and Social Democracy*, 3(3), 132–148

Cocq, C. (2014) 'Kampen om Gállok: platsskapande och synliggörande', *Kulturella perspektiv: Svensk etnologisk tidskrift*, 23(1), 5–12

Dean, C. (2010) 'A yarning place in narrative histories', *History of Education Review*, 39(2), 6–13

Dodson, M. (2004) 'Indigenous Australians', in ManneR. (ed.), *The Howard years*, Black Inc, Melbourne, Australia, 119–143

Ehn, B. and Löfgren, O. (2001) *Kulturanalyser*, Gleerups, Malmö, Sweden

Federal Court of Australia (2009) *Adnyamathanha No 1 Native Title Claim Group v The State of South Australia (No 2) [2009] FCA 359*30 March 2009http://www.austlii.edu.au/au/cases/cth/FCA/2009/359.html

Fredericks, B.L., Adams, K., Finlay, S., Fletcher, G., Andy, S., Briggs, L., Briggs, L. and Hall, R. (2011) 'Engaging the practice of yarning in Action Research', *Action Learning and Action Research Journal*, 17(2), 7–19

Fur, G. (2013) 'Colonialism and Swedish history: Unthinkable connections?', in Naum, M. and NordinJ.M. (eds), *Scandinavian colonialism and the rise of modernity*, Springer, New York, 17–36

Galtung, J. (1969) 'Violence, peace, and peace research', *Journal of Peace Research*, 6(3), 167–191

Galtung, J. (1990) 'Cultural violence', *Journal of Peace Research*, 27(3), 291–305

Galtung, J. (1996) *Peace by peaceful means*, Sage, London

Galtung, J. and Fischer, D. (2013) *Johan Galtung pioneer of peace research*, Springer, Heidelberg/New York/Dordrecht/London

Gammage, B. (2011) *The biggest estate on Earth. How Aborigines made Australia*, Allen & Unwin, Crows Nest, Australia

Hansen, L.I. and Olsen, B. (2006) *Samernas historia fram till 1750*, Liber, Stockholm

Hilson, G. (2002) 'An overview of land use conflicts in mining communities', *Land Use Policy*, 19, 65–73

Howlett, C., Seini, M., McCallum, D. and Osborne, N. (2011) 'Neoliberalism, mineral develoment and Indigenous people: A framework for analysis', *Australian Geographer*, 42(3), 309–323

Johansson, P. (2008) *Samerna – ett ursprungsfolk eller en minoritet? En studie av svensk samepolitik 1986–2005*, PhD thesis, Göteborgs universitet

Kowal, E. (2015) 'Welcome to Country: Acknowledgement, belonging and white anti-racism', *Cultural Studies Review*, 21(2), 173–204

Kuhmunen, L-E., Huuva, T-E., Nilsdotter, K., Wollmén, M., Ruder, L. and Aaro, L-E. (2013) 'Vi har olika intressen men vi kan samverka' (Eng. We have different interests but we can cooperate), *Aftonbladet*, 31 August 2013

Lantto, P. (2012) *Lappväsendet: Tillämpningen av svensk samepolitik 1885–1971*, Centre for Sami Research, Umeå University, Umeå, Sweden

Lantto, P. and Mörkenstam, U. (2015) 'Sametingets historiska och politiska kontext', in Nilsson, R., Dahlberg S. and Mörkenstam U. (eds), *Sametingsval: Väljare, partier och media*, Santérus, Stockholm, 45–76

Lewis, C. (2016) 'Indigenous peoples and the corporate responsibility to respect human rights', in LennoxC. and ShortD. (eds), *Handbook of Indigenous peoples' rights*, Routledge, New York, 201–222

Liddle, C. (2015) 'Why a connection to country is so important to Aboriginal communities', NITV, 22 October 2015http://www.sbs.com.au/nitv/article/2015/10/22/why-connection-country-so-important-aboriginal-communities

LKAB (2017) 'LKAB in brief' https://www.lkab.com/en/about-lkab/lkab-in-brief/

Löf, A. (2014) *Challenging adaptability: Analysing the governance of reindeer husbandry in Sweden*, PhD thesis, Umeå University

Loomba, A. (2015) *Colonialism/Postcolonialism*, 3rd edition, Routledge, London and New York

Lu, C. (2011) 'Colonialism as structural injustice: Historical responsibility and contemporary redress', *The Journal of Political Philosophy*, 19(3), 261–281

Marsh, J. (2010) *A critical analysis of decision-making protocols used in approving a commercial mining license for the Beverley Uranium Mine in Adnyamathanha Country: Toward effective Indigenous participation in caring for cultural resources*, PhD thesis, Department of Geographical and Environmental Studies, University of Adelaide

Marsh, J. (2013) 'Decolonising the interface between Indigenous peoples and mining companies in Australia: Making space for cultural heritage sites', *Asia Pacific Viewpoint*, 54(2), 171–184

Mörkenstam, U. (1999) *Om "Lapparnes privilegier" Föreställningar om samiskhet i svensk samepolitik 1883–1997*, Stockholm Studies in Politics 67, Department of Political Science, Stockholm University, Stockholm

NFCRC (Nuclear Fuel Cycle Royal Commission) (2016a) http://nuclearrc.sa.gov.au/#fndtn-external-commission-visits

NFCRC (Nuclear Fuel Cycle Royal Commission) (2016b) *Tentative findings*, http://nuclearrc.sa.gov.au/app/uploads/2016/02/NFCRC-Tentative-Findings.pdf

Nilsson, B. (2009) *Kiruna: Staden som ideologi*, Borea, Umeå, Sweden

Nordin, Å. (2002) *Relationer i ett samiskt samhälle: en studie av skötesrensystemet i Gällivare socken under första hälften av 1900-talet*, PhD thesis, Umeå University

O'Faircheallaigh, C. (2016) *Negotiations in the Indigenous world: Aboriginal peoples and the extractive industry in Australia and Canada*, Routledge, New York

Össbo, Å. (2014) *New waters, reflections of obscurity: Industrial colonialism through the Swedish hydropower development in the Reindeer Herding areas 1910–1968*, PhD thesis, Umeå University

Ramsbotham, O., Woodhouse, T. and Miall, H. (2011) *Contemporary conflict resolution*, 3rd edition, Polity Press, Cambridge, UK

Reid, J.B. and Taylor, K. (2011) 'Indigenous mind: A framework for culturally safe Indigenous health research and practice', *Aboriginal and Islander Health Worker Journal*, 35(4), 19–21

Reimerson, E. (2015) *Nature, culture, rights: Exploring space for Indigenous agency in protected area discourses*, PhD thesis, Umeå University

Reynolds, H. (2003) *The law of the land*, 3rd edition, Penguin Books, Camberwell, Australia

Rigney, L-I. (1999) 'Internationalization of an Indigenous anticolonial cultural critique of research methodologies: A guide to indigenist research methodology and its principles', *Wicazo Sa Review*, 14(2), 109–121

Samer (2017) 'Rennäring' http://samer.se/renn%C3%A4ring

Sametinget (2013) 'Uttalande från Sametinget om exploateringen av Sápmi'http://www.sametinget.se/61172

Sehlin MacNeil, K. and Marsh, J. (2015) 'Indigenous research across continents: A comparison of ethically and culturally sound approaches to research in Australia and Sweden', in Huijser, H., Ober, R., O'Sullivan, S., McRae-WilliamsE. and ElvinR. (eds), *Finding the common ground: Narratives, provocations and reflections from the 40 year celebration of Batchelor Institute*, Batchelor Press, Batchelor NT, Australia, 119–126

Sehlin MacNeil, K. (2015) 'Shafted: A case of cultural and structural violence in the power relations between a Sami community and a mining company in northern Sweden', *Ethnologia Scandinavica: A Journal for Nordic Ethnology*, 45, 73–88

Sehlin MacNeil, K. (2016) 'On equal terms? Traditional Owners' views regarding nuclear waste dumps on Adnyamathanha Country', *Journal of Australian Indigenous Issues*, 19(3), 95–111

Sehlin MacNeil, K. and Lawrence, R. (2017) 'Samiska frågor i gruvdebatten 2013 – nya utrymmen för ohörda diskurser?' in Liliequist, M. and CocqC. (eds), *Samisk kamp för kulturell överlevnad*, H:ströms förlag, Umeå, Sweden, 140–161

Sehlin MacNeil, K. (2017) *Extractive violence on Indigenous country: Sami and Aboriginal views on conflicts and power relations with extractive industries*, PhD thesis, Umeå University

Sehlin MacNeil, K. (2018) 'Let's name it: Identifying cultural, structural and extractive violence in Indigenous and extractive industry relations', *Journal of Northern Studies*, 12(2), (in press)

Sjöstedt Landén, A. (2017) '"'Gruvboom' kallade de det": Gruvkritik och kamp för alternativa samhällen', in LiliequistM. and CocqC. (eds), *Samisk kamp för kulturell överlevnad*, H:ströms förlag, Umeå, Sweden, 116–139

Skarin, A., Nellemann, C., Rönnegård, L., Sandström, P. and Lundqvist, H. (2015) 'Wind farm construction impacts reindeer migration and movement corridors', *Landscape Ecology*, 30(8), 1527–1540

Smith, L.T. (2012) *Decolonizing methodologies: Research and Indigenous peoples*, 2nd edition, Zed Books Ltd, London

SOU (2006) *Gränsdragningskommissionen: Samernas sedvanemarker*, Edita Sverige AB, Stockholm, 14

Stammler, F. and Ivanova, A., (2016) 'Confrontation, coexistence or co-ignorance? Negotiating human-resource relations in two Russian regions', *The Extractive Industries and Society*, 3, 60–72

Stoor, K. (2017) Vi följer renens vandringar: Skogssamiska manliga renskötares förhållande till landskapet, in LiliequistM. and CocqC. (eds), *Samisk kamp för kulturell överlevnad*, H:ströms förlag, Umeå, Sweden, 188–222

Svonni, C. (2015) 'At the margin of educational policy: Sámi/Indigenous peoples in the Swedish National Curriculum 2011', *Creative Education* 6(9), 898–906

Wilson, S. (2001) 'What is an Indigenous research methodology?' *Canadian Journal of Native Education*, 25(2), 175–179

9 Forest governance in post-agreement Colombia

Torsten Krause

Introduction

Decades of violence and a long armed internal conflict in Colombia forced millions of mostly small-scale poor farmers to abandon their homes in search of security and a more peaceful life (Kirk, 2009). After years of negotiations a peace agreement between the government of Colombia (referred to throughout the chapter as GoC) and the Revolutionary Armed Forces of Colombia (FARC – Fuerzas Armadas Revolucionarias Colombianas), the country's main guerilla group, was signed in 2016, marking a new era for the country.

Colombia's violent armed conflict can be traced back to the 1950s, but it originated in colonial times with unequal access to ownership of land and the absence of a comprehensive land reform that reverberates to the present. While approximately 68% of the rural population lives in poverty, an estimated 0.4% of the population owns 62% of the country's best land (USAID, 2017). This highly unequal distribution of land has been criticised by left wing intellectuals, Catholic radicals and local small-scale farmer self-defence groups, who have demanded a re-distribution of land. This gave rise to the formation of several armed groups, most famously the FARC and the National Liberation Army (ELN – Ejército de Liberación Nacional), which increasingly started to use violence in order to enforce a Marxist-Leninist political agenda. Throughout the decades the Colombian armed conflict varied in intensity with certain years such as the early and late 1990s being categorised as war (Gleditsch et al., 2002). In the beginning, both FARC and ELN depended on the support of small-scale farmers in order to fill the ranks of their groups. However, the conflict that started with the goal of re-distributing land more fairly instead led to the expansion of large landholdings and the forced and violent abandonment of rural areas by small-scale farmers in search of security (Beittel, 2015). Thus, despite having set out as the self-claimed liberators of the Colombian people from the oppressive elites, the FARC and the ELN themselves became principal agents of illegal activities, human rights violations and, in part, also environmental destruction.

A further spiral of violence emerged when organised cartels started to engage in narcotraffic fueling the expansion of illicit crops that provided a source of income for the different armed groups (Thoumi, 2002), and when wealthy landowners started to finance local paramilitary groups for protection against the guerilla groups in the 1980s which led to the formation of the United Self-Defense Forces of Colombia (AUC – Autodefensas Unidas de Colombia), the largest paramilitary group of Colombia until 2006. The Uppsala Conflict Data Program states that during the Colombian conflict three types of organised violence took place: intra-state violence between armed groups and the state, non-state violence between the different armed groups, and one-sided violence where armed groups targeted civilians (UCDP, 2017).

During the six decades of armed conflict, hundreds of thousands of civilians lost their lives, millions were displaced and uncountable human rights violations took place. Many indigenous groups suffered at the hands of the guerilla groups, the paramilitaries and the state security forces. Not only were their lands turned into battlefields of military action, they also became a target for exploiting land and natural resources (Beittel, 2015; Rodríguez, 2016). The production of illicit crops and mining for gold and other scarce minerals continue to provide a stable income source for the various armed groups and paramilitaries (Beittel, 2015; Guevara et al., 2016). Attempts by the GoC and the US initiated and led 'Plan Colombia' to eradicate coca plantations were futile and, after years of decreasing cocaine production, Colombia has again become the main producer of cocaine globally (UNODC, 2017; Rico, 2017).

Conversely, notwithstanding the often devastating social consequences, the armed conflict in Colombia has also provided a rather unintended protection for local ecosystems largely due to the lack of infrastructure construction and other external investments in rural areas during the armed conflict (Sanchez-Cuervo and Aide, 2013b). Compared to neighbouring countries Colombia has had a relatively low deforestation rate (FAO, 2012).

Colombia is a democratic, unitary and decentralised republic with autonomous territorial entities (Constitución de la República de Colombia, 1991) and one of Latin America's most decentralised environmental administrations (Aguilar-Støen et al., 2016). However, forest governance in Colombia is deficient, particularly in relation to its institutional capacities, unclear property rights and lack of enforcement of existing laws and the participation of stakeholders in processes and decision making around forests (Orozco et al., 2014). A major shortcoming for better forest protection is the lack of coordination and the institutional fragmentation at the national and regional levels (Martínez Salas et al., 2015).

This chapter analyses forest governance in a post-agreement context. The analytical focus moves across different scales and draws on examples from the Colombian Amazon. Below I will discuss how the post-agreement period has affected the region and its indigenous groups to now.

A brief history of natural resource conflicts in the Amazon

Colombia is one of the most biodiverse and culturally rich countries in the world (Myers et al., 2000). The Amazon region of Colombia covers approximately 450,000 km^2 and is relatively well preserved. Nonetheless, resources in and under the tropical forests have been exploited for more than two centuries, the effects of which still shape the social-ecological dynamics and conflicts in the Amazon to this day.

The extraction of rubber (*Hevea brasiliensis*) characterised the first economic boom in the Amazon. Starting at the end of the 19th century it was driven by growing car manufacturing. Thousands of rubber extractors, often working for private companies, entered the forests and forced indigenous tribes to collect the 'white gold'. Altogether, the rubber industry enslaved tens of thousands of indigenous people who suffered tremendously (Peluso, 2014). During the rubber boom, a major reconfiguration of indigenous territories took place as many ethnic groups were decimated or extirpated, while others fled into remote forest areas (Hecht and Cockburn, 2011).

In the beginning of the 20th century rubber plantations in Asia replaced Amazonian rubber, but hunting of Amazonian animals became a new boom and reached industrial scales. The trade of Amazonian hides was lucrative and lasted for several decades until the 1970s (Antunes et al., 2016). Although the trade is now prohibited, overharvesting for consumption, deforestation, forest fragmentation and illegal trade in wild meat continue to pose a threat to many species (van Vliet et al., 2014; Sarti et al., 2015).

The next wave of exploitation started in the 1950s when oil and gold were being extracted from beneath the forests (oil), rivers and soils (gold). Both activities are a driver of deforestation and forest degradation in the Amazon, polluting rivers and threatening human health (CESR, 1994; San Sebastián et al., 2001; Hurtig and San Sebastián, 2002; Alvarez-Berrios and Aide, 2015). While the Colombian Amazon has so far been largely spared from oil extraction, compared to the Ecuadorian and Peruvian Amazon (Rivard, 1982; Alvarez-Berrios and Aide, 2015), gold mining is a continuous threat to the ecosystem and people's health (Asner et al., 2013; Alvarez-Berrios and Aide, 2015).

In recent years the Colombian Amazon has received renewed attention both by national and international governments and organisations due to its biological and cultural richness and the relatively intact forests, that provide climate benefits and carbon storage (Buizer et al., 2014). However, this attention also creates new conflicts revolving around how to use and best manage the natural resources in and underneath the forest, by whom and to whose benefit. Given the signing of the peace agreement, several scholars point towards the potential negative impacts peace might have for Colombia's ecosystems (Sanchez-Cuervo and Aide, 2013a; Baptiste et al., 2017; Morales, 2017). In the subsequent sections, I present and analyse examples of these struggles over natural resources and land and how these are connected to the transition towards sustainable development in post-agreement Colombia.

Who owns the Amazon – Rights to forest land in Colombia

Clarifying collective rights to forest lands is key for effective and equitable forest governance and sustainable forest management. Devolving land tenure to local and indigenous communities leads to more sustainable forest resources use and reduces deforestation (Holland et al., 2014; Robinson et al., 2011; Ding et al., 2016; Blackman et al., 2017). Traditionally, indigenous forest ownership in the Amazon has been fluid and many indigenous groups lived semi-nomadic lifestyles. The onset of the rubber boom forced many groups to abandon their ancestral lands. Beginning in the 1980s, the GoC started to title indigenous lands as indigenous reserves (*resguardos indigenas*). Although these do not necessarily reflect the historic lands of specific groups, the strife for clarifying land tenure and forest ownership was also an opportunity for many indigenous groups to claim rights to the land where they had settled.

Colombia's constitution recognises the fundamental rights of indigenous people, for instance the right to self-governance (Constitución de la República de Colombia, 1991, Art. 330). Colombia's institutional and legal framework supports indigenous rights and land tenure and the GoC ratified two international agreements – the United Nations Declaration on the Rights of Indigenous Peoples (UNDRIP, 2008) in 2009 and the International Labour Organization's convention 169 (ILO, 1989) in 1991. In accordance with the ILO convention indigenous people have the right to land and resources, to participation in decision making, the right to self-determination and the right to consultation regarding any decisions or projects (private or publicly led) that might affect their rights.

Compared to other countries, Colombia has a relatively large share of indigenous and local community owned forest lands (see Fig. 9.1). Today almost half of Colombia's forests are collectively owned by indigenous and local communities, the majority of these areas being located in the Amazon region (ESRI, 2017).

Nevertheless, all nonrenewable natural resources belong to the Colombian state, which can undertake exploration and exploitation on its own or grant concession rights to private parties. The constitution specifies that the exploitation of natural resources in indigenous territories will be done without impairing the cultural, social and economic integrity of the indigenous communities and the government

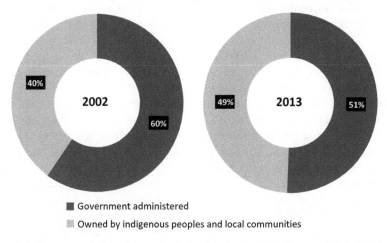

■ Government administered

▨ Owned by indigenous peoples and local communities

Figure 9.1 Forest ownership change in Columbia 2002–2014 (Source: RRI, 2017)

will encourage the participation of representatives of respective communities in case of planned natural resources exploration or exploitation projects (Constitución de la República de Colombia, 1991, Art. 80 and 330). However, numerous court cases between indigenous people, the state and private companies underline the struggles to ensure these rights are recognised, upheld and respected (Rodríguez, 2016; EJOLT, 2017; Semana, 2017b).

Post agreement, sustainable development and forest governance in the Columbian Amazon

Although past resource extraction has left an imprint on the social-ecological fabric of the Amazon, new developments might threaten the region like never before. Since 1990 Colombia has lost more than 6 million hectares of native forest cover and in 2016 alone, 178.597 hectares of forests were lost, an increase of 44% compared to the previous year (IDEAM, 2017). The Amazon region has the highest share and the largest extent of forest cover loss. The main drivers of deforestation are land-grabbing and land-speculation for agriculture (45%), illicit crops (22%), road infrastructure expansion (10%), forest fires (8%), cattle ranching (8%) and illegal mining (7%) (IDEAM, 2017). This complexity of drivers needs to be acknowledged and accounted for in attempts to achieve a more sustainable development.

Although this development is worrisome it has been expected since the drafting of the peace agreement (Mendoza, 2017; Baptiste et al., 2017). Yet, it jeopardises the government's zero deforestation target in the Amazon by 2020 and halting the loss of all natural forest by 2030. According to unpublished reports, the withdrawal of the FARC into demobilisation camps led almost immediately to a sharp rise in deforestation (Semana, 2017c). This is explained by the fact that the FARC exerted, paradoxically, an environmental control thereby limiting deforestation. With the move of the FARC to camps in late 2016, large landowners and small-scale farmers seized the opportunity to cut forests to expand cattle ranching or coca growing. Larger landowners further have the financial means to pay landless colonists to cut forests in order to subsequently claim them for themselves or sell them as part of a large ongoing attempt at land grabbing of forest lands.

The construction and expansion of roads opens up once remote and inaccessible forest areas to agricultural colonisation and land grabbing, currently the main drivers of deforestation in Colombia (Kirby et al., 2006; Ahmed et al., 2013; Carrasco et al., 2017). Behind this land grabbing are often large landowners who want to obtain more land for themselves. By paying poor landless farmers to start clearing forests these landowners are able to establish priority for claiming the land, based on speculating that the GoC will later on legalise these lands (Semana, 2017c). Scholars have long hypothesised the links between potential land reforms and the legalisation of claimed land together with cattle ranching on newly claimed lands that strengthen these land claims (Chadid et al., 2015).

The expansion of illicit crops, mainly coca, is currently a major cause of deforestation, driven by expectation of future incentives, such as money from the government to grow alternative legal crops (Castro-Nunez et al., 2016; IDEAM, 2017; Rico, 2017; Isacson, 2017), which is specified in the peace agreement (OACP, 2016). Yet, attempts to eradicate coca plantations have been fortuitous and small-scale farmers continue to grow coca and other illicit crops (Davalos et al., 2011; Rico, 2017; Chadid et al., 2015) as these are more profitable, easy to sell, and alternatives are hard to come by due to the distance of farms to markets and the lack of road access in remote areas (UNODC, 2017). In addition, agricultural colonisation in forest areas mainly through cattle ranching and the growing of profitable illicit crops (Sanchez-Cuervo and Aide, 2013a; Davalos et al., 2011) is used to access and enhance the value of marginal or conflict affected lands (Castro-Nunez et al., 2016; Castro-Nunez et al., 2017).

Examples from other countries, such as Peru or Liberia that underwent a transition from armed conflict to a post-agreement context provide valuable lessons for Colombia. Nevertheless, these examples also show the difficulty of preserving ecosystems and forests that are at risk from agricultural colonisation and natural resources exploitation, as these often are priorities for the government to foster economic development (Beevers, 2016; Baptiste et al., 2017). However, policies that are designed to provide alternative income sources, for example shifting from coca growing to legal crops, may turn out as a potential perverse incentive, due to small-scale farmers expanding coca plantations into forest areas in order to qualify for future programs providing subsidies for alternative crops (Rico, 2017). Moreover, alternative income sources might not be more environmentally friendly, but instead lead to even more environmental destruction. There is evidence that former coca growers are using the financial incentives provided by the government to invest in and expand cattle ranching activities (Palmer, 2017).

Another important driver of deforestation is gold and coltan mining, most of it illegal (Davalos, 2001; Armenteras et al., 2011; Armenteras et al., 2013; Wagner, 2016). Currently, the ELN, paramilitaries and other criminal groups are battling to control mining and trade of gold and coltan, to secure new forms of income (Guevara et al., 2016), leading to violence over access to and control of mines and the pollution of rivers and soils. Notably, the rise in deforestation coincides in those municipalities that experienced the highest levels of violence during the armed conflict (IDEAM, 2017).

The void left behind by the FARC complicates the situation and in the absence of the state illegal activities and resources exploitation takes place leading to environmental degradation and deforestation (Semana, 2017a). The peace agreement has led to an increase in deforestation rates, particularly in colonisation frontier areas bordering the Amazon region. The void left behind by the demobilisation and retraction of most FARC fighters into transition camps is a main reason. Where the FARC previously controlled land they enforced rules for land use, and in particularly critical or important places they limited forest conversion to a certain percentage of a land holding. Thus, in the absence of state control in these areas, deforestation is increasing and the dominant perception of farmers is to look at forest lands as 'unused new land'. Due to widespread rural poverty, small-scale farmers and landless colonists seek new land in order to survive. The lack of institutional control and the ongoing land grabbing resembles an open-access common-pool resource problem (Ostrom, 1999).

Complicating the situation for the indigenous and rural communities, often living in remote areas, the peace agreement between the FARC and the GoC might lead, paradoxically, to more insecurity and violence. Other guerilla groups like the ELN, paramilitary and other newly formed armed groups, as well as an onslaught of multinational companies are threating their lands and livelihoods (ONIC, 2017; Anderson, 2017). Paramilitary groups and dissident, former FARC fighters, are claiming control over previously FARC controlled areas since the peace agreement (Gaviria, 2017; RdC, 2017). Defending human and indigenous rights or the environment in Colombia is becoming increasingly dangerous and more than 230 human rights activists have been assassinated in the past two years, most of whom belonged to Afro-Colombian and indigenous groups and particularly in places that already suffered disproportionately due to the armed conflict (Global Witness, 2017; Moloney, 2017). Furthermore, it underlines that in order to achieve sustainable development the historic and present complexities surrounding control and use of land have to be accounted for and finding solutions for the real causes of current conflicts is crucial.

Figure 9.2 Recently cleared rainforest in the Guaviare Department of Columbia (Picture taken in June 2017 by the author)

An example of what might happen with the official end of the armed conflict between the FARC and the GoC is the changing land-use dynamics in the frontier regions of colonisation such as the Caquetá department where a substantial increase in forest clearings for cattle ranching and farming is observed (Semana, 2017c). In the neighbouring Guaviare department the peace agreement has led to new ambitions for building roads connecting remote towns with the departments capital. One such project is the expansion of a 135-km long paved road between the municipality of Calamar and the town Miraflores through a large natural forest area. Already the prospect of constructing the road has led to forest clearings, threatening the ancestral territory of the Nukak ethnic group (Volckhausen, 2017). However, expanding the road network is a crucial component of the national development plan and features in the official roadmap for constructing peace in rural areas by integrating remote settlements to markets (DNP, 2014).

Forest governance in a post-agreement Colombia – possible ways ahead

Before the peace talks were concluded, issues relating to forest conservation in the post-agreement period were already brought to the attention of the GoC (Orozco et al., 2014). Although the final agreement mentions the need for forest conservation and sustainable management in areas of special interest, it does so only superficially and without specifying where. Neither does it mention the adverse effects of the proposed land reform and the inevitable land use changes that will come with the peace agreement (OACP, 2016).

Despite all of the aforementioned challenges, the GoC created an ambitious plan for the Amazon with support from the governments of Germany and Norway. It is aptly titled *Visión Amazonica* and aims to reduce deforestation through alternative livelihoods and the strengthening of environmental governance and indigenous participation. Yet, Colombia's decentralised system with regional environmental authorities is unable to stop land grabbing, let alone the illegal construction of roads by local municipalities (Volckhausen, 2017; Baena and Correa, 2017).

Multi-layered governance implies that operational decisions are taken by landowners and right holders, such as indigenous people, while respecting national laws and forest codes. But, the reality is often very different from this imaginary reality and free, prior and informed consent and meaningful participation of indigenous people are often absent (Rodríguez, 2016). Just recently indigenous groups in the central Amazon region complained that the expansion of the Chiribiquete National Park lacked meaningful consultation of indigenous reserves whose territories either border or are within the new boundaries (Echeverri, 2016).

Governance is always a product of contestation, and stakeholders, such as the government, criminal groups, guerillas, farming communities, indigenous groups and international actors, countries and organisations, view forests in profoundly different ways, making forest governance almost always a deeply contentious process (Beevers, 2016). Farmers in Colombia hold a dominant view that forest lands are unused and need to be rendered profitable through agricultural expansion, in contrast to the dominant view held by indigenous groups. Experience from post-conflict countries such as Liberia shows the contention that underlines forest governance and how the diverse actors continuously shape the agenda and try to impose their interests in ways that influence the long-term trajectory of forest governance (Beevers, 2016).

Some scholars claim that Colombia needs to reconcile agricultural expansion, biodiversity and sustainable development through stronger regulatory and enforcement frameworks at different administrative levels, combined with incentive schemes focusing on smallholders (Boron et al., 2016). Furthermore, expanding certification schemes (for example shade-grown coffee and cocoa) might benefit both biodiversity and farmers (Tscharntke et al., 2015). However, these must be applied from the farm to the landscape level, particularly for those areas that are designated to be redistributed under the land reformation act. To sustainably manage forests in frontier areas, local livelihoods that respect and maintain forest ecosystems need to be combined with income opportunities, for instance through non-timber forest products (NTFP) (Morsello et al., 2012). The current expansion of intensive land use (for example oil palm) and extensive cattle ranching supported by policies must be revised (Aguilar et al., 2015). This requires a paradigm shift away from seeing large-scale agriculture as the main driver of development.

There is no question that ending a conflict that lasted more than half a century is a vital achievement for Colombia. Yet, achieving lasting peace and sustainable development is not easy. The challenge will be to not repeat the experiences of other countries that experienced the destruction of native ecosystems at the hands of uncontrolled expansion of unsustainable agriculture, mining and infrastructure projects such as road construction or hydropower dams (Laurance et al., 2014; Finer et al., 2015; Baptiste et al., 2017). Unfortunately, there is mounting evidence that Colombia is heading in a similar direction.

Conclusion

The Colombian peace agreement has been termed *Pax neoliberal* (Neoliberal Peace) and the structural reasons and inequalities that gave rise to the conflict in the first place have not been sufficiently addressed (Forero and Urrea, 2016). Furthermore, the GoC builds its vision for Colombia's future largely on 'sustainable' mining and green growth (DNP, 2014), which is a contradiction in terms. Peace cannot be extracted, nor can sustainable development be driven by inherently unsustainable practices such as large-scale mining (McNeish, 2017). However, the increasing application of public referendums on mining projects foretells a growing environmental and social awareness amongst the population no longer willing to buy the government's empty promises of wealth through natural resources exploitation.

In Colombia, reducing deforestation will ultimately depend on the ability to address historical reasons for violence rooted in inequality and grievances related to land ownership and forced displacement. Here, the existence of recognised collective land rights might be a key to reverse conflicts and achieve better forest management (Boron et al., 2016; Castro-Nunez et al., 2017). Achieving a lasting transition to peace without opening up new areas of social and social-ecological conflict remains a great challenge. Some recommendations provided so far are to strengthen and enforce regulatory frameworks at different administrative levels and to support innovations in agricultural production that are sustainable (Boron et al., 2016), such as agroforestry (Tscharntke et al., 2015), increase the value of standing forests through non-timber forest products, nature-based tourism or payments for reducing deforestation that are equitable and effective (Aguilar-Støen, 2015; Castro-Nunez et al., 2016), and to strengthen land rights of local and indigenous communities instead of indirectly incentivising the expansion of large land holdings, cattle ranching and illicit crops (Boron et al., 2016).

Crucially, at this point the void left behind by the demobilisation of FARC must be filled by the authorities and state security forces and not left to become a battlefield for other violent and criminal actors as is currently the case. Colombia is experiencing a dramatic increase in assassination of environmental and human rights defenders, which is partially explained by the inability of the GoC to control former conflict areas, but also by the onslaught of extractive industries and land speculation in former conflict areas. Without a robust territorial peace there is an increasing risk for a transformation of the armed conflict into numerous and persistent local environmental conflicts around the access and use of natural resources and lands, with old and new actors involved.

Finally, it is imperative to recall that a multitude of actors each with their own aspirations and visions shape forest governance and also the governance of natural resources in a broader sense. The global political economic system plays a crucial role as it is an accomplice and both directly and indirectly fuels the constant struggle to seize power and ownership over soils, minerals and forests in Columbia.

References

Aguilar, M., Sierra, J., Ramirez, W., Vargas, O., Calle, Z., Vargas, W., Murcia, C., Aronson, J. and Barrera Cataño, J.I. (2015) 'Toward a post-conflict Colombia: Restoring to the future', *Restoration Ecology*, 23, 4–6

Aguilar-Støen, M. (2015) 'Global forest conservation initiatives as spaces for participation in Colombia and Costa Rica', *Geoforum*, 61, 36–44

Aguilar-Støen, M., Toni, F. and Hirsch, C. (2016) 'Forest governance in Latin America: Strategies for implementing REDD', in De Castro, F., Hogenboom, B. and Baud, M. (eds), *Environmental governance in Latin America*, Palgrave Macmillan, London

Ahmed, S., Souza, C., Jr., Riberio, J. and Ewers, R. (2013) 'Temporal patterns of road network development in the Brazilian Amazon', *Regional Environmental Change*, 13, 927–937

Alvarez-Berrios, N.L. and Aide, T.M. (2015) 'Global demand for gold is another threat for tropical forests', *Environmental Research Letters*, 10, Number 1

Anderson, A. (2017) 'Colombian peace doomed if Human Rights Defenders not protected', *Irish Times*, 23 August 2017

Antunes, A.P., Fewster, R.M., Venticinque, E.M., Peres, C.A., Levi, T., Rohe, F. and Shepard, G.H. (2016) 'Empty forest or empty rivers? A century of commercial hunting in Amazonia', *Science Advances*, 2

Armenteras, D., Rodríguez, N., Retana, J. and Morales, M. (2011) 'Understanding deforestation in montane and lowland forests of the Colombian Andes', *Regional Environmental Change*, 11, 693–705

Armenteras, D., Cabrera, E., Rodríguez, N. and Retana, J. (2013) 'National and regional determinants of tropical deforestation in Colombia', *Regional Environmental Change*, 1–13

Asner, G.P., Llactayo, W., Tupayachi, R. and Luna, E.R. (2013) 'Elevated rates of gold mining in the Amazon revealed through high-resolution monitoring', *Proceedings of the National Academy of Sciences*, 110, 18454–18459

Baena, M.P. and Correa, P. (2017) 'La carretera con la que quieren pavimentar el Amazonas', *El Espectador*, 5 February 2017

Baptiste, B., Pinedo-Vasquez, M., Gutierrez-Velez, V.H., Andrade, G.I., Vieira, P., Estupiñán-Suárez, L.M., Londoño, M.C., Laurance, W. and Lee, T.M. (2017) 'Greening peace in Colombia', *Nature Ecology and Evolution*, 1, 0102

Beevers, M.D. (2016) 'Forest governance and post-conflict peace in Liberia: Emerging contestation and opportunities for change?', *The Extractive Industries and Society*, 3, 320–328

Beittel, J.S. (2015) *Peace talks in Colombia*, Congressional Research Services

Blackman, A., Corral, L., Lima, E.S. and Asner, G.P. (2017) 'Titling indigenous communities protects forests in the Peruvian Amazon', *Proceedings of the National Academy of Sciences*, 114, 4123–4128

Boron, V., Payán, E., Macmillan, D. and Tzanopoulos, J. (2016), 'Achieving sustainable development in rural areas in Colombia: Future scenarios for biodiversity conservation under land use change', *Land Use Policy*, 59, 27–37

Buizer, M., Humphreys, D. and De Jong, W. (2014) 'Climate change and deforestation: The evolution of an intersecting policy domain', *Environmental Science and Policy*, 35, 1–11

Carrasco, L.R., Nghiem, T.P.L., Chen, Z. and Barbier, E.B. (2017) 'Unsustainable development pathways caused by tropical deforestation', *Science Advances*, 3

Castro-Nunez, A., Mertz, O. and Quintero, M. (2016) 'Propensity of farmers to conserve forest within REDD+ projects in areas affected by armed-conflict', *Forest Policy and Economics*, 66, 22–30

Castro-Nunez, A., Mertz, O., Buritica, A., Sosa, C.C. and Lee, S.T. (2017) 'Land related grievances shape tropical forest-cover in areas affected by armed-conflict', *Applied Geography*, 85, 39–50

CESR (1994) 'Rights violations in the Ecuadorian Amazon: The human consequences of oil development', *Health and Human Rights*, 1, 82–100

Chadid, M., Dávalos, L., Molina, J. and Armenteras, D. (2015) 'A Bayesian spatial model highlights distinct dynamics in deforestation from coca and pastures in an Andean biodiversity hotspot', *Forests*, 6, 3828

Constitución de la República de Colombia (1991) *Constitucíon de 1991 con reformas hasta 2009*, Corte Constitucional, Bogotá

Davalos, L.M. (2001) 'The San Lucas mountain range in Colombia: How much conservation is owed to the violence?', *Biodiversity and Conservation*, 10, 69–78

Davalos, L.M., Bejarano, A.C., Hall, M.A., Correa, H.L., Corthals, A. and Espejo, O.J. (2011) 'Forests and drugs: Coca-driven deforestation in tropical biodiversity hotspots', *Environmental Science and Technology*, 45, 1219–1227

Ding, H., Veit, P.G., Blackman, A., Gay, E., Reytar, K., Altamirano, J.C. and Hodgdon, B. (2016) *Climate benefits, tenure costs – The economic case for securing indigenous land rights in the Amazon*, World Resources Institute, Washington, DC

DNP (2014) *Bases del plan nacional de desarrollo 2014–2018*, Government of Colombia, Bogotá

Echeverri, J.Á. (2016) 'Amazonía 2020, sin visión indígena', *UN Periódico*, Universidad Nacional de Colombia, Bogotá

EJOLT (2017) 'Environmental justice atlas – Colombia', Environmental Justice Organisations, Liabilities and Tradehttps://ejatlas.org/country/colombia

ESRI (2017) 'Resguardos indigena Colombia' ESRI.com

FAO, (2012) *State of the world's forest 2012*, Food and Agriculture Organization of the United Nations, Rome

Finer, M., Babbit, B., Novoa, S., Ferrarese, F., Pappalardo, S.E., Marchi, M.D., Saucedo, M. and Kumar, A. (2015) 'Future of oil and gas development in the Western Amazon', *Environmental Research Letters*, 10, Number 2

Forero, L.F. and Urrea, D. (2016) 'Territorial peace and land grabbing in Colombia', Transnational Insitute, Amsterdamhttps://www.tni.org/en/article/territorial-peace-and-land-grabbing-in-colombia

Gaviria, R.M. (2017) 'Qué se sabe de la disidencia del frente primero de las FARC?', *El Colombiano*, 10 April 2017

Gleditsch, N.P., Wallensteen, P., Eriksson, M., Sollenberg, M. and Strand, H. (2002) 'Armed conflict 1946–2001: A new dataset', *Journal of Peace Research*, 39, 615–637

Global Witness (2017) 'Environmental Activists', Global Witness, Londonhttps://www.globalwitness.org/en/campaigns/environmental-activists/#more

Guevara, E.L., Duarte, N. and Salcedo-Albarán, E. (2016) *Introduction to trafficking of gold and coltan in Colombia. The global observatory of transnational criminal networks*, Research Paper No.1 – VORTEX Working Papers, Vortex Foundation, Bogotá

Hecht, S. and Cockburn, A. (2011) *Fate of the forest: Developers, destroyers, and defenders of the Amazon*, University Of Chicago Press, Chicago

Holland, M.B., De Koning, F., Morales, M., Naughton-Treves, L., Robinson, B.E. and Suárez, L. (2014) 'Complex tenure and deforestation: Implications for conservation incentives in the Ecuadorian Amazon', *World Development*, 55, 21–36

Hurtig, A.-K. and San Sebastián, M. (2002) 'Geographical differences in cancer incidence in the Amazon basin of Ecuador in relation to residence near oil fields', *International Journal of Epidemiology*, 31, 6

IDEAM (2017) *Esfuerzos del país se concentran en alcanzar meta de zero deforestación*, Colombian institute of hydrology, meteorology and environmental studies (IDEAM), Bogota

ILO (1989) *C169 – Indigenous and tribal peoples convention, 1989*, International Labour Organization, Geneva

Isacson, A. (2017) 'Colombia's peace accords point the way to a solution But will they be implemented?', Brookings Institution, Washington, DChttps://www.brookings.edu/blog/order-from-chaos/2017/04/28/colombias-peace-accords-point-the-way-to-a-solution-but-will-they-be-implemented/

Kirby, K.R., Laurance, W.F., Albernaz, A.K., Schroth, G., Fearnside, P.M., Bergen, S., Venticinque, E.M. and Da Costa, C. (2006) 'The future of deforestation in the Brazilian Amazon', *Futures*, 38, 432–453

Kirk, R. (2009) 'Colombia: Human rights in the midst of conflict', in Babbitt, E.F. and Lutz, E.L. (eds), *Human rights and conflict resolution in context: Colombia, Sierra Leone, and Northern Ireland*, Syracuse University Press, Syracuse, New York, 23–45

Laurance, W.F., Sayer, J. and Cassman, K.G. (2014) 'Agricultural expansion and its impacts on tropical nature', *Trends in Ecology and Evolution*, 29, 107–116

Martínez Salas, M.D.P., López Arévalo, H.F. and Sánchez Palomino, P. (2015) 'Subsistence hunting of mammals in the eastern sector of Tuparro Biosphere Reserve, Vichada (COLOMBIA)', *Acta Biológica Colombiana*, 21, 16

McNeish, J.A. (2017) 'A vote to derail extraction: Popular consultation and resource sovereignty in Tolima, Colombia', *Third World Quarterly*, 1–18

Mendoza, M.L. (2017) 'La paz: reto y oportunidad frente a la deforestación', *El Tiempo*

Moloney, A. (2017) 'Colombia rights activists facing danger, U.N. says', Reuters.com

Morales, L. (2017) 'Peace and environmental protection in Colombia – Proposals for sustainable rural development', The Dialogue – Leadership for the Americas, Washington, DC

Morsello, C., Ruiz-Mallèn, I., Diaz, M.D.M. and Reyes-Garcìa, V. (2012) 'The effects of processing non-timber forest products and trade partnerships on people's wellbeing and forest conservation in Amazonian societies' *PLOS ONE*, 7, e43055

Myers, N., Mittermeier, R.A., Mittermeier, C.G., Da Fonseca, G.A.B. and Kents, J. (2000) 'Biodiversity hotspots for conservation priorities', *Nature*, 403, 7

OACP (2016) *Acuerdo Final Para la Terminación del Conflicto y la Construcción de una Paz Estable y Duradera*, Government of Colombia, Bogotá

ONIC (2017) 'Pueblos indígenas en el Chocó entre el fuego cruzado de actores armados legales e ilegales' http://www.onic.org.co/comunicados-regionales/2012-pueblos-indi genas-en-el-choco-entre-el-fuego-cruzado-de-actores-armados-legales-e-ilegales

Orozco, J.M., Mogrovejo, P., Jara, L.F., Sánchez, A., Buendia, B., Dumet, R. and Bohórquez, N. (2014) *Tendencias de la Gobernanza Forestal en Colombia, Ecuador y Perú*, TRAFFIC International, Cambridge, UK, 152

Ostrom, E., Burger, J., Field, C.B., Norgaard, R.B. and Policansky, D. (1999) 'Sustainability – Revisiting the commons: Local lessons, global challenges', *Science*, 284, 278–282

Palmer, L. (2017) '"It's a perverse system": How Colombia's farmers are reforesting their logged land', *The Guardian*, 29 December 2017, https://www.theguardian.com/ environment/2017/dec/29/its-a-perverse-system-how-colombias-farmers-are-refor esting-their-logged-land

Peluso, D. (2014) 'Shajaó—Histories of an invented savage', *History and Anthropology*, 25, 102–122

RdC (2017) 'Paras' están ocupando territorios que dejamos: Jefe de las FARC en zona veredal del Meta', Centro Nacional de Memoria Histórica, Fundación ConLupa, Verdad Abierta, http://rutasdelconflicto.com/noticias/detalle_noticias.php?noticia=17

Rico, D.M. (2017) 'No veo la estrategia para enfrentar los cultivos de coca', 3 March 2017https://www.semana.com/nacion/articulo/experto-en-narcotrafico-daniel-rico-critica-politica-de-cultivos/517393#

Rivard, G. (1982) 'Oil and colonization in Ecuador', *Geoscope*, 13, 54–67

Robinson, B.E., Holland, M.B. and Naughton-Treves, L. (2011) *Does secure land tenure save forests? A review of the relationship between land tenure and tropical deforestation*,

CCFAS Working Paper No.7, CGIAR Research Program on Climate Change, Agriculture and Food Security (CCAFS), Copenhagen

Rodríguez, G.A. (2016) *Los conflictos ambientales en Colombia y su incidencia en los territorios indígenas*, Editorial Universidad del Rosario, Bogotá

RRI (2017) 'Tenure data and tool – Colombia', Rights and Resources Initiative, Washington, DChttps://rightsandresources.org/en/work-impact/tenure-data-tool/#. Wk5mto7A1nE

San Sebastián, M., Armstrong, B., Córdoba, J.A. and Stephens, C. (2001) 'Exposures and cancer incidence near oil fields in the Amazon basin of Ecuador', *Occupational and Environmental Medicine*, 58, 6

Sanchez-Cuervo, A.M. and Aide, T.M. (2013a) 'Consequences of the armed conflict, forced human displacement, and land abandonment on forest cover change in Colombia: A multi-scaled analysis', *Ecosystems*, 16, 1052–1070

Sanchez-Cuervo, A.M. and Aide, T.M. (2013b) 'Identifying hotspots of deforestation and reforestation in Colombia (2001–2010): Implications for protected areas', *Ecosphere*, 4

Sarti, F.M., Adams, C., Morsello, C., van Vliet, N., Schor, T., Yag,E. B., Tellez, L., Quiceno-Mesa, M.P. and Cruz, D. (2015) 'Beyond protein intake: Bushmeat as source of micronutrients in the Amazon', *Ecology and Society*, 20

Semana (2017a) 'Deforestacíon en las puertas de la Amazonía', *Semana Sostenible*

Semana (2017b) 'Indígenas denuncian vulneraciones a sus derechos', *Semana*

Semana (2017c) 'Las mafias de la deforestación en el Guaviare', *Semana*

Thoumi, F.E. (2002) 'Illegal drugs in Colombia: From illegal economic boom to social crisis', *The Annals of the American Academy of Political and Social Science*, 582, 102–116

Tscharntke, T., Milder, J.C., Schroth, G., Clough, Y., Declerck, F., Waldron, A., Rice, R. and Ghazoul, J. (2015) 'Conserving biodiversity through certification of tropical agroforestry crops at local and landscape scales', *Conservation Letters*, 8, 14–23

UCDP (2017) 'Colombia', Uppsala Conflict Data Program – Department of Peace and Conflict Researchhttp://ucdp.uu.se/#country/100

UNDRIP (2008) *United Nations Declaration on the Rights of Indigenous Peoples*, United Nations

UNODC (2017) *Colombia – Monitoreo de territorios afectados por cultivos ilícitos 2016*, United Nations Office on Drugs and Crime, Vienna

USAID (United States Agency for International Development) (2017) 'Colombia – Property rights and resource governance' https://www.land-links.org/wp-content/up loads/2016/09/USAID_Land_Tenure_Colombia_Profile-1.pdf

van Vliet, N., Quiceno Mesa, M.P., Cruz-Antia, D., Neves De Aquino, L.J., Moreno, J. and Nasi, R. (2014) 'The uncovered volumes of bushmeat commercialized in the Amazonian trifrontier between Colombia, Peru and Brazil', *Ethnobiology and Conservation*, 3, 7

Volckhausen, T. (2017) 'Rebel road expansion brings deforestation to remote Colombian Amazon', in Erickson-Davis, M. (ed.) *Global Forest Reporting Network*, Mongabay

Wagner, L. (2016) 'Organized crime and illegally mined gold in Latin America', The Global Initiative against Transnational Organized Crime, Geneva

10 To change, or not to change? The transboundary water question in the Nile Basin

Ana Elisa Cascão

Introduction

Transboundary water conflict/cooperation is a widely covered topic by academic literature with studies of more than 200 rivers around the world that are shared by two or more countries, and how this sharing increases the complexity of decisions on how to manage, develop and allocate water (cf. review of literature on transboundary water conflict/cooperation in Zeitoun and Mirumachi, 2008; Zeitoun et al., 2011; Zeitoun et al., 2016). It is particularly complex in places such as the Middle East, a region already experiencing physical water scarcity – where water availability cannot anymore respond to demands – in particular in the case of the highly water-consumptive agricultural sector. African river basins are also experiencing an escalation of complexity due to higher demands for water access and infrastructure associated with fast-growing economies, increasing living standards, urbanisation and industrialisation processes and rising demands for food and energy security. The Nile Basin is at the crossroads between these different hydropolitical realities.

This chapter aims at providing an analysis of the 'conflict of interests and approaches' (called paradigms hereby) in the Nile Basin, shared between 11 countries (Burundi, Democratic Republic of Congo, Egypt, Ethiopia, Eritrea, Kenya, Rwanda, South Sudan, Sudan, Uganda and Tanzania). The specific focus will be on the transboundary water interactions while not ignoring that they are ultimately influenced by dynamics at the national and sub-national levels. The national water availability, demands and developments are determinant in the definition of countries' water-related national interests and the relations with the neighbouring riparians. Besides, the outcomes of transboundary interactions (be it conflict, negotiations, collaboration and/or cooperation) will in return eventually influence the national and sub-national dynamics, as examples provided in the next sections will illustrate.

This chapter considers whether the fundamental question in the Nile Basin can be defined as a *conflict between two different (and often understood as divergent) major paradigms*: a) a paradigm that appeals to the maintenance of the current state of affairs, i.e. maintaining the existing pattern of utilisation and distribution of the Nile water resources; and, b) a paradigm that calls for shifts away from the current situation. It discusses how these two paradigms do not necessarily have to be divergent.

Background – a century of regime building and contestation

One hundred years ago, most of the Nile Basin states – including Egypt, Sudan and several of the Equatorial Nile countries – were part of the British Empire in Africa. The British have built systematic knowledge about the river, its geography and hydrology, and had, to a great extent, identified the relevant potential for irrigated agriculture and associated storage capacities along the Nile's multiple tributaries. The comprehensive and ambitious Nile's 'Century Storage Plan' was built based on decades of detailed studies carried out by British and Egyptian engineers (Tvedt, 2004). The main goal of the Plan was to achieve full control over the Nile, namely by regulating its extremely uneven flows, to optimise the water development potential in order to increase the agricultural output of large-scale agriculture projects in Egypt and Sudan (Waterbury, 1979). The Owen Falls Dam in Uganda and the Sennar and Jebel Aulia Dams in Sudan are projects that were built at different stages to serve those purposes. The big absence in the Century Storage Plan was Ethiopia's section of the Nile, because this country was an independent state. This absence was not at all trivial, as already by then there was clear awareness of Ethiopia's contribution of around 85% to the total Nile flows.

In successive stages starting from Egypt's independence in 1922, the 'Century Storage Plan' was side-lined and later overthrown in the 1950s when President Nasser decided that the best (and the only possible) large-scale storage of Nile waters would be the one located within the administrative borders of Egypt. The process of independence of Sudan from the Anglo-Egyptian Condominium (1952–1956) was crucial to Nasser's decision to move forward with the construction of the High Aswan Dam (HAD), a massive over-year storage dam. This was the beginning of a new regime in the Nile more in line with Egypt's national plans. The strongest pillar of that rising water regime was the 1959 Nile Waters Agreement, signed between Egypt and the newly independent Sudan. This agreement made possible the construction of the HAD and defined clearly the allocations – often called 'historical rights', of the two signatory countries (Agreement, 1959). For the past 60 years, this agreement has been the one guiding the bilateral hydropolitical relations between Egypt and Sudan and, as a by-product, influencing the relations between them and their neighbours upstream.

Meanwhile upstream, during the same long period of time, the changes have been numerous, such as processes of independence in the 1960s, internal civil conflicts and some interstate conflicts in the 1970s, the region was involved in Cold War alliances and proxy wars in the 1980s, the region has had fast-growing populations throughout the half century, increasing demands for economic development in the 1990s, and already in the 21st century a batch of new water development plans (Cascão, 2009). In the last decade, plans for developing the Nile have increased due to a growing inflow of national and foreign direct investment, including towards large-scale hydraulic infrastructure such as hydropower dams and irrigation schemes – and this is likely to have major impacts (Sandström et al., 2016). A common characteristic to these upstream countries is as follows: they did not recognise the water regime agreed by the downstream neighbours, as they were not signatories to the 1959 Agreement. Ethiopia, in particular, has contested it systematically as in practice it has contributed to preclude the development of projects in upstream countries (Salman, 2010).

Historical/current uses *versus* future uses: Two conflicting paradigms?

The long-lasting assumptions behind the paradigms

The argument hereby is that the main source of conflict in the Nile Basin is related to the long-lasting coexistence of two concomitant paradigms. There are two main assumptions that underpin this ideational process: first, the assumption that the Nile might be experiencing 'basin closure', i.e. that there are no more utilisable flows left in the basin, because all water resources are already allocated. Some authors alert for the fact that often basin closure is artificially created by over-committing water resources (Molle et al., 2010). Second, the assumption that water-related issues are a political matter and as such they can jump the queue of political priorities and be framed as a matter of national security (Zeitoun and Warner, 2006).

The combination of these two assumptions have strong impacts in decision-making processes over transboundary water resources – as decisions might not necessarily be guided by technical/economic rationality, but often by political agendas. The deconstruction of these assumptions is needed in order to find lasting solutions that serve the interests of all parties involved. On the one hand, the Nile riparians can jointly demystify the 'basin closure' assumption by embracing basin-wide solutions towards optimal utilisation of available water resources. On the other hand, riparian countries should jointly work towards a 'regional water security' agenda, to replace the nationalist and fragmented approaches that so far have contributed little to find holistic solutions.

Historical/existing uses paradigm

Often used average calculations refer to a total of 84 billion cubic meters (bcm) of Nile water per year as measured at Aswan in Egypt. As any average, it hides enormous variations in the hydrological system. For example, the intra-annual variability due to uneven rainfall patterns that results in a runoff very much dependent on 2–4 months of rainfall in the upstream catchments, in particular in the Blue Nile and Atbara river basins (see Fig. 10.1). Besides, the average conceals an inter-annual variability characterised by long periods of drought as those experienced in the 1970s and 1980s, but as well by periodic extreme

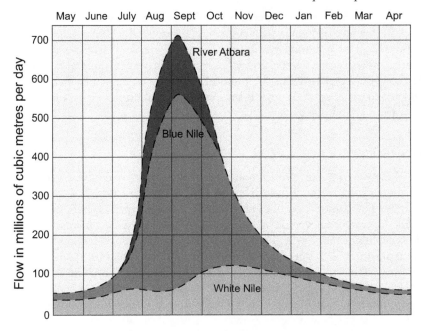

Figure 10.1 Variability of Nile flows (Source: Sutcliffe and Parks, 1999)

flood events. Therefore, some authors are extremely careful in using 84bcm as an annual average and suggest that it can actually be higher than that (Water-bury 1979; Blackmore and Whittington, 2008; Whittington et al., 2014).

The different views on the calculation of the annual water flow is relevant for this discussion because the 84bcm/year average has been adopted under a *ceteris paribus* principle, i.e. there is a rigid assumption that all other variables remain constant. It does not consider that many variables can change (e.g. climate extreme events/change, new water withdrawals, evapotranspiration rates in new projects) and thus influence the calculations of annual averages in a significant manner. But these variables cannot be overlooked.

For the proponents of the 'historical rights' paradigm, the 84bcm/year is the figure to be used in all analysis and debate over the Nile waters. It is also this figure that informs the 1959 'Agreement for the *Full Utilization* of the Nile Waters' (Agreement, 1959). The title of the agreement is in itself very clear – it aims to fully allocate the total flows, and the negotiated breakdown was: 55,5bcm to Egypt, 18,5bcm to Sudan and 10bcm for evapotranspiration at the reservoir of HAD once it would be built (see Art. 2(4), in Agreement, 1959). No allocations for other countries were contemplated, although the Agreement establishes procedures on how to deal with future upstream claims, namely that 'the accepted amount shall be deducted from the shares of [Egypt and Sudan] in equal parts' (see Art. 5(2) in Agreement, 1959). In this sentence, there is a tacit assumption that the upstream riparians would recognise and accept the Agreement, which has proven to be a delusion.

For Egypt, the figures, agreements and procedures described above are the baseline for any dialogue and negotiation regarding the Nile waters, and the backbone of its positionality *vis-à-vis* all its neighbours. The Nile is the main source of freshwater for this arid country and since time immemorial the Nile has played a crucial role in the political economy of Egypt, in social, cultural and economic terms. But what is the current contribution of the Nile water for Egypt's food and energy security?

Food security

The Nile waters sustain a massive and complex irrigation system that is responsible for the agricultural production that partially contributes to Egypt's national food security. The construction of the HAD has allowed Egypt to benefit from 'timely water' (instead of uneven flows), and to expand threefold the agricultural production output since the 1970s. The agricultural sector is nowadays responsible for 25% of employment in Egypt, although the sector only contributes around 12% to the national GDP – in contrast with 55% and 30% respectively back in 1971 (World Bank, 2017). Even after processes of economic diversification in the 1980s and 1990s, the employment rate in the agricultural sector keeps being a main pressure factor in Egypt's Nile policies. However, as regards food security *per se*: since the 1970s, the Nile-dependent agriculture has not been enough to guarantee Egypt's food self-sufficiency. According to the forthcoming new National Water Plan, it is calculated that Egypt imports around 35bcm of virtual water (water embedded in food crops) per year from the global food market (equivalent to more than 1/3 of Egypt's total current water needs). This fact has been long discussed widely in academic circles, but only recently officially recognised by the Egyptian government.

Energy security

If the Nile is key for Egypt's employment and partially its food security, the same cannot be said about its contribution to national energy security. Hydropower currently represents around 12% of the total installed power generation in Egypt (Ibrahim, 2012). Already by the time of planning and construction of the HAD, hydropower was only a by-product whereas irrigation expansion was the major objective. In brief, hydropower is not a central factor in Egypt's definition of national water security.

Storage security

The maintenance of an unchanged storage of Nile waters at the HAD – calculated at 169bcm total – keeps being the central piece of Egypt's water policy. The HAD provides Egypt with an over-year storage that allows the country to store and manage its annual historical rights, but also any water surplus in the system. For the past four decades, thanks to the HAD Egypt has actually benefitted from the unused water by Sudan (which did not use its 18,5bcm/year quota so far), as well as any surplus of water when annual average has surpassed the 84bcm (which has been registered in many years, e.g. in the 1990s). In practice, it means that Egypt's de facto current uses have been above the 'historical rights' as defined in the 1959 Agreement.

The short description above highlights the key features of Egypt's understanding of 'water security' – maintenance of the current utilisation of the Nile waters (or at least the 'historical rights') and safeguarding the HAD will keep being the main storage facility in the Basin.

Future uses paradigm

In theory, the paradigm described above has been translated into a foreclosure of future uses of the Nile water resources, i.e. by preventing future uses of water through the prior use of, and the claiming of rights to such water (Salman, 2010). This is so because the 1959 Agreement established a regime for the 'full utilization' of the Nile waters, and not giving any space for future withdrawals and therefore crafted a situation of 'basin closure'. However, it did not prevent major economic and hydropolitical changes upstream. Changes in the political economies upstream indicate an ever-increasing demand for developing and utilising more systematically the Nile water resources (NBI, 2012). Upstream countries advocate their right to use these resources for their national economy development, to satisfy the increasing needs of their citizens, as well as national and foreign companies investing in water-related projects (Sandström, 2016). Hydropower and storage dams and large-scale agriculture featured high in the political agendas of Ethiopia, Uganda, Kenya, Tanzania and Rwanda – all of them increasingly attractive as business hubs for foreign investment. In Sudan, recent changes in the political economy lead to the expansion of commercial agriculture, which is expected to increase water demands beyond the current use (Cascão and Nicol, 2016a).

Increasing water withdrawals

Figures show that current water withdrawals upstream have been extremely limited – varying from 0,2/0,3bcm in the case of Rwanda/Burundi to around 5bcm in the case of Ethiopia or Tanzania (NBI, 2012; numbers are for all rivers and not just Nile). For the past decade, upstream countries have been witnessing fast-growing economic processes, including expansion of large-scale commercial agriculture. But more often than not, these projects are rainfed agriculture or irrigated agriculture outside of the Nile Basin catchments (Zeitoun et al., 2009). In brief, upstream countries have been mainly exploiting their 'green water' (water embedded in soil moisture) potential but not directly increasing their use of 'blue water' (Nile waters) – therefore not affecting the downstream water flows (Cascão, 2017). Even if all upstream countries would fully develop their irrigation potential, it is not expected this could have a significant impact on the water flows – even in the case of Ethiopia, where the potential for irrigation in the Nile Basins is relatively small (McCartney et al., 2012).

According to McCartney et al. (2012) it is Sudan – the midstream Nile riparian country – which has the biggest potential and plans to increase the withdrawals of 'blue water'. As mentioned earlier in this chapter – already in the British studies (Tvedt, 2004) the extraordinary potential of Sudan for development of large-scale agriculture was identified and exploited. The Gezira scheme, initiated by the British – around 400,000 hectares of land – was by then the largest agricultural project in Africa, possibly because of the storage at the Sennar Dam (Waterbury, 1979; Tvedt, 2004). After independence, and the building of the Roseires Dam (around 3bcm storage capacity), the Gezira scheme was extended – an extra 400,000 hectares of land (Conniff et al., 2012) – with a potential to utilise several billion cubic meters of water.

Official numbers put the current utilisation of Sudan at a total of 12/14bcm of water per year (cf. Cascão and Nicol, 2016a), which is the maximum Sudan has reached since its independence – but the Sudanese government and private sector has been developing many other schemes and have several additional plans to expand, in particular in Blue Nile Basin (Cascão and Nicol, 2016a). Plans for expansion only became possible after the heightening of the Roseires Dam

Table 10.1 Summary of land and water requirements of the Blue Nile irrigation schemes in Sudan

	Land	Water
Current irrigation (with Old Roseires and Sennar storage)	**1.3 million ha of land** Total area currently under irrigation = Gezira + Managil: 882,000ha + Raha: 148,293ha + Suki: 29,827ha + upstream Sennar: 77,177ha + downstream Sennar: 167,200ha = 13,305,037ha	**± 3bcm/year** Total reservoir capacity: Old Roseires Dam: 3.3bcm + Sennar: 0.9bcm = 4.2bcm/year, but significant storage losses (around 85% in Sennar and 35% in Roseires) due to sedimentation
Full-development scenario	**Additional 0.9 million ha of land** Total area of extended and new schemes = extension of Rahad I: 19,740ha + Rahad II: 210,000ha + Suki full extension: 2,940 +3,361ha + extension of upstream Sennar: 39,910ha + extension of downstream Sennar: 44,110 +6,804ha + New Kenanas (II & III): 420,093ha + New South Dinder: 84,019+48,318ha = 879,295ha	**Additional 10bcm/year** Total average annual water demand of extended and new schemes: Rahad: 2.43bcm + Suki: 2.2bcm + upstream Sennar: 0.75bcm + downstream Sennar: 1.5bcm + Kenana II & III: 2.35bcm + South Dinder: 0.85bcm = 10.08bcm/year

Source: Cascão and Nicol, 2016a

(2012), located just upstream of these potential projects and from where irrigation canals can be connected. Table 10.1 above summarises the main existing and potential irrigation schemes in the Blue Nile in Sudan and respective water demands (Cascão and Nicol, 2016a based on McCartney et al., 2012).

In a nutshell, a scenario wherein Sudan fully develops its agricultural potential would require much more water than the threshold of 'historical right' of 18,5bcm of water per year, as defined in the 1959 Agreement. Besides, these figures about Sudan's agricultural potential shed light on the most significant threat to the paradigm on historical and existing uses: Sudan is (by far) the Nile riparian country with the largest capacity to reduce significantly the total water flows arriving to Aswan. Egypt knows it too well, and this is also the reason why the 1959 Agreement is so sacrosanct – it is the instrument to contain Sudan's future water demands/utilisation.

Increasing storage capacity

One of the limiting factors of Sudan's ambitions to expand irrigated agriculture further has always been the lack of storage capacities. Box 10.1 shows the installed storage capacity in the Nile Basin, including the four Sudanese dams. Sudan has exhausted its capacity to build new or upgrade existing large storage facilities in the Blue Nile. Therefore, Sudan is very supportive of development of storage upstream in the Blue Nile that could provide 'timely water' to its future agricultural plans. The GERD can actually be one of these projects, as discussed below. However, Sudan's current official position is that it has no intentions to go beyond the 18,5bcm threshold (cf. Cascão and Nicol, 2016a; 2016b).

Box 10.1 Main storage capacities in the Nile Basin, in bcm

Dam, Tributary, Country, (Year of completion), aprox. storage capacity in bcm water

High Aswan Dam, Main Nile, Egypt (1971): 169bcm
Merowe Dam, Main Nile, Sudan (2009): 12,39bcm
Khashm El-Girba, Atbara River, Sudan (1964): 0,8bcm
Tekezze Dam, Atbara River, Ethiopia (2009): 9,29bcm
Sennar Dam, Blue Nile River, Sudan (1925): 0,05bcm
Roseires Dam, Blue Nile River, Sudan (1966, heightened 2012): 5,9bcm
Grand Ethiopian Renaissance Dam, Blue Nile River, Ethiopia (under construction): 74bcm
Jebel Aulia, White Nile River, Sudan (1937): 3bcm
Owen Falls Dam, White Nile River, Uganda (1954): neglible storage
Bujagali Dam, White Nile River, Uganda (2012): 0,75bcm

Sources: Awulachew et al., 2012; NBI, 2012; NBI, 2014

The GERD – pictured still empty in Fig. 10.2 – will have a total storage capacity of 74bcm. In itself this dam would not have to be considered as a challenge to the historical/current uses paradigm, because it is a hydropower dam and therefore non-water consumptive (although during the filling period some changes in the flows can occur, dependent on the filling strategies to be agreed between the three countries). Several studies show that if the three Eastern Nile countries can agree on a coordination mechanism to jointly operate the existing reservoirs – for both the filling and long-term operation periods – the impact of GERD's hydropower production in the total Nile flows could be minimised (Whittington et al., 2014; Wheeler, 2016; Jeuland et al., 2017).

An important detail in this complex situation is: the GERD in itself is not water-consumptive, but it will assist Sudan in its strategy to move from the current under-utilisation of its Nile water quota to its full utilisation (from 12–14 to 18,5) – because it allows Sudan to proceed with its irrigation expansion plans in the Blue Nile. This also means that Egypt will stop benefitting from the water surplus it has benefitted from since the construction of the HAD. This is not minor as it comes to shed light on the fact that: historical and current uses do not mean the same thing and as such should not be used interchangeably. 'Historical' uses means the quotas as defined by the 1959 Agreement, and 'existing' uses are the actual withdrawals by Egypt and Sudan.

Storage – current and future – has a significant role in any discussion regarding conflict and cooperation in the Nile Basin. Increasing storage capacity can guide discussions on how to maximise and optimise the common resources. Joint discussions and decisions on the best locations and magnitudes are

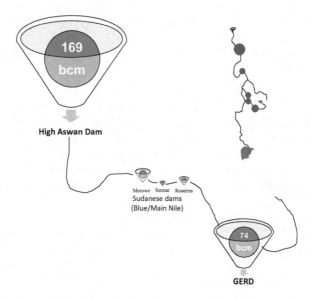

Figure 10.2 Storage magnitudes in the Blue Nile and Main Nile basins (Source: author)

fundamental to prevent and mitigate conflicts of interests. Besides, it should inform any negotiation process on current and future uses of the Nile waters. The discussion should also consider a common challenge that needs to be included in the decision-makers' equation – climate change and its impacts. Recent studies point out that potential changes in the flow of the Nile River as a result of climate change may complicate an already critical situation (cf. Siam and Eltahir, 2017). Studies show that the deviation describing inter-annual variability of total Nile flow could increase by 50%, but that extreme events such as drought and floods will become more recurrent (ibid.). These authors alert for the fact that in order to deal with the projected inter-annual variability, the decision-makers must re-evaluate the adequacy of current water storage capacity and also plan for additional storage capacity in the basin (ibid.).

In conclusion, be it human-induced or nature-induced (such climate) changes, it does not look like the current water regimes are taking them into account. Therefore, proponents of the second paradigm consider that sooner rather than later these changes need to be accounted for. Any sustainable and forward-looking regime will require parties to embrace these changes as opportunities to build a robust but flexible regime that can protect the interests of all parties – countries, economic sectors, and ultimately the final users. This new regime should be the result of a reflective process wherein decision-makers move towards the convergence of paradigms, while at the same time adopting policies and approaches that deal with fast-changing settings resulting from climate change.

Conflict resolution and transformation in the Nile Basin

The previous sections outlined the coexistence of two main paradigms in the Nile Basin. These next sections analyse what has been done so far to address the apparent divergences and to promote convergence between them towards a joint approach. This section analyses two ongoing processes – the trilateral cooperation process specific to the GERD (2011–2017) and the multilateral cooperation process through the Nile Basin Initiative (NBI) (1999–2017). The analyses of both processes highlight that conflict and cooperation in the Nile Basin co-exist – but that the countries have been engaging to find solutions for a convergence between paradigms.

The trilateral process

This section looks at how Ethiopia, Egypt and Sudan have been working closely in order to address the current and future conflict of interests. In April 2011, the Ethiopian government announced to the world the ambition to build its first national large-scale dam in the Blue Nile River in Ethiopia, the GERD – a 4,5 billion dollar self-financed dam with a 6,500MW energy potential and a reservoir capacity of 74bcm raised alarms in the region and in the international community. Since then, much has been written about the 'new' conflict that a project of this dimension could bring (cf. several contributions in Yihdego et al., 2016; 2017). But in effect the GERD is just bringing the 'old' conflict (the one between two paradigms) back to the surface. Simultaneously it can also be seen as a unique opportunity to move towards a constructive trilateral cooperation process.

Since mid-2011, the three Eastern Nile countries have engaged in the following processes (from Cascão and Nicol, 2016b; Tawfik, 2016):

- 2011–2013: The formation of a trilateral technical joint committee that discussed all issues pertaining to the dam, including the establishment of an International Panel of Experts (IPoE) that produced a report on the main critical issues (e.g. design, safety and stability of the dam, hydrological studies, environmental and social impacts, etc.) based on Terms of Reference also jointly defined;
- 2013–2014: Technical and political talks on how to take forward and address jointly the main recommendations by the IPoE, namely the need to have more elaborated studies on the hydrological and other impacts of the dam during and after the filling period;
- 2014–2015: Preparatory high-level legal and political negotiations that led to the signature of a trilateral agreement – the Declaration of Principles (DoP) signed at the highest political level by the three heads of state in March 2015, plus a supporting document (Khartoum accord) signed in December 2015 to cement the DoP resolutions;
- 2016–2017: Lengthy and regular meetings between technical and political parties to define the scope of the studies, put a team of consultants together and initiate the studies – which have meanwhile started but are facing delays because of disagreements over interpretation on what is the baseline to study impacts (which brings again the discussion about past/current and future uses to the centre of the discussion).

The difficulties and dilemmas associated with these processes are vast and should not be overlooked – at the end, they mirror or encapsulate decades of divergent views on how to manage the Nile water resources. However, these difficulties should also not overshadow some important discursive and action-oriented achievements such as:

- Egypt's bold recognition of the right of Ethiopia (or other upstream countries) to develop hydraulic infrastructures for their own economic development;
- Ethiopia's commitment to build and finalise the dam without causing significant impacts to the two downstream neighbours;
- Sudan's commitment not to increase its water utilisation beyond what is defined in the 1959 agreement, despite the fact that the GERD storage capacities might allow Sudan to go beyond it;

- Detailed discussions on current and future sectorial allocations and trade-offs, including how to do it in the spirit of regional cooperation and integration;
- Deep engagement of the three countries to have a legal framework (jointly negotiated and signed) to guide the filling and the future operations of the GERD.

However, these achievements are not yet sufficient to build a paradigm convergence, and it is not yet even a complete process. It already includes a number of steps forward towards a conflict transformation. The year of 2018 was bound to be a tipping point – there were high expectations that countries would reach a negotiated final solution for the pending issues, although this has not materialised. The drawback of this trilateral process is: it is a piecemeal approach, as it will only address the dilemmas regarding the GERD. It is project-specific and only focuses on the storage capacity in the Blue Nile and besides it is just between three of eleven Nile riparians, and it does not offer any institutional solution. A robust multilateral all-inclusive institution to deal with other future changes/challenges is needed more than ever.

The multilateral process

It was back in the mid-1990s that all the Nile Basin countries, with the support of the international community, initiated an ambitious multilateral process to promote transboundary water cooperation in the basin (NBI 1999; 2014). This cooperation process consisted of two parallel but complementary tracks: 1) the technical track with the establishment of the Nile Basin Initiative (NBI) in 1999, a transitional institutional arrangement with the final aim 'to achieve sustainable socio-economic development through the equitable utilization of, and benefit from, the common Nile Basin water resource' (NBI, 1999); and, 2) a political track initiated in 1997 aimed at paving the way for a new Nile Cooperative Framework Agreement (CFA) that could establish the general legal principles and provide an institutional framework for the establishment of a permanent basin commission. These two processes were expected to establish a new regime for the Nile – one that could transform the long-lasting conflict of interests in the Nile into a basin-wide and fully-fledged cooperation process. Ultimately this is to be translated into:

- the building of a permanent institution, owned by the Nile riparians, with the capacity of supporting and influencing decision-making processes related to the management and development of the common water resources, based on internationally-recognised principles of international water law;
- a joint decision-making process, including the investment on infrastructure projects, based on a regional and common assessment of the options, optimisation of resources, minimisation of risks, trade-offs, joint studies, implementation and operations, etc., and that can ultimately deliver socio-economic benefits for all countries;

- implicitly, it was expected countries would move away from unilateral, uncoordinated and fragmented plans towards a multilateral decision-making process that would reduce significantly the threats and risks associated with unilateral action, while at the same time making the best use of the common resources to promote regional water security.

An in-depth analysis of the trajectory of the multilateral cooperation process highlights that a lot has been achieved. Countries have been building a common basis of understanding, improved dramatically the knowledge base about the river and its development options, and developed crucial tools for policy-making, identification and implementation projects with multiple benefits for several countries. However, there are still some setbacks to this ambitious basin-wide approach, namely because the political track (CFA) is not completed and as such the NBI is still a transitional institutional arrangement. The NBI is not yet a permanent institution that could be more pro-active in bringing to the forefront jointly agreed projects.

Conclusions on the way forward

The chapter analysed how two different paradigms on the past/current and future utilisation of the Nile waters have marked more than a century of transboundary hydropolitical relations, and which have been basically translated into fragmented approaches to the management of the common water resources at the expenses of a holistic approach. The tailored basin-wide approach put forward by the British at the beginning of the 20th century was later replaced by national hydraulic missions, characterised mainly by the development of infrastructure projects only aimed at guaranteeing 'water-food-energy security' at national levels. This limited scope led to a situation where water resources have been allocated without an integrated approach to all uses and users. This has led to an over-allocation of water resources in the downstream catchments of the basin, and any development upstream is considered to be a risk to the existing utilisation.

A century later, regional cooperative mechanisms were initiated with the ambitious goal of bringing back the basin-wide perspectives in the decision-making process. Implicitly, the objective now is to have the two paradigms converging: promoting future water uses for food and energy production in the upstream countries that can be beneficial (rather than detrimental) for all the countries, including the two downstream riparians who are the current main users. As analysed in the previous sections, the attempts to promote basin-wide approaches were not yet fully successful – mainly because the two paradigms are still understood as mutually exclusive. However, it does not have to be the case, because there is still water in the system: there are ways of increasing the yield through optimisation processes; infrastructures can be in place to minimise system losses and increase water availability and productivity; and – ultimately – current uses do not have to be significantly impacted by new/

future uses. In brief, by having a jointly-regional-multilateral approach in place, the Nile Basin countries can protect the interests and fulfil the needs of both downstream and upstream riparians – the major challenge is really to change the inflexible perceptions associated with the two paradigms.

A move towards a constructive and inclusive basin-wide thinking is likely to require major changes in perceptions among the political leadership in the Nile countries – including above all the adoption of a forward-looking approach. The complex dynamics and rapid changes occurring at the national and regional levels in the Nile Basin require more sophisticated analytical perspectives that can assist decision-makers in their policy formulation and/or implementation. This will have to include an in-depth discussion about future 'water security' scenarios in the Nile Basin, to anticipate the main challenges ahead and ultimately to mitigate common risks through a regional approach to water security (Cascão, forthcoming). In conclusion, the Nile riparian countries ultimately need to expand the 'solution space' to deal with anticipated multiple changes (societal, climate, economic, political), instead of sticking to rigid positions – arriving to such a goal demands joint work towards the adoption of robust, resilient and comprehensive agreements and institutions.

References

Agreement (1959) *Agreement between the Republic of the Sudan and the United Arab Republic for the full utilization of the Nile waters*, signed at Cairo, Egypt, 8 November 1959

Awulachew, S. B., Smakhtin, V., Molden, D. and Peden, D. (eds) (2012) *The Nile River Basin: Water, Agriculture, Governance and Livelihoods*. Routledge, New York

Blackmore, D. and Whittington, D. (2008) *Opportunities for cooperative water resources development on the Eastern Nile: Risks and rewards. An independent report of the scoping study team to the Eastern Nile Council of Ministers*, World Bank, Washington, DC

Cascão, A.E. (2009) 'Changing power relations in the Nile River Basin: Unilateralism vs. cooperation?' *Water Alternatives*, 2(2), 245–268

Cascão, A.E. and Nicol, A. (2016a) 'Sudan, 'kingmaker' in a new Nile hydropolitics: Negotiating water and hydraulic infrastructure to expand large-scale irrigation', in Sandström, E., Jägerskog, A. and Oestigaard, T. (eds), *Land and hydropolitics in the Nile River Basin: Challenges and new investments*, Routledge, London, 89–116

Cascão, A.E. and Nicol, A. (2016b) 'Grand Ethiopian Renaissance Dam (GERD): New norms of cooperation in the Nile Basin?' *Water International*, 41(4), 550–573

Cascão, A.E. (2017) 'Food, fodder and flowers:
The critical role of global and regional virtual water trade in the Nile Basin'. Presentation at the 5th Nile Basin Development Forum, Kigali, Rwanda, October 2017

Cascão, A.E. (forthcoming) 'Water security in the Nile Basin: Understanding and expanding the "solution space"', *Water International*, Special Issue

Conniff, K., Molden, D., Peden, D. and Awulachew, S.B. (2012) 'Nile water and agriculture: Past, present and future', in Awulachew, S.B., Smakhtin, V., Molden, D. and Peden, D. (eds), *The Nile River Basin: Water, agriculture, governance and livelihoods*, Routledge, New York, 5–29

Ibrahim, A. (2012) 'Renewable energy sources in the Egyptian electricity market: A review', *Renewable & Sustainable Energy Reviews*, 16(1), 216–230

Jeuland, M., Wu, X. and Whittington, D. (2017) 'Infrastructure development and the economics of cooperation in the Eastern Nile', *Water International*, 42(2), 121–141

McCartney, M., Alemayehu, T., Easton, Z. and Awulachew, S. (2012) 'Simulating current and future water resources development in the Blue Nile River Basin', in Awulachew, S.B., Smakhtin, V., Molden, D. and Peden, D. (eds), *The Nile River Basin: Water, agriculture, governance and livelihoods*, Routledge, New York, 269–291

Molle, F., Wester, P. and Hirsch, P. (2010) 'River basin closure: Processes, implications and responses'. *Agricultural Water Management*, 97(4), 569–577

Nile Basin Initiative (NBI) (1999) *Policy guidelines for the Nile River Basin strategic action program*, NBI, Entebbe, Uganda

Nile Basin Initiative (NBI) (2012) *State of the Basin Report*, NBI, Entebbe, Uganda

Nile Basin Initiative (NBI) (2014) *Nile cooperation: Opportunities and challenges*, NBI Flagship Paper, NBI, Entebbe, Uganda

Salman, S.A. (2010) 'Downstream riparians can also harm upstream riparians: The concept of foreclosure of future uses' *Water International*, 35(4), 350–364

Sandström, E., Jägerskog, A. and Oestigaard, T. (eds) (2016) *Land and hydropolitics in the Nile River Basin: Challenges and new investments*, Routledge, London

Siam, M.S. and Eltahir, E.A.B. (2017) 'Climate change enhances interannual variability of the Nile river flow', *Nature Climate Change*, 7, 350–354

Sutcliffe, J.V. and Parks, Y. (1999) *The hydrology of the Nile*, IAHS Special Publication 5, IAHS Press, Wallingford

Tawfik, R. (2016) 'The Grand Ethiopian Renaissance Dam: A benefit-sharing project in the Eastern Nile?' *Water International*, 41(4), 574–592

Tvedt, T. (2004) *The River Nile in the age of the British – Political ecology and the quest for economic power*, IB Tauris, London

Waterbury, J. (1979) *Hydropolitics of the Nile Valley*, New York University Press, Syracuse

Wheeler, K.G., Basheer, M., Mekonnen, Z.T., Eltoum, S.O., Mersha, A., Abdo, G.M., Zagona, E.A., Hall, J.W. and Dadson, S.J. (2016) 'Cooperative filling approaches for the Grand Ethiopian Renaissance Dam' *Water International*, 41(4), 611–634

Whittington, D., Waterbury, J. and Jeulan, M. (2014) 'The Grand Renaissance Dam and prospects for cooperation on the Nile', *Water Policy*, 16, 595–608

World Bank (2017) World Bank Open Data – Arab Republic of Egypt https://data.worldbank.org/country/egypt-arab-rep

Yihdego, Z., Rieu-Clark, A., and Cascão, A.E. (eds) (2016) 'The Grand Ethiopian Renaissance Dam: Legal, political and scientific challenges', *Water International*, Special Issue, 41(4), 503–651

Yihdego, Z., Rieu-Clark, A., and Cascão, A.E. (eds) (2017) *The Grand Ethiopian Renaissance Dam and the Nile Basin: Implications for transboundary water cooperation*, Routledge, London

Zeitoun, M. and Warner, J. (2006) 'Hydro-hegemony – a framework for analysis of interstate water conflicts' *Water Policy*, 8(5), 435–460

Zeitoun, M., and Mirumachi, M. (2008), 'Transboundary water interaction I: Reconsidering conflict and cooperation', *International Environmental Agreements: Politics, Law and Economics*, 8(4), 297–316

Zeitoun, M., Allan, J.A. and Mohieldeen, Y. (2009) 'Virtual water 'flows' of the Nile Basin, 1998–2004: A first approximation and implications for water security', *Global Environmental Change*, 20(2), 229–242

Zeitoun, M., Mirumachi, N., and Warner, J. (2011), 'Transboundary water interaction II: Soft power underlying conflict and cooperation', *International Environmental Agreements: Politics, Law and Economics*, 11(2), 159–178

Zeitoun, M., Cascão, A., Warner, J., Mirumachi, N., Matthews, N., Menga, F., and Farnum, R. (2016) 'Transboundary water interaction III: Contest and compliance', *International Environmental Agreements: Politics, Law and Economics*, 17(2), 271–294

Part III

Transforming natural resource conflicts

11 Benefit sharing for project risk–conflict reduction and fostering sustainable development: Current understanding and mechanisms

Shivcharn S. Dhillion

Introduction

The surge and growing focus on renewable energy as a viable and sustainable source of energy is increasingly seen as a key component of planning for future energy needs. Renewable energy plays an important role in reducing greenhouse gas emissions and its increasing use is reducing demand for fossil fuels. Unlike fossil fuels, non-biomass renewable sources of energy like hydropower, geothermal, wind and solar do not directly emit greenhouse gases. Then why don't we use more renewable energy? In general, renewable energy is more expensive to produce and use than fossil fuel energy. Favourable renewable resources are often located in remote areas, and it can be expensive to build power lines from the renewable energy sources to the cities that need the electricity. In addition, renewable sources are not always available, e.g., dry periods can reduce the water available for hydropower production, electricity is reduced from solar power generators during cloudy periods and wind velocity affects rotation of wind turbine blades. This chapter will focus on experiences with hydropower projects (HPPs).

Hydropower development occupies a special niche in the current mode of environmental governance – as a low carbon solution to the rising energy demands and social inclusion when international standards of performance are practised (www.worldbank.org; www.ifc.org; www.adb.org). This is particularly so in low to middle income nations where infrastructure has historically limited and hindered development, and thus energy demand. In many nations with mountain areas providing the hydraulic head (height for the fall of water for power generation needs) and abundant water resources, like in Vietnam, Bhutan, East-Timor, Nepal, Lao PDR (Laos), Indonesia, Lesotho, Papua New Guinea and Ethiopia, hydropower power is emerging as a reliable, sustainable and economically viable source of energy. Those countries are now attracting foreign investments and seeing a growth in national developers.

Hydropower like other renewable energy resources requires a large land area for the infrastructure required for generation purposes, associated structures (including access roads) and/or for accumulation/storage of water in the form of reservoirs. There are various types of HPPs including those called the run-of-river which work to minimise the land-take for the project, nevertheless land has to be acquired for facilities. Hydropower projects require a fall in the height of the water to generate energy (turn turbines) – the greater the fall and availability of water, the more rapid and longer the turbines turn, the greater amount of energy that can be produced. Projects are often located in remote mountainous locations where harnessing water is possible for power generation and these HPPs supply energy where required (usually far from the physical location site of the project, nationally or internationally). Pressure of land and water resources is high and returns (including power supply) to the local communities can vary. Hydropower development requires that water and land resources are available and can be obtained from either state or private actors.

Proponents or developers of HPPs can be governmental and/or private (including joint-ventures). The proponents affect how the local affected actors are compensated and how natural resources (including biodiversity on land and water) are managed. Developers complying with international standards and requirements usually strive to ensure that fair and equitable measures are used and that sustainable development is a goal. Such developers include several multinational energy developers (state and private) and are often supported through loans by international development/financing agencies and at times development agencies of donor nations. Increasingly national or regional banks are opening portfolios for such developments (e.g., Indonesia Infrastructure Finance, India Infrastructure Finance Corporation). Development agencies can be involved in rather stringent due diligence processes requiring adherence and monitoring of projects as can the multilateral financing agencies with the aim of reducing financial, environmental and social risks. Less serious proponents generally do not adhere to international practice and these are the ones which are often laden with conflicts rooted in unsound impact assessments, non-inclusive practices and poor stakeholder participation and incomprehensive compensation and livelihood restoration measures. The lack of inspection (due diligence), monitoring and evaluation processes lend to projects risks and unresolved conflicts.

Opponents claim that there is mounting evidence that there exist modern non-hydropower renewable technologies with the capacity to meet a substantial proportion of the global electricity demand. Hydropower installations have grave consequences to natural resources and local community livelihoods, often causing disintegration of social networks, unsuccessful relocation and devastating impact on environments (land and particular fishes/fisheries in managed water ways). In addition, it exploits the rights of people to their ancestral resources. Affected people are rarely informed in full, in time or included in decision making. One of the most relevant critics to HPPs has been associated to the unequal distribution of costs and benefits. A large share of costs are carried by the local communities – usually in isolated and rural areas – and most of the benefits are being accrued to urban populations and industries. This feature constitutes a 'structural' challenge to the hydropower industry. The 'structural challenge' has to do with the fact that most hydropower projects are physically located in isolated, rural, poor areas – whereas the 'benefits' of electrification often are 'exported' to urban (often far-away) areas. Under these conditions, then, the rationale for benefit sharing in the sector is a must for the long-term social-economic-environmental sustainability of the investments. Serious proponents learning from HPPs related unfair social practices and environmental catastrophes have recently turned to instill requirements for benefit sharing going beyond the obligatory (legal) mitigation and compensatory requirements.

History, rationale and concept of benefit sharing

The concept of benefit sharing can be traced back to its origin in two UN resolutions[1] 1979 and 1982 and has lingered in development arenas. Benefit sharing was introduced as a core concept in the objectives of the Convention on Biological Diversity (UNEP, 1992) to point to the potential need to share equities/royalties from the sales of biodiversity-related drugs/medicines. This concept hinged on the premise that biodiversity is based in biological abundant environments which is likely be home to rural or forest-dwelling communities who not only depend on the natural resources around them but have profound knowledge of the resources. This knowledge is likely to be developed over generations (imbedded in local cultural intellectual knowledge and practice) and is referred to as traditional 'ecological' knowledge (TEK) (Svarstad and Dhillion, 2000; Dhillion et al., 2002; Berkes, 1999). In the context of infrastructure, developers require land and water resources both in terms of a source of energy and space for establishing the physical structures needed. The land-take thus can include forested or vegetation-covered land, land in use by local communities, and ecosystems rich in terrestrial, avain and aquatic habitats infringing on ecosystem services and watershed/basin integrity (Ahlers, et al., 2015; Dhillion, 2017).

Origins of benefit sharing in the hydropower sector

Social and environmental impacts from HPPs became recurrent and have captured the attention of public opinion and NGOs since the late 1980s. Prominent arguments are: flooding of productive agricultural land and wildlife habitats, the displacement of indigenous groups, the submergence of communities and/or cultural heritage sites, the effects of construction and operating regimes of hydropower facilities on fish/aquatic habitats and slow-occurring cumulative effects. In addition to the above, the emergence of environmental concerns related to the use and exploitation of natural resources led to a closer focus towards social and environmental sustainability in the hydropower industry. Following this recognition, different efforts have been made by the industry to overcome criticisms. In particular, there were at least two relevant efforts that aimed to improve the social performance of hydropower investments that introduced the concept of 'benefit sharing': International Energy Agency (IEA, 2000) and World Commission on Dams (WCD, 2000).

Benefit sharing principles

The extractive sector (mining) has a long history and more established benefit sharing regime based on two important principles which also work for the renewable energy sector and particularly hydropower. According to the first *principle of derivation*, the revenue is shared by derivation when a percentage of the revenues is allocated upfront to the producing territory (area of origin) which may be local community institutions, local and regional governments. This is the case in, for example, Bolivia, Brazil, Colombia, Indonesia, Papua New Guinea, Mexico, Chile and Ghana that have adopted the derivation principle in sharing the benefit among stakeholders involved in the extractive sector. The second principle known as *principle of need* suggests that resources should be distributed based on need so that those with greater need will receive a greater share – this is the case for Botswana, for example. It is noteworthy that Norway has decided not to spend revenues received from the oil sector and they are kept in a sovereign fund. Either geared towards derivation or need, it is important to note that mineral-rich countries have considered the use of Foundations, Trusts and Funds (FTFs) as vehicles for sharing the benefits of mining operations with the surrounding communities (Wall, 2014).

Correa (2010) outlines the underlying principles derived from these initiatives that are relevant for benefit sharing in hydropower/multipurpose development. In short, revised, these are: (i) equitable and fair sharing of benefits arising from resource use; (ii) appropriate sharing arrangements and access to resources by those who contribute directly and indirectly to the exploitation and use of the resource and; (iii) priority access and special consideration on benefit sharing to those in a disadvantaged position related to the utilisation of the resource. Fields (in Sweco, 2011) proposed 'A framework to maximize and distribute benefits across stakeholders, consistent with the principles of sustainability' as a practical working definition of benefit sharing. These concepts, illustrated in Table 11.1, build on the idea of the use of one natural resource for a single output which feasibly may allow for multiple interventions across a landscape with potential development effects. The scalar aspects are important in defining benefit sharing although regional and national benefit sharing measures cannot overshadow local affected people or community interventions.

Conflicts around hydropower and, in general, large-scale infrastructure development

The key actors involved in conflicts related to hydropower development are developers and the affected people. NGOs, development agencies and financing agencies can play a vital role in surfacing conflicts, and assure that the appropriate processes and safeguards are in place to reduce conflicts. It has been

Table 11.1 Interpretation of various aspects of benefit sharing across issues and scales

From single output .... to multiple interests at different scales		
Single output	**Local** → to	**Regional** → **National** → **Transboundary**
ENERGY as output Source: water, nat-ural resource use: water and land	*Upstream and downstream project* Aquatic ecosystems & fisheries Irrigated agriculture, forestry Domestic – liveli-hoods, local commu-nity infrastructure Wildlife and river bank Ecosystem services Mobility	Irrigation Flood management Watershed management Environmental protection/conservation Regional electricity transmission Infrastructure development (e.g., roads for mobility and access)
Benefit sharing	Weak definition.......... moving to ....Strong definition (more obligatory ....not mandatory (unless regulated))	

Various scalar aspects of types of benefit sharing interventions possible based on an energy source

well documented that large-scale HPPs have considerable consequences for the environment and groups of people living both upstream and downstream of hydropower installations. In many developing countries, dams are built without the full participation and consent of local inhabitants and without the proper environmental and social impact assessments. Local populations rarely receive the necessary compensation for their loss of habitat and livelihood. The sub-sequent energy that is produced by the dams often bypasses local populations and is sent to regional and national hubs where it is used predominantly to power industrial demands. In addition, the power produced is often too expensive for the majority of rural inhabitants. Some of the key challenges (not all-encompassing) are listed in Table 11.2.

Global financing for hydropower projects and the surge for using benefit sharing approaches

After the publication of the World Commission on Dams (WCD, 2000) report the hydropower sector suffered from a period of low investments by multi-lateral and regional financial institutions and critics from different stakeholders. The pivotal report pointed clearly to uplifting requirements (standards) for hydropower development targeted at proponents (developers/owners) and solutions for reducing adverse effects on humans and the environment. Projects'

Table 11.2 Key challenges faced in hydropower project development and the role of benefit sharing in addressing these challenges

Examples of challenges causing conflicts due to inadequate adherence to requirements or weak/ vague national policies	*Role that benefit sharing can play*
Assuring adequate resettlement/relocation compensation is provided by project owners, i.e., in agreement with affected households and land owners. Not doing this has resulted in dissatisfaction creating risk for developers where projects are stopped or halted by affected people (or their representatives, e.g., NGOs), by protests, locking of gates to project sites, blocking of roads, violence and robbing of sites of equipment.	This is usually a project-based action and benefit sharing does not come into play. Here the authorities and due diligence processes have to keep this in check. Enhancing the livelihood measures through benefit sharing funds can help ease tension and conflicts and often allow parties to discuss terms.
Ensuring that a range of livelihood restoration measures are used and affected communities and households accept these and have the knowhow to use them. Inadequate measures can lead to risk for developers as mentioned above due to the devastation of livelihoods and subsequent increase in poverty levels. It must be understood that not all affected persons/households are able to easily bounce back after being relocated in hydropower projects – the impacts are high and multifaceted, including psychological.	Benefit sharing measures can extend and enhance the magnitude of livelihood measures through financial allocations for capacity building related to agriculture methods, machinery, long-term follow-up, creating SMEs and providing resources for assuring markets for produce, etc.
Adequate measures for securing that forest and water ecosystem services are not lost and if reduced alternative options substituting these are included in project environmental and social management plans.	Benefit sharing can provide financial means for the set-up of trusts and funds for watershed management institutions.
Ensuring that all affected people, particularly the vulnerable, are included in decision making and agreed targeted measures are in place.	Benefit sharing can assure added funds for vulnerable groups in building-up livelihood means, for example training women for SME set-up and management, assuring their inclusion for health and education, providing land ownership to assure that livelihoods are manageable.
Lack of local (community-based) or regional institutions to partake in decision making in the above issues and also in the follow-up monitoring processes.	Funds through benefit sharing regimes go beyond the usual environmental and social management plans to provide for trust funds, project development loans, forest management committees and women groups for decision making at the local level.

Examples of challenges causing conflicts due to inadequate adherence to requirements or weak/ vague national policies	*Role that benefit sharing can play*
Lack of national and/or project policy or strategy and action plans which call for safety-nets (safeguards) to come into play when affected people fail to regain livelihoods.	Benefit sharing has in a number of countries been introduced through national policy and/or project strategy to provide additional development input to the project going beyond the usual project level required (nationally mandatory) environmental and social mitigation and enhancement.

proponents needed to be responsible for mitigation of impacts: fairly compensating, restoring livelihoods and making sound environmental conservation decisions – aiming to sustainable development. It was through the WCD report that the hydropower sector was introduced to the potential need for employing benefit sharing regimes for enhancing or going beyond required mitigation measures – so that firstly revenues or royalties from the sales of power could be shared with stakeholders. This resulted in changes in requirements internationally (multilateral banks, donor nations and some national governments) and investments in HPPs have gradually changed in the last decade.

There is growing evidence that to mitigate and minimise existing and future resource conflicts especially related to livelihoods and cultural heritage, approaches and pathways that transform brewing conflicts are looked for by developers (and proponents). One key pathway is that of benefit sharing regimes coupled with communication, which can nurture and enforce collaboration necessary for any form of sustainable development. The spatial localisation (far from those who pay for the power and which proponents tend to focus on) of the HPPs can limit the trickle down of benefits unless specific social development investment programs are undertaken in the area impacted by the project (the project footprint). In this context, hydropower companies and governments must often take action to share benefits at the local level – an action which can only be feasible through project-based policy/strategy, national legal requirements and/or requirement of loan providers.

Current status of hydropower development and new paradigms – fostering conflict minimisation and sustainable development

After many years of gradual dampening of pugnacious opposition to dam constructions, hydropower is back on the international donor and financial institutions agenda. International Finance Institutions and Multilateral Development Banks[2] are renewing their investments in hydropower: parallel to the development of new paradigms and instilling of new policies. Starting with the World Commission on Dams (WCD, 2000) which pushed for stringent regulations for hydropower development across financing institutions, there have been a range of now anchored initiatives – including integrated resource management, sustainability, cumulative and strategic assessment guidelines – all pointing to the recognition of the requirements of sustainability. The IPCC (2011) report clearly supported hydropower as a vital renewable energy vehicle that can contribute to mitigating climate change, recognising that social and environmental issues will remain challenging. While some of the old debates on environmental impact are being revisited, new narratives and discourses on processes, structuring and value of benefit sharing at national to local levels are being placed upfront in infrastructure development.

The contemporary discourse on infrastructure development and benefit sharing parallels a broader reframing of hydropower development as an important trigger for sustainable development. Resource use beyond biological resources includes water-land-cultural resource use and loss/dilution, particularly to indigenous communities. Here other sectors have included the following issues into benefit sharing regimes: property rights and entitlement to resources (water, land, public goods) and access, which are also beginning to surface as pertinent and, in some cases, formidable issues of concern both to proponents, donors and local communities in hydropower projects. Within this context, hydropower development is also seen as a path for working towards resolving embedded issues of social and environmental equity in resource use and environmental governance within water and climate realms. Thus, benefit sharing is seen as a vehicle to transform conflicts and fulfil expectations of mitigation to a greater extent than before (Fig. 11.1). In the case of weak governance, poor environmental and social impacts assessment resulting in poorly developed mitigation and compensation action plans, the well-being of communities is jeopardised and actions can lead to conflicts and resentment towards project development. For proponents of HPPs, private or non-private, securing a *social licence to operate* (SLO) is also increasingly seen as an integral part of hydropower development and for achieving trust and legitimacy with affected people.

Framing benefit sharing

Hydropower and related multipurpose development is increasingly recognised as providing multiple opportunities to significantly enhance development of communities at local levels but also at regional and transboundary levels if planned, designed and implemented in a sustainable manner. However, it is also widely recognised that for hydropower projects to contribute effectively to poverty alleviation and social development, the quality of projects must be enhanced and driven by imperatives of sustainable development with a strong focus on broader development goals. In general, there is no dispute that for many HPPs and, specifically, multipurpose dams, there may be a significant number of possible options that can derive benefits to wider stakeholder groups. The need to consider multiple, and often conflicting, objectives for a large number of stakeholders, and across a broad spectrum of scales constrained by geographical location, of the infrastructures and remoteness, means that a

A. Limited measures and intangible well-being based on inadequate environmental and social impact assessment and prescribed management for minimising, mitigating and resettlement compensation.

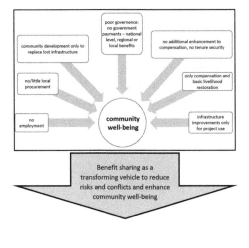

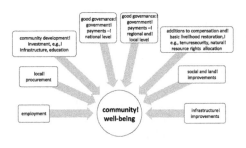

Challenges that create conflicts and jeopardise well-being:

The national requirements in most nations do not call for benefit sharing measures. Strict mitigation and compensation measures are to adhere to national legal requirements which may have limitations.

Governments want to keep similar levels of mitigation across projects as those applying elaborate measures (like those prescribed by the World Bank or development agencies) may create tension across sectors and communities. Proponents and investors are eager to develop projects and have little time for detailed stake-holder/community involvement to design proper mitigation/resettlement.

Importantly the environmental and social impact assessment conducted is not comprehensive and lacking elements that allow sound management of impacts which is required for tangible benefit sharing to be developed.

The lack of recognition/inclusion of indigenous people, vulnerable groups and gender leading to unagreed compensation and mitigation.

Lack of land for relocation of affected people (resettlement).

Unfair compensation for loss of physical and livelihood losses, including that associated with ecosystems (terrestrial and aquatic) and biodiversity.

B. Potential areas of project developers' social and economic contributions often anchored in both required environmental and social mitigation and additional enhancement – ideal areas that proponents could develop under benefit sharing regimes to instill well-being. Some of the funds allocated go via government royalty contributions trickling back via targeted allocations to regional and local levels (government or community-based organisations).

Note that keeping clarity between obligatory measures (those required by law for compensation and mitigation) and enhancement through benefit sharing is important (although not always easy) so that communities are informed as to the nature of the measures and their rightful entitlements.

Figure 11.1 Main categories of project owner contribution (A) that affect community well-being and where benefit sharing regimes (B) can transform the quality of well-being

huge number of decision variables and constraints may need to be considered. Our experiences in these arenas are still new and uncharted across nations and projects. This is mainly due to the benefit sharing measures required going beyond the obligatory measures of mitigation and compensation which do not necessarily encompass sustained social development.

Disentangling benefit sharing and mechanisms

Project promoters may share project benefits through two broadly obvious mechanisms: monetary and/or non-monetary mechanisms. Most common forms of *monetary benefit sharing mechanisms* include:

Revenue sharing
Development funds
Equity sharing
Property taxes/Royalties/Resource fees
Preferential electricity rates

Through these mechanisms the benefits from investment projects are being shared with local communities. One important aspect to consider is that some of these mechanisms do not target directly or exclusively affected populations but may be used to finance long-term local/regional development initiatives. As such these mechanisms may also support the creation of long-term partnership between developers and concerned communities, a core approach of Corporate Social Responsibility (CSR) regimes.

Non-monetary mechanisms are probably more common as they are usually part of Environmental and Social Management/Action Plans (ESMPs/ESAPs) in the form of mitigation and compensation packages. Most common forms of non-monetary benefit sharing mechanisms are listed in Table 11.3. Hydropower companies and governments manifest their socially responsible behaviour through diverse mechanisms aiming at (Égré, 2007; Roquet and Durocher, 2006; Dhillion, 2014; Nair, 2014; Ahlers et al., 2015):

- **compensation** of project-affected populations usually by means of monetary compensation for lost assets and loss of access to resources
- **restoration** of the livelihoods of project-affected populations living in the vicinity of a hydropower development by means of non-monetary or monetary benefit sharing mechanisms
- **enhancing and improving** the livelihoods of project-affected populations living in the vicinity of a hydropower development by means of non-monetary or monetary benefit sharing mechanisms

In the case of the two last types of mechanisms it is often difficult to draw a strict line to distinguish between what corresponds to mandatory mitigation commitments (i.e., to restore existing pre-project conditions) and what goes beyond it, to

Table 11.3 Monetary and non–monetary instruments used in hydropower development to manifest socially responsive behaviour

Main mechanism/ instruments	*Main objective – obligatory and non-obligatory*	
	Mitigation and restoration (obligatory)	*Enhancing local development (Benefit sharing programs, non-obligatory)*
Monetary	Monetary compensation for lost assets or access to resources	Revenue sharing Development funds Equity sharing Property taxes/Royalties/Resource fees Preferential electricity/water-related rates Payment for Environment/Ecosystem Services (PES)
Non-monetary	Livelihood restoration and enhancement Community development (health, education, mobility) Concessions for natural resource use Catchment/watershed development	

improve existing conditions. Benefit sharing initiatives deal mostly with the third type of mechanism, mechanisms that go beyond the monetary compensation for lost assets and/or loss of access to resources, namely, non-monetary and monetary local development enhancing mechanisms. Since in the case of non-monetary mechanisms some instruments usually aim simultaneously to restore and to improve existing conditions, there is a need to advance towards a concept that is more operational.

From an overall development framework, it can be argued that all the instruments included as 'enhancing local development' in Table 11.3 can act as local development drivers. Both monetary and non-monetary instruments can contribute to local development initiatives. There are at least two (interrelated) criteria under which one could classify these instruments according to potential for contributing to local development. The first criteria would be the degree of targeting that can be expected from the instrument, whether the beneficiaries should be restricted to exclusively or mostly restricted to the project-affected population. For instance, a regional development fund would most likely promote regional development and thus benefit both project-affected and not-affected populations. The second criteria would be the degree of centralisation (regional-national vs local) of the funds/initiatives being part of the benefit sharing program.

From an economic point of view, the positive externalities that may be triggered by both types of instruments can improve the welfare of the beneficiary communities, if applied and monitored. Improved road access, improved access and quality of health and education centres, strengthening of local private and public organisations, etc., all have a positive contribution to local development. Monetary instruments are more intangible when provided directly to affected households – where there is danger of mismanagement and distribution among household members.

Both instruments are used as part of typical ESMPs and also as part of benefit sharing programs, as it can be seen that non-monetary instruments can be used indistinctively as part of mitigation/restoration packages (in ESMPs) and as part of benefit sharing programs. From an overall development perspective, considering both types of mechanisms (monetary and non-monetary) as actual contributions to enhance local development appears as a reasonable approach. From an operational perspective it will be a challenge to be able to disentangle non-monetary benefit sharing mechanisms from plain mitigation and compensatory measures. Detailed studies of HPPs show that directly affected communities were not always clear on the difference between compensation and livelihood restoration measures and those considered as additional (IIED, 2014; Sweco, 2011). When benefit sharing measures are intertwined with obligatory compensations, expectations from communities appear to be lifted to levels where larger contributions from the proponent increasingly include benefit sharing measures (Table 11.3), thus including non-obligatory measures. The result of this was a confusion of expectations and the actual nature (e.g., proponent's contribution of revenues) of benefit sharing.

Benefit sharing mechanisms – typology

Major categories of benefit sharing mechanisms employing either monetary or non-monetary instruments, or both, can be categorised as presented in Table 11.4. The typology requires consideration of geographical scale, that is, the segment of society likely to be affected by a given mechanism (Figure 11.1; Table 11.4). Beneficiary groups can be defined at many levels; each application of the suggested typology may thus be tailored to specific circumstances and local/national/regional-transboundary conditions. The mechanisms can be reached via a range of entry points and the portfolio of measures is wide and varied (Tables 11.3, 11.4 and 11.5; Box 11.1). CSR is an entry point based on reports mainly related to private proponent initiative, whether reactive or proactive in nature (Table 11.4).

Box 11.1 Examples of benefit sharing mechanisms across countries

Countries and mechanisms used in hydropower projects

Burkina Faso Fixed tax on infrastructure value paid to local government

Canada Trust Fund from revenues specific to Columbia basin HPP projects; Equity sharing: in Cree Nation payments from the State Government for all types of resource extraction

Colombia 3% of gross hydropower sales each to environmental authority and local municipality: local employment; infrastructure development; local institutional and capacity building

Costa Rica Payment of Environmental Services, watershed management instruments

Ghana Resettlement Trust Fund
India Preferential electricity rates
Lao PDR Revenues to Government; Environmental/Watershed Protection programs; livelihood capacity building programs
Lesotho Fund for community development
Mali Royalties, 60% to municipality and 40% to province/region
Nepal Royalties (10% of revenues) paid to national government for distribution to local level: local development programs (education, health); community fund; community/household shares in local electrification schemes
Norway 28% tax on profits, property taxes, natural resource taxes, licence fees towards business development fund; preferential electricity rates
Philippines CSR fund – voluntary contributions to 3 national funds
South Africa Educational, mobility and land use support
Vietnam Local development fund – community based

Sources: IIED, 2014; Sweco, 2011; Wang, 2012; Dhillion (personal observations, 2011–2018)

Concluding key elements and enablers of benefit sharing

Underlying principles derived from experiences and practices relevant for benefit sharing in hydropower development that transform conflicts and reduce risks are:

- Equitable and fair sharing of benefits arising from resource use
- Appropriate sharing arrangements and access to resources by those who contribute directly and indirectly to the exploitation and use of the resource are necessary to ensure sustainable development and affected persons' well-being
- Special consideration on benefit sharing to those in a disadvantaged position related to the utilisation of the resource
- Landscape/ecosystem transformation requires compensation and mitigation assuring that affected persons are not rendered disadvantaged post-hydropower (infrastructure) development
- Affected persons are included in the decision-making processes. Communication is informed and participatory.

Benefit sharing can work against communities as learned from a number of HPPs, for example, where money can land up in a few hands, or if benefit sharing is done rapidly and is non-inclusive of gender and vulnerable groups, and when it goes unmonitored. There is an absolute need to involve those directly affected in the design of benefit sharing regimes.

Table 11.4 Typology of mechanisms and potential entry points for benefit sharing

Mechanism	Entry points for benefit sharing (enablers)	Description
Project design and operations	Policy and Regulatory Instrument at feasibility evaluation stage	Maximise benefits of flexible infrastructure and integrated resource management, e.g., multi-purpose infrastructure (flood control, irrigation), managed flows, watershed management
Ancillary investments	Local–regional development plans CSR Mitigation instruments (enhancement)	Investments outside core infrastructure to broaden reach of benefits, e.g., social infrastructure (including access to resources), community programs (social, education, health, agriculture), conservation, ecosystem services and catchment treatment
Financial allocations (Including royalty and equity investments)	Policy instrument CSR	Distribute economic rents, e.g., taxes, development funds, preferential rates, joint ownership (equity investment, local share offers in HPPs). Royalty regimes and equitable electricity access. Institutional frameworks can act as enablers.
Institutions	Local, regional and national development plans including institutional framework development CSR Mitigation instruments (enhancement)	Build enabling environment for leveraging benefits, e.g., (i) knowledge sharing, river basin organisation, SME development, development planning capacities at regional and national levels, and (ii) knowledge sharing, stakeholder–community organisations/ institutions (agriculture, infrastructure, health and education, gender, youth) and thematic local focus groups.
Policies	National strategic plans	Building and assuring requirements for benefit sharing through a range of mechanisms including institutional frameworks
Capacity building	Development plans CSR Mitigation instruments (enhancement)	Building required knowhow for designing, implementation and monitoring benefit sharing measures. Community-level capacity to manage funds both on household levels (small-scale industry; women-run businesses) is required when measures are aimed at increasing household fund management and security.

Adapted from: World Bank 2009; IIED 2014

Table 11.5 Example of benefit sharing targeted at local community well-being and environmental protection

Lao PDR. The Nam Theun 2 project set by various capacity building programs for enhancing livelihoods through testing new systems and seeds via agricultural training programs.

An extensive health care and improvement program was implemented and has improved general health levels.

This is usually only possible with additional funds going beyond the usual mitigation requirements. Here benefit sharing is a viable tool.

Integrated Community Health Center at Sop On, a village of resettled households

The Nam Theun 2 (NT2) project also set up a trust for environmental protection and an institution for watershed management to safeguard forest resources – protecting biodiversity and ecosystem services.

A community-based forest management plan was also set up providing local communities a 70-year concession for forest use.

Increasing health-care awareness among women

Nepal. Through benefit sharing the project owner in the Khimti hydropower project, the project initiated a partnership with an international NGO (UNDP) and local communities where a local electrical energy supply cooperative was set up where each household had an equal share. The cooperative is managemed and run by local communities where expert management training has been provided.

In addition, an ambulance system and use of the project health clinic (for workers) for local communities is fully functional. Furthermore, an extensive irrigation system financed by the project owner has been set up by governance through local institutions (user-groups).

Project health clinic for workers also allowed access to villages. It is used by villages beyond the project's footprint (area of impact) thus benefiting a wider area.

A number of scholarships for higher education (university level) are also made available for qualified students from the communities.

The actions of the project owner were part based on its own Corporate Social Responsibility strategy and not a government requirement.

These actions, among others, led to high acceptance of the hydropower project and reduced risk for the project owners.

Source: Photographs taken by author. See also Lao PDR, Nam Theun 2 (NT2) HPP (https://www.namtheun2.com/); Nepal, http://hpl.com.np/projects/khimti-power-plant/; Wang, 2012; Sweco, 2011; Dhillion, 2014.

Today many governments and proponents (hydropower developers) shy away from benefit sharing going beyond the minimum required compensation and mitigation – thus there is still much ground to cover in terms of learning how benefit sharing can work in the long run, how it is to be framed, if legal requirements are the only way to assure benefit sharing, and if it justifies the argument for large-scale infrastructure developments like dams and ultimately sustainable development. In many countries there is the issue of corruption and thus instilling transparent management of funds related to benefit sharing regimes is challenging and at times not possible. Further, benefit sharing returns in investments by the community may end up as 'elite capture'.

Proponents can face unjustifiable demands due to misunderstandings of the nature and scope of benefit sharing which is largely non-obligatory (Fig. 11.2). Of relevance is to realise that, in practice, it is difficult for project owners to draw a categorical line between obligatory and non-obligatory aspects, for example compensation and livelihood restoration, where extra funds through benefit sharing enhance the planned livelihood measures and work as extensions of compensation and associated enhancement measures (Wang, 2012; Dhillion, 2017).

Social acceptance to operate hydropower projects

Social risks arise because the expectations of external stakeholders are broader or different than those defined by legislation, regulatory approvals and/or the conditions of project financing. While it is universally accepted that a legal

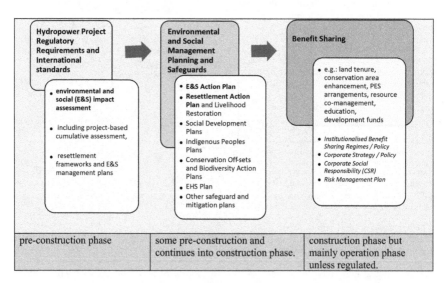

Figure 11.2 Hydropower project development and required, obligatory and non-obligatory measures

licence is required from the relevant government agencies, project proponents are also acknowledging the importance of obtaining a *social licence to operate* (SLO). Establishing good relationships with stakeholders and focusing on their concerns can generate significant positive opportunities for the project and proponent. It is critical that project stakeholders are not just seen as a source of negative risks to projects. The bottom line is that with a proper approach the potential social risks can be converted into potential social opportunities, requiring a systematic approach to managing both aspects (risks and opportunities).

Undoubtedly, community engagement is part and parcel of a successful social responsibility strategy (Wynberg et al., 2009; Dhillion and Granfelt, 2010; Dhillion, 2014; Dhillion, 2017; Dhillion, 2018). Some developing nations (like Lao PDR, Nepal, Vietnam and Bhutan) are starting to include benefit sharing and social responsibility – accountability – into policy regimes. There is also a significant amount of theory building up around the issue of CSR and its sustainability (e.g., Reinhardt, et al., 2008; IIED, 2014). However, the mechanisms and assessments required for stakeholder understanding require deeper understanding from a practical standpoint. Although arguably approaches and mechanistic processes may be case specific there are likely processes that are applicable globally.

Making benefit sharing plans tangible

Benefit sharing plans and precise measures may be agreeable to all parties involved but their implementation and success can be hinged on the following:

- Policy and Regulatory frameworks. Institutional presence and establishment.
- Presence and type of implementation arrangement. Responsibilities of parties involved, procedures/protocols and operational plans required. Monitoring and evaluation.
- Institutional agreements.
- Communication policy and strategy, including complaint management.
- Community representation, engagement and mobilisation, indigenous cultures.
- Funding arrangements and clarity in purpose and flow of funds. Partnerships.
- Capacity building for implementation and management of benefit sharing plans. Technical and human resource needs.

Without doubt, benefit sharing is now viewed as a vital component of sustainable hydropower development and management – aiming to assure well-being, gain acceptance locally and as a practical instrument for encouraging cooperation among differently-positioned stakeholders. It is a new key enabling mechanism to many environmental and social safeguard arrangements. It is however only practised by a few serious actors and needs to gain ground to show it is a viable mechanism for sustainable hydropower development. At this stage our experiences are few but there is promising potential when projects actually go beyond the basic obligations of mitigation and compensation.

Notes

1 The Agreement governing the activities of states on the Moon and other celestial bodies (1979) and the Convention on the Law of the Sea (1982).
2 The World Bank upgraded its E&S Framework and safeguard policies in 2017. http://www.worldbank.org/en/programs/environmental-and-social-policies-for-p rojects/brief/environmental-and-social-safeguards-policies

References

Ahlers, R., Budds, J., Joshi, D., Merme, V. and Zwarteveen, M. (2015) 'Framing hydropower as green energy: Assessing drivers, risks and tensions in the Eastern Himalayas', *Earth System Dynamics*, 6, 195–204

Berkes, F. (1999) *Sacred ecology: Traditional ecological knowledge and resource management*, Taylor & Francis, London

Correa, E. (2010) *Benefit sharing vs. local sustainable development: Providing meaning of benefit sharing into a local sustainable development framework*, Draft Report, The World Bank, ID 423

Dhillion, S.S., Svarstad, H., Amundsen, C. and Bugge, H.C. (2002) 'Bioprospecting: Effects on the environment and development', *AMBIO* 31(6), 491–493

Dhillion, S.S. and Granfelt, T. (2010) 'Enhancing stakeholder participation: Mainstreaming global threats and, cumulative and trans-boundary impacts', *The International Journal of Hydropower and Dams*, ASIA 2010, E-publication, www.hydrop ower-dams.com

Dhillion, S.S. (2014) 'Benefit sharing and enhancing development', in 'Resettlement, rehabilitation and benefit sharing in infrastructure development', Nair, R. (ed.), *Journal of Management*, 44(1), 51–53

Dhillion, S.S. (2017) 'Informed consultations and participation (ICP): Legacy, IPs, livelihoods', IAIA and Inter-American Dev Bank, Washington, DChttp://conferences.ia ia.org/wdc2017/presentations.php

Égré, D. (2007) *Benefit sharing issue, Compendium on relevant practices* – Dams and Development Project, United Nations Environment Programme, Geneva

IEA (2000) 'Hydropower and the environment: Present context and guidelines for future action', in *IEA technical report*, Annex III, Vol. I: Summary and recommendations, Paris

IIED (2014) 'Redistribution of revenues from hydropower dams', IIED, Londonwww. iied.org/pubs

IIF (2018) http://iif.co.id/en/

IPCC (2011) 'Summary for policymakers', in *IPCC special report on renewable energy sources and climate mitigation*, Cambridge University Press, Cambridge, UK

Nair, R. (ed.) (2014) 'Resettlement, Rehabilitation and Benefit Sharing in infrastructure Development', *Journal of Management*, 44(1), 41–46

Reinhardt, F.L., Stavins, R.N. and Vietor, R.H.K. (2008) 'Corporate social responsibility through an economic lens', *Review of Environmental Economics and Policy*, 2(2), 219–239

Roquet, V. and Durocher, C. (2006) *Compensation policy issue, Compendium on relevant practices* – Dams and Development Project, United Nations Environment Programme, Geneva

Svarstad, H. and Dhillion, S.S. (eds) (2000) *Responding to Bioprospecting: from biodiversity in the South to medicines in the North.* Spartacus Press AS, Oslo.

Sweco (2011) *Synthesis report – Benefit sharing and hydropower: Enhancing development benefits of hydropower investments through an operational framework,* Lillehammer, L., San Martin, O. and Dhillion, S.S. (eds), World Bank

UNEP (1992) *Convention on biological diversity*https://www.cbd.int/convention/

Wall, E. (2014) 'Benefit sharing in the extractive sector', *Journal of Management,* 44(1), 41–46

Wang, C. (2012) *A guide for local benefit sharing in hydropower projects,* World Bank Social Development Working Paper No. 128, June 2012

WCD (2000) *Dams and development: A framework for decision making,* Earthscan, London

World Bank (2009) *Benefits sharing and hydropower: Enhancing development benefits of hydropower investment through an operational framework – Concept note,* World Bank, Washington, DC

Wynberg, R., Schroeder, D. and Chennells, R. (2009) *Indigenous peoples, consent and benefit sharing,* Springer, New York

12 Power and knowledge use in coastal conflict resolution

Olga Stepanova

Introduction

Coasts are complex nodes of interrelated synergies of human activities and development, the scale and rate of which is unprecedented in human history (Šunde, 2008; IOC/UNESCO, 2011). Coasts are now a frontline area of the sustainability crisis with the majority of the world's population and economic activity situated there (Šunde, 2008; IOC/UNESCO, 2011). With two thirds of the megacities of the world situated on the coast, rapid urbanisation and population growth are the development trends that contribute to the growing pressure on coastal natural resources (Pelling and Blackburn, 2014; Barragán and de Andrés, 2015). Urban development on the coast creates an intensification of resource use, and subsequently competition for access to limited resources, which in turn leads to conflicts among different stakeholders involved such as residents, commuters, tourists, enterprises, political actors, public administrations and other organisations. Conflicts, competition for and access to resources are likely to become more severe in the future, especially in coastal areas (Weinstein et al., 2007). This calls for more attention to be given to conflict and its resolution in coastal resource management.

Coastal conflicts are complex and include ecological and environmental components together with social, cultural, political and economic ones (Cadoret, 2009). In their social component, for example their management and resolution methods, coastal conflicts are not so different from any other resource use conflicts. Normative components of rights, interests, responsibilities, positions and worldviews of different stakeholders are intertwined with competing forms of resource use, internal and external power relations, for example through local political and economic contexts that affect the development of conflicts. However, conflicts in coastal areas are specific in their spatial delimitations, in their ecological components related to the coastal ecosystems, the services they provide, their sensitivity to environmental change, and in the intensity of responses to growing anthropogenic pressure (Brown et al., 2008).

Non-violent, local natural resource use conflicts and their resolution at European urbanised coasts are the focus of this chapter. The discussion is based on a summary of the analysis of three conflict cases from Belgium, the UK and Sweden, studied within the international project SECOA 'Solutions to Environmental Contrasts in Coastal Areas' (2009–2013) funded by the European Commission 7th Framework Programme 2007–2013[1]. I discuss the importance of themes of knowledge use, in particular knowledge integration, and power inequalities for more lasting and long-term oriented local conflict resolution. I also identify one case where conflict was transformed into a more cooperative mode and reached an accepted solution. It is emphasised that more attention needs to be paid to power inequalities and practices of knowledge use in processes of conflict resolution along with making flexible conflict resolution integral to management and planning.

Coastal conflicts

In recent studies of fisheries, aquaculture and coastal land use, conflicts are seen as a natural part of coastal social-ecological dynamics when many different users with heterogeneous interests use the resources (Seijger et al., 2014; Stepanova, 2014; 2015; Tuda et al., 2014). For the term 'conflict', I use the delimitation criteria that include local, coastal and non-violent conflict between organised actor groups. I differentiate between 'environmental conflicts' and 'resource use conflicts' where the former refers to the broader concept of natural environment and climate (Leal Filho et al., 2008), and the latter refers to particular living and non-living natural resources (for example water, land, fish). I use the notion of 'resource use conflict' because the conflicts referred to here have clear connections to certain natural resources, primarily land.

Broadly defined, resource use conflicts should have at least two parties simultaneously striving to acquire a set of limited resources (Jarvis and Wolf, 2010). For local coastal resource use conflicts, a more specific definition may be used. It suggests that multi-dimensional and multi-stakeholder coastal conflicts are characterised by case specific social and ecological complexity where conflicting interests, positions, rights and perceived responsibility of conflicting parties are among the main factors that determine this complexity (Stepanova and Bruckmeier, 2013). Therefore, these factors require special attention when studying conflict resolution practices.

Conflict resolution and transformation

In the field of natural resource management, conflict resolution is understood as a continuous iterative process that is closely connected with other requirements of sustainable (coastal) resource management, which needs to be long-term, cross-scale and integrative (Brown and Raymond, 2014; Bruckmeier, 2014). At the same time, conflict resolution is part of the challenges and complexity of coastal and resource management (Nobre, 2011). In practice, conflict resolution can take different forms from formal legal and court-based procedures, (participatory) spatial planning routines (for example opportunities for the public to appeal against changes in land use), to informal mediation, stakeholder forums and dialogues. Outcomes of different resolution strategies also differ. Some may have only a short-term effect, resolve an immediate issue (for example legal formal solution) but initiate another spin of conflict development in the long run (protests and appeals). Others may lead to more long-term accepted solutions, for example strategies that include informal, learning and cooperation-based approaches such as mediation, informal stakeholder forums and dialogues. Despite the fact that conflict resolution is case and context specific, recent studies on natural resource management show that there are some common aspects, which are important for successful conflict resolution. Along with well-known requirements for cooperative, collaborative and participatory settings (Blackmore, 2007; Leys and Vanclay, 2011; Blythe and Dadi, 2012), aspects of knowledge use (joint learning and integration) and changes of power imbalances are seen as central for achievement of lasting solutions in natural resource management (Arnold et al., 2012; Bremer and Glavovic, 2013; Stepanova, 2014; 2015; Jentoft, 2017).

Since conflict resolution as a term includes a very broad variety of approaches and strategies with different (sometimes negative) outcomes, the term conflict transformation seems more appropriate to use if we understand conflict resolution as a necessary part of sustainable resource management. Referring to conflict resolution I define it as a dynamic iterative *process* that aims at conflict *transformation* towards *lasting cooperation* among the actors through (a combination of) methods like mediation, negotiation, power equalisation, participation, knowledge sharing and other forms of cooperation that aim at integrating stakeholders' interests, needs, values and knowledge.

The notion of conflict transformation stems from peace and conflict studies (Lederach, 2003; Miall, 2004) and constitutes an approach to conflict in its dynamics that addresses both immediate and long-term goals and issues, not only material ones but also relations between stakeholders (Madden and McQuinn, 2014). Conflict transformation '... focuses on the dynamic aspects of social conflict. At the hub of transformational approach is a convergence of the relational context, a view of conflict-as-opportunity, and the encouragement of creative change processes' (Lederach, 2003, p.15; Madden and McQuinn, 2014). Conflict transformation gives attention to relationship components of conflicts, strives to strengthen them and create constructive and positive decision-making processes (structural change), for example through empowerment, improved communication, sense of responsibility, respect and trust (Mitchell, 2002; Madden and McQuinn, 2014). It also takes into consideration actors' views and values with the aim to understand and reconcile or positively change negative relationships through long-term continuous engagement with the actors (Madden and McQuinn, 2014). That is, conflict resolution is not simply a final target, but a continuous process of positive change and an integral component of resource management.

Operationalising conflict resolution through the notion of conflict transformation gives an opportunity to acknowledge the initiatives and capacities of the actors to resolve conflicts rather than leaving it only to professionals such as courts and mediators. It also takes into consideration the use of formal and informal resolution approaches, which eventually broaden the capacity of decision making.

Power and knowledge in conflict resolution

In natural resource management, knowledge and power are interconnected and interrelated (Jentoft, 2017, Van Assche et al., 2017). For instance, some scholars refer to knowledge as 'a key resource in exercises of power' which is 'used by both dominant parties and by those resisting action' (Adger et al., 2006, p. 7); others conceptualise it as the meta-condition of power, as something that conditions the exercise of power (Avelino and Rotmans, 2011, p.802). The focus on the relation between knowledge and power in natural resource management is central to understanding practical outcomes of management efforts (Van Assche et al., 2014; 2017; Jentoft, 2017). As Van Assche et al. (2017, p. 245) put it: '… focus on knowledge follows from the facit that certain types of knowledge, certain ways of constituting and understanding the natural resource, might lead to specific ways of managing or governing it'.

Power has different roles in resource use conflicts. Sometimes it underlies the causes of conflicts, for instance, when there is unequal access to resources or asymmetric power relations, sometimes it is used to resolve conflicts, for instance, in cases where power relations are transformed and there is a redistribution of power, or when resolution is initiated and controlled by a powerful stakeholder (for example, the municipality).

In a municipal planning context, conflicts occur when a planned change in land use infringes upon the interests and/or values of some stakeholders to such a degree that they cannot accept the change without negotiation (for example nature protection, biodiversity conservation vs. economic development). Discussion of power relations in conflicts that develop within municipal planning becomes especially relevant because the municipality combines the roles of being one of the most powerful actors and a decision-maker responsible for conflict resolution. On the one hand, the municipality may initiate a change in resource use, which potentially may become a source of conflict; on the other hand, it is responsible for initiation and managing of conflict resolution by choosing the approaches and tools to be applied. Power inequalities also become visible within the processes of formal and informal conflict resolution, for example with formal legally based solutions and formal participatory approaches within municipal planning versus informal participatory settings (for example open stakeholder forums). To address this complexity, the notion of 'structural power' becomes especially relevant. The term relates to the unequal power relations created through the systems and structures of societies, and political and economic systems (for a critical overview see Guzzini, 1993). This type of power as expressed through capital and markets, or power relations between institutions cannot be changed or transformed through local projects and processes that aim at temporary conflict resolution in resource management. The problem of dealing with structural power becomes obvious in local participation processes that are often used in conflict resolution. Local participation may change power relations among actors only temporarily and for specific purposes, but it does not change the structural power relations that exist independently between particular actors. In the context of conflict resolution, it is important to consider the implications of structural power relations when choosing reso-lution strategies. That is, power relations[2] cannot be transformed only through participation, knowledge integration and learning, thus a better institutionalisation of conflict resolution as a systematic routine for local resource management at multiple levels is needed.

The interconnectedness of power and knowledge plays out explicitly and implicitly in conflicts, for instance in situations where knowledge of the less pow-erful actors is ignored or not taken into consideration, or when less powerful actors are excluded from negotiation and decision-making processes. The processes of joint learning and knowledge integration in particular are among the key processes for conflict resolution in natural resource management (Bremer and Glavovic, 2013; Seijger et al., 2013). Learning as a process where new, shared and individual knowledge emerges most clearly shows the important changes that happen during conflicts and in conflict resolution, for example through changes in the beliefs, values and behaviours of actors (Henry, 2009, p. 134). Knowledge integration as an integral part of joint learning among the participating actors is present in every phase of the conflict development, as part of both the individual and group learning (Stepanova, 2015). In conflicts, knowledge integration may be expressed through the change in the positions of the conflicting actors towards a compromise/trade off. The results of knowledge integration may be visible in the documented agreements, minutes from the meetings and reports from the municipal planning. Knowledge integration may also happen between formal/informal participation and actual decision making. This type of integration may be articulated through implementation of alternative land use plans jointly produced by the conflicting parties. However, knowledge integration may lead to a change of stakeholders' perceptions, which may or may not be in favour of conflict resolution. New knowledge acquired in the process of joint learning may lead to the reinforcement of the initial conflicting positions of the actors thus reinforcing the conflict. The role of power imbalances and practices of knowledge use for conflict resolution is exemplified below in the three cases of coastal conflicts, which developed in the context of municipal planning. Description of the three cases is followed by the analysis of resolution practices summarised in Table 12.1.

Three conflicts from Belgium, the UK and Sweden[3]

Expansion of the inland harbour, Zeebrugge, Belgium

This conflict is about the government-supported plan to expand the inland harbour of Zeebrugge, Belgium, to increase the goods transportation capacity, over a 362-hectare area protected by local and European nature protection and biodiversity conservation policies and laws (European Bird protection, RAMSAR) (Wiedemann et al., 2011). The harbour expansion plans included a construction of a new railway track bundle near a local village. This is a conflict between economic development, nature protection and biodiversity conserva-tion, together with the dimension of quality of living (for example noise

Table 12.1 Conflict characteristics, resolution practices and their deficits in three coastal conflicts from Belgium, the UK and Sweden

Conflict case	Main conflict characteristics: core issues, key stakeholders	Resolution practices	Problems, deficits and outcomes of conflict resolution practices
Expansion of the inland harbour of Zeebrugge, Belgium	Chronic, multi-scale, multi-stakeholder conflict Issues of economic development (harbour), nature protection/conservation (biodiversity, habitat), quality of resource (increased noise levels due to planned railway) Key stakeholders: local residents, general public, the municipality and the government	*Formal resolution*: legal administrative procedures, policies and regulations, i.e., nature compensation *Formal participation*: formal public consultation within municipal planning *Informal participation*: Local information meetings voluntarily organised by the opponents of the plans No organised conflict resolution efforts	Institutional mechanisms for mediation are lacking Processes of formal resolution are not transparent and not inclusive; opportunities for dialogue and open communication are missing Power inequalities among stakeholders are significant and not addressed in resolution practices. Local residents feel excluded from the decision-making process Opportunities for informal participation and knowledge integration are largely missing Unlikely that the conflict will be settled with an accepted solution in the near future; conflict transformation limited

Conflict case	Main conflict characteristics: core issues, key stakeholders	Resolution practices	Problems, deficits and outcomes of conflict resolution practices
Regeneration and development of coastal land, Portsmouth, UK	Chronic, multi-scale, multi-stakeholder conflict. Issues of nature protection/conservation (sea level rise, decontamination of land), urban development. City council is among the key stakeholders. Great number of NGOs with mediating positions	*Formal participation* through development planning system – a public consultation process. *Informal participation*: Advisory Network to City Council's Planning Committee with no executive power	Formal participation is limited to informing; not inclusive; vertical information flow, no open dialogue or discussion. Resolution is heavily based on scientific and managerial knowledge, does not include local ecological knowledge. Lack of knowledge integration and joint learning to deal with competing knowledges: difficulties to achieve common understanding of problems and find possible solutions. Power inequalities affect consulting within the informal network – difficulties in reaching agreement. Unlikely that the conflict will be settled with an accepted solution in the near future; conflict transformation limited

| Gothenburg port expansion in Torsviken, Sweden | Multi-dimensional, multi-stakeholder, multi-scale conflict: local and regional aspects dominate; complex core conflict between national and regional interests in industrial and economic development (port expansion) and local, national and international interest in nature protection (Natura 2000 protected area, EU Bird and Habitat directives) Key stakeholders: the municipality is the main actor, environmental NGOs, the city port (a major enterprise), local leisure and recreation associations; 22 directly involved actors, some actors without articulated positions | *Formal resolution:* formal public consultation within municipal planning, legal procedures *Formal participation:* formal public consultation within municipal planning *Informal participation:* An informal open stakeholder forum, professional mediation, dialogue with stakeholders, and a stakeholder working group | Formal public consultation within municipal planning does not allow for a meaningful conflict transformation due to its formal format (limited opportunities for transformation of power relations, learning and knowledge integration) An informal open stakeholder forum, mediation and a stakeholder working group facilitated transformation of interests, positions and strategies through dialogue, joint learning and knowledge integration at different levels, e.g. through a jointly written alternative land use plan for the area. Power relations transformed through informal participation and mediated dialogue (open forum); also due to willingness of most powerful actors to share power with other actors in an informal dialogue; different knowledge types were integrated in the decision-making process (jointly written land use plan). Openness and dialogue changed the top-down approach, fostered trust and promoted cooperation among stakeholders. Conflict was successfully resolved/transformed |

Adapted from: Wiedemann et al., 2011 (the Belgian case), Evans and Witting, 2011 (the UK case) and Stepanova, 2015 (the Swedish case)

pollution and landscape change) of the nearby residents. The most powerful stakeholders in this case included the Flemish governmental authorities and the port authority (who together with the governmental department for Mobility and Public works initiated the project). Another governmental department of Environment, Nature and Culture was responsible for nature compensations, which were part of the proposed development project, but had a less powerful position as it had to follow the governmental decisions, which were initially in favour of the project (adapted from Wiedemann et al., 2011). Among the less powerful but most active stakeholders who were in opposition to the plan were an action committee that represented the local residents that were in opposition to the location of the planned railway track bundle (300 m from the village), and an environmental NGO, which was concerned with inadequate nature compensation propositions. The committee argued for an alternative location of the railway track due to the projected rise of noise levels and negative impact on the quality of living due to the landscape and green area change (ibid.).

The governmental agencies and the port authority were the most powerful actors and argued for their own interests through legal administrative paths. According to these, the plan to expand the harbour was legally sound because in the national harbour development plan the natural site in question had been allocated for harbour activities, which had also been a national priority for the last 10–15 years (ibid.). Formally, the opponents had no legal power to object to the project, nor against the destruction of natural sites. The government believed that the nature-related values could be fully replaced at another location through nature compensation. Therefore, the objections to the harbour expansion were seen as ungrounded. However, environmental opposition saw available and suitable places for nature compensation sites as limited both in their quality and in quantity (Wiedemann et al., 2011).

Despite all parties claiming dialogue as the most important instrument to resolve the conflict, the local residents represented by the action committee expressed that they felt ignored by the government (ibid.). Major power inequalities among stakeholders, competing and conflicting knowledge about possibilities for nature compensation and lack of participatory, informal and integrative approaches to conflict resolution were among the major impediments used in order to transform this conflict into a cooperative approach. For detailed analysis, see Table 12.1.

Regeneration and development of contaminated land, Portsmouth, UK

This conflict developed in a municipal process of planning for decontamination, regeneration and intensive development of industrial land in the coastal zone of Portsmouth (Tipner). Tipner is 'the largest "undeveloped" site available in Portsmouth and has been the subject of successive (failed) planning applications in the past' (Evans and Witting, 2011). Despite high contamination, Tipner is partly a wildlife/habitat protection site according to local and European policies and laws. The main conflict has been between economic and urban development (housing) and long-term environmental protection (wildlife habitats) (ibid.). The site is also prone to flooding from surface water drainage, storms and the rise of sea level, which fuels the debate around the quality of prospected housing and risk of pollution if no protection is approved as part of the development plan. The conflict is complex with multiple stakeholders who nevertheless share the common aim to decontaminate and develop the site (ibid.). However, the stakeholders have different priorities and development goals, which add to the conflict's complexity.

The most powerful stakeholders include Tipner Regeneration Company and South East England Development Agency, a developer/landowner who shares development interests with another landowner – Portsmouth City Council. Both were initiators of the plan proposal. The municipality of Portsmouth had a double role acting simultaneously as both a decision and policy maker. The municipality has also been responsible for decisions concerning both economic development and environmental protection, aims where there are often conflicts of priority. The complexity of this conflict stems to some extent from the difficulty of balancing between the different municipal roles and responsibilities as the formal procedures of conflict resolution should have been initiated within the planning procedure of the municipality.

Other key stakeholders included three environmental NGOs with interests in nature protection and conservation, landscape and natural heritage. One of them was a very powerful NGO with highly influential members concerned with protection of reserve habitats and wild bird protection (ibid.). Other stakeholders included an environmental agency (executive non-departmental public body) with interests in environmental protection and adaptation to sea level rise; a governmental agency responsible for operating, maintaining and improving strategic road networks in England; a housing association aiming to maximise opportunities to develop accessible/affordable housing; and local residents with interest in protecting natural and landscape values (Evans and Witting, 2011).

The most powerful stakeholders (the Portsmouth municipality, the development companies and governmental agencies) pursued their interests through the formal statutory process of municipal planning. Interests and priorities of other stakeholders were considered in the process of formal public consultation. However, their proposals/objections were dismissed, as they did not comply with the current city plan and development policies. The discussion was based on institutional expertise, with little room for other knowledge types and sources (Evans and Witting, 2011). As conflict resolution in this case was very formalised and limited to planning procedures, the opposing stakeholders did not have much room to negotiate. 'Stakeholders did not develop a universal understanding of what constituted the problem and, therefore, could not come up with appropriate solutions' (ibid). Moreover, there was another issue related to representation and inclusion of potential stakeholders in the case of land use change from industrial to residential – the future residents of the proposed residential area. 'The planning consultation process has been limited to vested interests including those concerned with the natural habitat, birds and amenity

with, as already noted, little obvious room for manoeuvre or trade-offs proposed by either side' (Evans and Witting, 2011, p. 236). Major power imbalances among stakeholders, as well as conflicting values, priorities and
understandings of what the problem was, remained unaddressed in the very
formal resolution process. Neither were any informal, participatory or collaboration oriented processes applied to resolve this conflict. Thus, transformation of the conflict into a more cooperative mode in the current context was
unlikely (see Table 12.1).

The Gothenburg port expansion in Torsviken, Sweden

This case of port expansion in the Natura 2000 protected area (according to the
EU Bird and Habitat Directives) in Gothenburg, Sweden, represents a conflict
between industrial and economic development, nature protection, conservation
and recreation. The area is an important wintering and resting area for endangered and protected bird species. It is also a coastal area with high value for
open-air activities. Port expansion would negatively affect biodiversity, conservation and landscape values in the area (Stepanova, 2015). Among the 22
stakeholders identified in the conflict, the most powerful were the municipality
of Gothenburg – the main landowner, stakeholder and decision-maker also
responsible for formal conflict resolution – and the Gothenburg Port – the
largest port in Northern Europe and one of the most important local and
regional economic development nodes, partly owned by the municipality.
Among the less powerful stakeholders were local and national environmental
NGOs (the Swedish Ornithological Association and Gothenburg Ornithological Association) and local leisure and recreation associations, which were in
strong opposition to the development plans originally supported and initiated
by the port and the municipality. A combination of formal and informal participatory and non-participatory approaches was applied in order to resolve the
conflict. After a series of (failed) attempts to resolve the conflict formally within
the statutory procedures of municipal planning, for example through public
consultation, more articulated cooperation-oriented strategies were applied.
Three main stakeholders (the municipality, the port and the local ornithological
association) signed an agreement of cooperation in order to create a meaningful
stakeholder dialogue (Stepanova, 2015). Within this agreement, an informal
participatory open stakeholder forum with regular meetings was established. To
help establish trust and organise the dialogue, professional mediation was called
for. The stakeholder forum provided a platform for knowledge sharing,
exchange of experiences and ideas, inclusion of different values (ibid.). These
informal dialogues resulted in an alternative land use plan formulated by a stakeholder working group with representatives from all stakeholder groups. This
alternative land use plan was further considered in the municipal decision
making. The conflict was finally settled with a decision not to use the Torsvi-
ken protected area for port expansion. The decision was a compromise accepted by all the stakeholders.

Discussion

The three conflict cases have several common characteristics: they have a clear land use related profile and the resolution processes took place primarily within municipal and regional planning where the municipality acted as one of the most powerful stakeholders, and as a decision-maker responsible for the conflict resolution. Such context has direct implications for power distribution among the stakeholders and for conflict resolution processes. Formal and informal resolution strategies were applied in the three conflicts: municipal and regional planning, public consultation, legal resolution through the court (Belgium, UK, Sweden), participation, discussion, dialogue, mediation (Sweden), informal stakeholder working groups with advisory functions (Sweden) and open stakeholder forum (Sweden). Formal methods of conflict resolution prevailed. Only in the Swedish case of port expansion was a long-lasting, fully accepted solution reached due to the inclusion of informal resolution approaches, which sought to establish trust and informal dialogue and served as a platform for knowledge exchange and integration. In two other cases from the UK and Belgium, a successful resolution seemed unlikely due to the lack of systematic resolution efforts, lack of processes seeking to address power imbalances among the stakeholders, limited possibilities to use and integrate knowledge from different actors, and overall absence of informal resolution approaches.

The key findings may be summarised as follows:

- Formal participation inbuilt in planning procedures did not help to resolve complex conflicts of resource use.
- Power inequalities among stakeholders were impeding conflict resolution.
- Lack of opportunities and platforms for informal joint learning, knowledge use, exchange and integration appeared as major impediments for conflict resolution (along with the above-mentioned unaddressed power inequalities and prevalent formal procedures).
- Joint learning and integration of knowledge into decision making had a positive effect on the acceptance of management solutions.

Looking at the case of successful conflict resolution/transformation (the Swedish case) it may be argued that the joint learning of stakeholders and efforts to integrate knowledge can improve cooperation, trust and decision making for sustainable resource management when they become part of *all* the stages of resource management – from planning to decision making and practical execution. At the same time, providing opportunities for knowledge integration (for example through mediation) is not a panacea. Knowledge-based, participatory approaches to conflict resolution need to be complemented with other context specific formal and informal resolution methods. Furthermore, conflict resolution depends on the institutional arrangements that facilitate or impede power equalisation, knowledge integration and application. In the conflicts, less powerful stakeholders representing for instance environmental NGOs, outdoor recreation unions or local residents, expressed their concerns about their opinions being ignored and not listened to in the participatory processes that were aimed at conflict resolution and/or decision making.

Based on the three conflict cases two major weaknesses in conflict resolution that takes place within the context of municipal planning can be identified. The first weakness is related to the procedures of municipal planning that, although not designed for conflict resolution, framed and shaped resolution practices. Within the process of public consultation, knowledge sharing and information exchange are limited, as the municipality communicates separately with each stakeholder. Due to the formal and rigid nature of this framing process and the inbuilt imbalance of power between the municipality and other stakeholders, opportunities for joint learning, knowledge integration and coproduction are reduced and become insufficient for a lasting resolution of complex conflicts. The formal public consultation can even reinforce power inequalities due to the lack of transparency in decision making and of open, informal communication, thus resulting in intensification of the existing tensions between the stakeholders. However, the significance of open public consultations should not be diminished or seen as insignificant for conflict resolution. Being by nature a platform for informing the public about planned changes in land use, it often unveils competing and conflicting interests. The second weakness, also connected to municipal planning practices, is the neglect of power relations and inequalities among stakeholders, when seeking for resolution. More specific deficits, such as lack of informal participation, open communication, knowledge integration and learning, as well as willingness to cooperate, are often connected with the two deficits mentioned above.

Transformation of power imbalances seems to happen easier through processes of informal participation where the setting is different from a negotiation. Knowledge coproduced as a result of knowledge integration among the actors in informal and non-hierarchical processes can be used in decision making for conflict resolution at higher levels of municipal planning, and also fulfil the function of a link between different scales of resource management.

Hierarchical and power-based approaches such as legal ones were the least effective, as they did not lead to long-term solutions. Formal, court-based solutions can be seen as a temporary solution in a situation where conflict resolution would otherwise be blocked. The most effective were flexible case specific combinations of formal (participatory/non-participatory) and informal approaches, such as informal participatory forums for stakeholders and mediation.

Conclusions

In order for participatory resource management to become effective, further efforts to transform the unequal power relations among the stakeholders are necessary. In particular, integrative approaches to conflict resolution need to address, transform and better include the changing power relations and their close interconnection with practices of knowledge use among stakeholders. In the case of European municipal planning, there is a need for development of institutional mechanisms and routines for *systematic* conflict resolution.

Further, the institutions involved need to develop procedures for the inclusion of knowledge produced during informal processes into different levels of decision making. The view of conflict resolution as instrumental, mechanical and terminal, which is characteristic for formal procedures, narrows and oversimplifies the problems and the resolution processes, and does not adequately account for the social, economic and environmental dynamics and context where conflict resolution is happening. After decades of experimenting, (informal) participatory resource management as a form of empowerment of stakeholders is still an exception. Addressing power relations and knowledge integration practices beyond local management and single cases is also required to enable the advancement of the transformation of resource management towards sustainability.

Notes

1 The SECOA project (www.projectsecoa.eu) included partners from universities from eight countries, five of which were European (Italy, Belgium, Portugal, the UK and Sweden). In the project, 17 case studies in urban coastal areas were carried out in the participating countries and 26 conflicts were analysed in depth. For details, see Khan et al. (2011).
2 For the current discussion of local resource use conflicts, I follow Avelino and Rotmans (2011) and conceptualise power as exercised by actors in interplay with institutions and social systems.
3 The detailed analyses of the three conflict cases were earlier published in Stepanova (2014, 2015, Swedish case), Khan et al. (2011, an overview).

Acknowledgements

The author gratefully acknowledges the financial support of the European Commission through the research project SECOA – Solutions to Environmental Contrasts in Coastal Areas (7th Framework Programme 2007–2013, Grant Agreement no. 244251).

References

Adger, N.W., Brown, K., Tompkins, E.L. (2006) 'The political economy of cross-scale networks in resource co-management', *Ecology & Society*, 10(2):9
Arnold, J.S., Koro-Ljungberg, M. and Bartels, W.L. (2012) 'Power and conflict in adaptive management: Analyzing the discourse of riparian management on public lands', *Ecology & Society*, 17(1)
Avelino, F. and Rotmans, J. (2011) 'A dynamic conceptualization of power for sustainability research', *Journal of Cleaner Production*, 19(8), 796–804
Barragán, J.M., and de Andrés, M. (2015) 'Analysis and trends of the world's coastal cities and agglomerations', *Ocean & Coastal Management*, 114, 11–20

Blackmore, C. (2007) 'What kinds of knowledge, knowing and learning are required for addressing resource dilemmas? A theoretical overview', *Environmental Science & Policy*, 10(6), 512–525

Blythe, J. and Dadi, U. (2012) 'Knowledge integration as a method to develop capacity for evaluating technical information on ocean currents for integrated coastal management', *Environmental Science and Policy*, 19–20, 49–58

Bremer, S. and Glavovic, B. (2013) 'Mobilizing knowledge for coastal governance: Reframing the science–policy interface for integrated coastal management', *Coastal Management*, 41(1), 39–56

Brown, A.C., NordstromK., McLachlan, A., Jackson, N.L. and Sherman, D.J. (2008) 'Sandy shores of the near future', in Polunin, N.V.C. (ed.), *Aquatic Ecosystems*, Cambridge University Press, Cambridge. UK, 263–280

Brown, G. and Raymond, C.M. (2014) 'Methods for identifying land use conflict potential using participatory mapping', *Landscape and Urban Planning, 122*, 196–208, https://doi.org/10.1016/j.landurbplan.2013.11.007

Bruckmeier, K. (2014) 'Problems of cross-scale coastal management in Scandinavia', *Regional Environmental Change*, 14(6), 2151–2160

Cadoret, A. (2009) 'Conflict dynamics in coastal zones: A perspective using the example of Languedoc-Rousillon (France)', *Journal of Coastal Conservation*, 13, 151–163

Evans, G. and Witting, A. (2011) 'UK case studies', in Khan, A., Wiedemann, T., Le, Q.X., Corijn, E. and Canters, F., *Synoptic report on conflicts of uses at coastal urban areas*, (research report), SECOA project deliverable 4.2, Vrije Universiteit, Brussels202–292

Guzzini, S. (1993) 'Structural power: The limits of neorealist power analysis', *International Organization*, 47(03), 443–478

Henry, A.D. (2009). 'The challenge of learning for sustainability: A prolegomenon to theory',. *Human Ecology Review*, 16(2), 131–140.

IOC/UNESCO (2011) *Blueprint for ocean and coastal sustainability*, An inter-agency paper by IOC/UNESCO, IMO, FAO and UNDPA towards the preparation of the UN Conference on Sustainable Development (Rio+20), IOC/UNESCO, Paris

Jarvis, T., and Wolf, A. (2010) 'Managing water negotiations and conflicts in concept and in practice', *Transboundary Water Management: Principles and Practice*, 125–141

Jentoft, S. (2017) 'Small-scale fisheries within maritime spatial planning: Knowledge integration and power', *Journal of Environmental Policy & Planning*, 1–13

Khan, A., Wiedemann, T., Le, Q.X., Corijn, E. and Canters, F. (2011) *Synoptic report on conflicts of uses at coastal urban areas*, SECOA project deliverable 4.2, Vrije Universiteit

Leal Filho, W., Brandt, N., Krahn, D. and Wennersten, R. (eds) (2008) *Conflict resolution in coastal zone management*, Environmental education, communication and sustainability, Vol. 28, Peter Lang GmbH, Internationaler Verlag der Wissenschaften, Fankfurt am Main

Lederach, J.P. (2003) *Little book of conflict transformation*, Good Books

Leys, A.J. and Vanclay, J.K. (2011) 'Social learning: A knowledge and capacity building approach for adaptive co-management of contested landscapes', *Land Use Policy*, 28 (3), 574–584

Madden, F. and McQuinn, B. (2014) 'Conservation's blind spot: The case for conflict transformation in wildlife conservation', *Biological Conservation*, 178, 97–106

Miall, H. (2004) 'Conflict transformation: A multi-dimensional task', in *Berghof handbook for conflict transformation*, Berghof Research Center for Constructive Conflict Management, Berlin

Mitchell, C. (2002) 'Beyond resolution: What does conflict transformation actually transform?', *Peace and Conflict Studies*, 9(1), 1–23

Nobre, A.M. (2011) 'Scientific approaches to address challenges in coastal management', *Marine Ecology Progress Series*, 434, 279–289

Pelling, M., and Blackburn, S. (eds) (2014) *Megacities and the coast: Risk, resilience and transformation*, Routledge

Seijger, C., Dewulf, G., Otter, H. and van Tatenhove, J. (2013) 'Understanding inter-active knowledge development in coastal projects', *Environmental Science & Policy*, 29, 103–114

Seijger, C., van Tatenhove, J., Dewulf, G. and Otter, H.S. (2014) 'Responding to coastal problems: Interactive knowledge development in a US nature restoration project', *Ocean & Coastal Management*, 89, 29–38

Stepanova, O., and Bruckmeier, K. (2013) 'Resource use conflicts and urban–rural resource use dynamics in Swedish coastal landscapes: Comparison and synthesis', *Journal of Environmental Policy & Planning*, 15(4), 467–492

Stepanova, O. (2014) 'Knowledge integration in the management of coastal conflicts in urban areas: Two cases from Sweden', *Journal of Environmental Planning and Management*, 53(11) 1658–1682

Stepanova, O. (2015) 'Conflict resolution in coastal resource management: Comparative analysis of case studies from four European countries', *Ocean & Coastal Management*, 103, 109–122

Šunde, C. (2008) 'The open horizon: Exploring spiritual and cultural values of the oceans and coasts', in Patterson, M. and Glavovic, B. (eds), *Ecological economics of the oceans and coasts*, Edward Elgar, Cheltenham, 166–183

Tuda, A.O., Stevens, T.F., Rodwell, L. D. (2014) 'Resolving coastal conflicts using marine spatial planning', *Journal of Environmental Management*, 133, 59–68

Van Assche, K., Duineveld, M. and Beunen, R. (2014) 'Power and contingency in planning', *Environment and Planning A: Economy and Space*, 46 (10), 2385–2400

Van Assche, K., Beunen, R., Duineveld, M. and Gruezmacher, M. (2017) 'Power/ knowledge and natural resource management: Foucaultian foundations in the analysis of adaptive governance', *Journal of Environmental Policy & Planning*, 19(3), 308–322

Weinstein, M.P., Baird, R.C., Conover, D.O., Gross, M., Keulartz, J., Loomis, D.K., Naveh, Z., Peterson, S.B., Reed, D.J., Roe, E., Swanson, L., Swart, J.A.A., Teal, J. M., Turner, R.E. and van der Windt, H.J. (2007) 'Managing coastal resources in the 21st century', *Frontiers in Ecology and the Environment*, 5(1), 43–48

Wiedemann, T., Khan Mahsud, A.Z., Le, X.Q., Corijn, E. and Canters, F. (2011) 'The Belgian case studies', in Khan, A., Wiedemann, T., Le, Q.X., Corijn, E. and Canters, F., *Synoptic report on conflicts of uses at coastal urban areas*, (research report), SECOA project deliverable 4.2, Vrije Universiteit, Brussels, 107–167

13 Environmental conflicts

Towards theoretical analyses of social-ecological systems

Karl Bruckmeier

Natural resource use conflicts: The research problems

Empirical knowledge from conflict research and theoretical concepts from social-ecological theory are used in this chapter to discuss the possibilities of resolving environmental and natural resource use conflicts. In the discourse of sustainable development in science and politics it became necessary to deal with the difficulty that sustainable development remained an idea with many different interpretations, and to reflect the connections between the terms of conflict and sustainability. The social-ecological perspective and terminology can be useful for the clarification of the concepts and for interdisciplinary knowledge integration: social ecology studies the interaction between social and ecological systems empirically and theoretically, e.g., with the concept of coupled social-ecological systems. Framing the analysis of environmental conflicts in such analyses of systems helps to study the contexts generating or influencing environmental conflicts more systematically, thus creating chances for improved conflict mitigation.

In the discourse of sustainable development conflicts are a marginal theme; sustainability appears as a diffuse idea for which no consensus can be achieved in science or politics (Bruckmeier, 2009; 2016, p. 125 cont; Princen, 2010; Wullweber, 2015). The idea of intra- and inter-generational solidarity remains abstract; it does not provide a conceptual basis for the integration of the manifold and different forms of conflicts studied in empirical research. The generalised intergenerational resource use conflict implied in sustainable development does not appear and cannot be mitigated as such, only in manifold activities, through more limited, local and actor-specific conflicts. It is necessary to specify conflicts, their causes, courses, consequences, contexts and forms of resolution, thus showing that the creation of solidarity requires – continuously – the resolving of resource use conflicts. Interpreting sustainability as a 'win-win solution' for everyone's advantage seems to ignore the manifold conflicts on the way towards sustainability. After the report 'The Limits to Growth' (Meadows and Meadows, 1972), the global overuse and scarcity of key resources was discussed as a conflict-related theme, for example, the overfishing of the oceans, the deforestation of tropical rain forests, the scarcity of oil and agricultural land and further natural resources. In this context sustainability appears as enforced by multiple conflicts about access to and use of resources.

Environmental conflict research intensified after 1990, especially in the political sciences, with the security and scarcity themes (Toronto school of conflict research: Homer-Dixon, 1999; Swiss ENCOP-Project: Spillmann, 1995; Bächler, 1999). In the debate about global change, including climate change, it became clear that the connected processes of social and environmental change resulted in intensifying conflicts, even militarisation of resource conflicts, wars and civil wars (Gleditsch, 2004; Welzer, 2008; Dyer, 2011). The broadening of conflict research was accompanied by new practices of conflict resolution, e.g., mediation or various forms of informal conflict resolution. Nature and causes of conflicts, larger societal contexts of the transition to sustainability in which conflicts happen, and design of policies and strategies of conflict mitigation: these themes require interdisciplinary knowledge synthesis, moreover, theoretical analyses of the interaction of nature and society and the coupling of social and ecological systems.

Conflicts between different interests and aims of humans as resource users have normative meanings all the way from the emergence to the resolution: conflicts may be rooted in different worldviews, cultural values and social norms, in specific material interests, and in basic human needs such as food, shelter and health. In the political discourse and in policy processes, conflicts appear in normative views and interpretations – through the attribution of interests, claims, aspirations, rights of access to and property of resources, perceptions and valuations of conflicting parties, owners or citizens. In conflict mitigation, the normative dimensions are visible in the struggles about definition, interpretation, aspiration, legitimation, rejection of claims and interests, and contestation of formal or informal norms.

To deal with the inherent normativity of conflicts more is required than the identification of worldviews, cultural values or clashes of values of the conflicting parties. How is mutual recognition, cooperation and mitigation possible, when the conflicts are rooted in the structures and processes of complex social and ecological systems? To find answers, the knowledge basis, the concepts and the methodological problems of environmental conflict research are described below; the knowledge used is from different disciplines, methods of conflict research and conflict resolution, and integrative theories. The recently developing discourse of social-ecological transformation gives a possibility for the further integration of conflict research, including the broader societal contexts of resource use conflicts.

The knowledge basis of environmental conflict research

Specialised environmental conflict research includes psychology, sociology, cultural anthropology, social geography, political science, economics, human ecology, peace and development research, and a field of interdisciplinary environmental conflict research with inexact contours. Except their quality as social-scientific research, the fields of conflict research do not have much in common. Within the disciplines conflict research can be found at sub-disciplinary

184 Bruckmeier

levels, research where the complexity of conflicts is fragmented through extreme specialisation. This implies two difficulties for environmental conflict research: to deal with the multi-dimensional social and ecological aspects of conflicts, and with interdisciplinary knowledge synthesis.

Empirical research – the phenomenology of resource use conflicts

Conflicts about natural resources appear as conflicts between persons, smaller or larger social, cultural, political and economic groups, organisations or institutions. The resource concept, although specified in types of natural resources, is a broad and inexact economic and ecological term. Studying resource use in environmental conflicts shows the necessity to specify the natural and social resources involved. Sometimes the classes of resources are differentiated as forms of capital (social, cultural, human, economic, financial, natural capital). Such metaphorical notions do not create a more operational terminology; rather they add further abstract terminologies and classifications to the ones existing.

The examples and studies of conflicts of natural resource use in this book illustrate important and recurring conflict forms known from many countries. To describe and analyse such conflicts more systematically requires the concepts summarised in Box 13.1.

Box 13.1 Concepts for empirical studies of environmental and resource use conflicts

The following synopsis differentiates three perspectives for the conceptual framing of conflict analyses: nature of conflicts in terms of scales and resource types, types of actors involved and their perceptions, and processes and procedures to describe the course of conflicts and their resolution.

Scope of conflicts and resource types

1 *Scales and political levels of the conflicts:* local, regional, national and transboundary or international, multi-scale and global conflicts
2 *Natural resources that give rise to conflicts:* biotic resources including living and organic material; abiotic resources including water, air, soils, metals; biodiversity; renewable and non-renewable resources
3 *Social resources:* economic, especially money and capital; political, especially power and influence; legal, especially ownership rights and citizen rights; different forms of knowledge; cultural ideas and perceptions, especially worldviews

Actors – their perceptions and views

4 *Actors or stakeholders:* local, national and international political actors and organisations, including governmental and non-governmental organisations; private and public, national and international enterprises; civil society

associations including social and environmental movements; cultural and religious institutions; professional associations, associations for nature protection, producer and consumer associations, scientific organisations, and others

5 *Secondary stakeholders:* many resource use conflicts are not limited to two conflicting parties, but include a larger number of stakeholders that position themselves in a conflict, although they are not directly affected (e.g., local inhabitants, interest groups, professional associations and associations for nature protection, political parties, scientific organisations)

6 *Perception and definition of conflicts by the actors:* value conflicts, interest conflicts, conflicts about rights, struggles for subsistence and livelihood, cultural conflicts, conflicts because of power asymmetries

Processes – course of conflicts and their resolution

7 *Intensity of conflicts:* low intensity, non-violent or 'soft conflicts'; non-mitigated and mitigated conflicts; violent and militarised conflicts, civil wars and wars

8 *Process and course of the conflicts:* duration, directions of development such as broadening or redefinition, intensification and escalation, phases, efforts and forms of intervention and mitigation

9 *Methods of conflict resolution:* different types of policy instruments – political, administrative, legal, economic instruments and informal instruments as mediation, negotiation, arbitration, civil society action, symbolic action as moral persuasion, or ethical debates about different values and world views-sSources: own inquiry; Stepanova and Bruckmeier, 2013

Aspects of conflict analysis as described in Box 13.1 are illustrated in several chapters in this book and in other studies (e.g., Leal Filho et al., 2008; Klenke et al., 2013; SECOA project on resource use conflicts in coastal areas: www.projectsecoa.eu/, accessed 30 October 2017). The conflict types are, in one form or another, related to scarcity and unequal distribution of or access to various kinds of natural resources (Box 13.2).

Box 13.2 Typology of natural resource use conflicts

In a social-ecological perspective, natural resource use conflicts appear in the *social forms and consequences of natural resource use in human society.*

1 *Conflicts about pollution of water, soil, air and other environmental damages* (pollution rights and the cleaning or restoration of ecosystems; conflicts through environmental disasters, inundations, storms): key conflicts of the industrial society

2 *Conflicts within and between different social types of natural resource use* (fishing, agriculture, industry, transport and trade of resources, recreational resource use, nature and species protection): inter-sectorial conflicts, related to the organisation of the economy

3 *Conflicts about access to and use of the natural resources that provide the subsistence basis for humans* (water and land and water- or land-based living resources like fish, game, crops, or abiotic physical resources): subsistence-related conflicts

4 *Conflicts about competing resource claims of different user groups, especially local and non-local users* (e.g., local fishermen and large-scale fishing industry; conflicts about the use of agricultural land between local peasants and farmers, external owners, international corporations, conflicting forms of land use – agriculture, industry, mining, settlement, recreation, nature protection): inter-group conflicts about user rights

5 *Conflicts caused through illegal use of natural resources* (illegal hunting, mining, use of water, land, forests): conflicts about user rights and distribution of resources

6 *Ecological distribution conflicts* as multi-scale conflicts where the conflicting parties are not in direct contact with each other and may not even see a conflict (e.g., in the cases of water-polluting shrimp production in Asian countries for export to European consumers, or of non-legitimated use of non-patented user rights of medical plants by pharmaceutical companies in the territories or aborigine populations and first nations): long-distance conflicts as a consequence of the globalisation of economy, of global trade and exchange of resourcesSources: own inquiry; Martinez-Alier, 2009; Klenke et al., 2013; Stepanova, 2015; SUCOZOMA-project: tmblma c19.tmbl.gu.se/Sucozoma/default.html (accessed 29 October 2017)

A broader and controversial debate of environment- and resource-related conflicts is about conflicts between humans and animals as users of natural resources, or ecological communities that share natural resources. Such conflicts are articulated differently and hardly integrated with research on resource conflicts. The conflicts are not always discussed as conflicts, but as problems of different kinds: justice and fairness between species (Cooper and Palmer, 1995), social relations between humans and animals, inter-species relations between humans and wild and domestic animals (Myers, 2003), interaction of humans and animals in theoretical analysis (Haraway, 2008), humanity's cooperative and conflictive relations with other species (Moore, 2015), human–animal interaction in agriculture (Tovey, 2003), and further spheres such as industry, medicine, science, defence (Tedeschi, 2016), human social lives with animals (Cudworth, 2013), relations between humans and endangered species (Hoffmann, 2004), conflicts between humans and wildlife (Klenke et al., 2013; O'Rourke, this book), humans and farm animals (Blokhuis, 2008), specific forms of working relations between humans and animals, and other forms of inter-species relations. The different themes cover many forms of relations, and also conflicts.

Conflicts originating in relations between humans and animals are often considered in terms of mistreating, suffering, cruelty, changing the life conditions of animals, etc. Conflicts in animal husbandry and about farm animals, especially in large-scale farming and mass production of animals, are mainly discussed as not species-specific animal keeping, as modifying and manipulating life conditions and animals for purposes of human consumption. These conflicts and their mitigation are addressed indirectly, as also in conflicts between humans and wild animals: whereas the origin of the conflicts can be traced back to competing and conflicting needs and behaviour forms of humans and animals, the discussion of the conflicts and their solutions are transformed into forms of advocacy (including animal rights, animal protection and governmental or legal programs), human care, responsibility and protection of animals, and articulated in normative perspectives.

The studies mentioned above imply three types of potential conflicts: between humans and wild animals, humans and domesticated animals, and between different animal species, which relates to the discipline ecology. Sometimes a classification is attempted with the terms of intra-species conflicts (as conflicts between one species, for example, humans) and inter-species conflicts (as conflicts between two or more species), for which the context of analysis needs to be broadened to include social and ecological systems (Mehta and Quellet, 1995, p. 112). That the conflicting needs, subsistence and foraging practices of humans and animals are described in different terminologies is part of the problem that emerges in interdisciplinary studies of resource use conflicts: how to systematise, connect or integrate the terminologies? This is hardly discussed; even the conflict term remains controversial in conflict research. Another conceptual problem is that theoretical classifications and concepts for the analysis of environmental conflicts come sometimes from older and other, not environment-related, conflict research, or from disciplinary specialised research (for example, classification of intra- and inter-personal conflicts, value and interest conflicts). The terminology is inhomogeneous, using several, or abstract and diffuse concepts that cannot be seen as creating conceptual integration – this implies continuous difficulties in interdisciplinary conflict research.

Methods of conflict resolution

The design of case studies or comparative studies of conflicts can evoke methodological controversies regarding data collection through qualitative or quantitative and statistical data. Yet, the methodological key problem is: how to provide knowledge for conflict resolution. Conflicts, especially violent conflicts and political conflicts, are often studied with the motivation that they need to be solved, for which effective tools of conflict resolution are required. Conflict resolution depends on science; however, the knowledge for conflict resolution is not exclusively scientific knowledge.

Different knowledge forms can be useful and need to be combined in mitigation processes, requiring knowledge integration and cooperation of actors: experience-based managerial and professional knowledge, applied scientific knowledge from monitoring and evaluation studies, normative knowledge from ethical discourses, juridical knowledge about legal norms, tacit personal knowledge, everyday knowledge of certain actors involved in conflicts, local ecological knowledge. Scientific and other knowledge forms cannot always be clearly differentiated, as they are often interwoven in the practices of conflict resolution.

Tools of conflict resolution are, for their acceptance by the conflicting parties, not only dependent on the experience, power and qualification of the experts trying to solve conflicts (governmental actors, legally mandated institutions for conflict resolution like courts and lawyers, police, military, coast guards, other mandated actors like mediators, negotiators, arbitrators). Increasingly the quality of tools of conflict resolution depends on their scientifically assessed effectiveness and efficiency, on their acceptance, on the costs, or the sustainability of solutions.

After all, certain conflicts cannot be solved, or only indirectly, partially and temporarily; others may not require active mitigation and can be solved by the conflicting parties themselves. To see conflicts as socially, economically or physically destructive and requiring prevention, suppression or mitigation may be justified for violent and military conflicts. Yet, the majority of natural resource conflicts are local, non-violent or soft conflicts, only seldom escalating to physical violence, military forms, civil wars or wars. With increasing scarcity of natural resources it is possible that conflicts escalate more often to violent forms, including symbolic and physical violence – examples are from many countries, in fishery, forestry and mining. But there is still a difference between single violent events and continued military violence in forms of wars and civil wars. In sociology and political science, where the conflict–power nexus is a main theme, it has long been discussed that conflicts are drivers and consequences of social and economic development and change, of political, economic and technological modernisation. With that opens a wider view of conflict resolution than in prevention, suppression or mitigation.

Based on these considerations, methods and policy instruments for conflict resolution cannot be assessed without analysing the social and ecological contexts of the conflicts. The toolbox for resolving environment-related conflicts shows only a variety of potential instruments which can be classified in four broad groups:

1   Political and administrative instruments

Political instruments: political programming and regulation, governmental decisions
Legal repression and violence: police, military, coast guard
Right-based instruments: conflict regulation by law and courts, sanctions and punishment
Administrative instruments: conflict regulation through public planning and resource management

2   Economic instruments

Monetary and market-based regulation of conflicts: compensation payments for damages, economic incentives and disincentives, taxes, tradeable quota or pollution rights

3   Instruments of collaboration and collective action

Collaboration: mediation, negotiation, arbitration, co-management through governmental institutions and resource users
Civil society action: participation of resource users and citizen groups, self-organisation of conflicting parties

4   Instruments of symbolic action

Ethical and moral debates: moral persuasion, ethical debates about different values and world views

The methods and policy instruments for conflict resolution need to be critically assessed and revised for further application and potential combinations; this can be seen as a main purpose of conflict research. Although informal methods and collaboration are seen as suitable for solving natural resource use conflicts, in practice often several methods are attempted, or combined.

Theoretical knowledge – frameworks for conflict research

Classifications and generalisations are a step to develop more systematic conceptual frameworks for conflict analysis. For the study of natural resource use conflicts, interdisciplinary concepts and frameworks that trace the development and ramification of conflicts in interactions between social and ecological systems seem useful. Ostrom (2009) formulated a multi-tier framework with a social-ecological systems perspective for analysing practices of natural resource use and their connections with the use of social resources. Her typology includes external contexts (social, political, economic settings, ecosystems), action situations and outcomes, connected through causal links and feedbacks between four components: resource systems, resource service units, governance systems and actors.

Ostrom's framework (similar: Manderson, 2006) does not provide theoretical explanations, but is a step of theory construction with the help of classifications. It has heuristic value for analysing resource use conflicts and identifying potential solutions. The key concepts for the formulation of integrative and interdisciplinary frameworks for conflict research include: (1) basic concepts of resource and conflict types, (2) activities and the actors, (3) processes, and (4) contexts of environmental conflicts.

1   Basic concepts

Resources and resource use problems causing conflicts
Types and degrees of conflict: violent/non-violent, political/non-political, scale (local, regional, national, international/global, trans-boundary, multi-scale)

2   Activities and actors

Human activities causing conflicts: mining, industrial production, trade and transport, and other activities
Actors involved in conflicts: conflicting parties are often more than two, including further groups, movements, public and private organisations – with their interests and aims

3   Processes

Courses of conflicts and attempts to conflict resolution: temporal differentiation of phases (chronologies of escalation, negotiation, resolution)

4   Contexts of conflicts

Normative contexts of worldviews, values, ideologies, social norms, laws, regulations, policies
System contexts of natural resource use conflicts, their linkage to social, political, economic and ecological systems

Each specific conflict is embedded in a broader context that includes social and ecological systems and different scale levels of action and interaction. Abstract descriptions of natural resource use conflicts as 'conservation vs. economic production' or 'ecology vs. economy' do not show how the conflicts between actors are interwoven with social systems and structures, modes of production and social-ecological regimes.

The following approaches from environmental conflict research can be applied in the analysis of natural resource use conflicts (more details in Stepanova and Bruckmeier, 2013, p. 25):

1   Policy-related theories and conceptual frameworks

Focus on aspects of peace, security, violence and scarcity (Bächler, 1999; Homer-Dixon, 1999; Ohlsson, 1999; Gleditsch, 2004)

2   Interdisciplinary approaches

Studies of common pool resources and social-ecological research with focus on specific forms of nature–society interaction (Ostrom, 1999; 2009)
Human-ecological and sociological approaches, especially on fisheries management (McCay, 2001; 2002; McCay and Jentoft, 1998)

3   Systemic approaches

Political economy (Schnaiberg, 1994, political economy of environment and natural resource use; Wallerstein, 2000, world system analysis) and critical environmental sociology (Rice, 2007, ecological unequal exchange in the economic world system)

Ecological economics, social and political ecology focusing on power structures and distribution of resources (e.g., Martinez-Alier, 2009, ecological distribution conflicts, Warlenius, 2017)

4   Applied research

Conflict transformation and resolution focusing on forms of negotiation, cooperation, participation of resource users in conflict resolution (Wittmer et al., 2006; Mason and Muller, 2007)
Ecological research on resilience (Folke, 2006; 2016) and conflicts related to or caused by disasters and catastrophes

These approaches and theoretical frameworks are sometimes competing, sometimes overlapping, cannot always be integrated and synthesised. Their main advantage is that they highlight specific aspects of environmental or natural resource use conflicts, or of their resolution with the key terms of political and economic power, transformation, regulation, resolution and conflict mitigation. A step of further codification can be found in interdisciplinary approaches that make use of several theoretical concepts and perspectives in system analyses of social and ecological systems and of multi-scale conflicts (e.g., the approaches of Ostrom, Martinez-Alier, Schnaiberg, Rice, see references above). For these approaches it is necessary to combine systematically empirical and theoretical knowledge, e.g., through the interpretation of conflicts with theoretically formulated concepts as that of ecological distribution conflicts. Further advances in theory development for natural resource use conflicts come with broader theories of human relations with nature and nature–society interaction. Such research, developing in social ecology (Fischer-Kowalski and Haberl, 2007; Bruckmeier, 2013; 2016), is focused on transition or transformation paths and processes, not primarily on conflicts; conflicts of natural resource use appear as a specific component of the manifold, complicated and extended processes of transformation to sustainability.

Integrating conflict research – interdisciplinary and social-ecological perspectives

The lack of knowledge integration in environmental conflict research and management

Overarching and long-term perspectives for conflict management and resolution require analyses of social, economic, ecological systems and contexts in which conflicts occur. The only overarching perspective established and widely accepted in environmental research, environmental policies and global environmental governance is, up to now, that of sustainability or sustainable development. The complicated discourse of sustainable development was reviewed several times (Du Pisani, 2006; Fischer-Kowalski and Haberl, 2007; Bruckmeier, 2009; Leach et al., 2012; Brand, 2015). How far do the debates of sustainable development take up research and solution of environmental conflicts?

The discourse of sustainable development is the latest variant of a debate on global development and North–South interaction and integration. Before that the unequal development process was discussed more critically, for example, in the UNCTAD-Declaration of Cocoyoc, Mexico, 1974, in the Dag Hammarskjöld report from 1975, or in the eco-development discourse in the 1970s and 1980s, and the dependency debate of the 1970s. There the systemic conflicts were more visible than in the Brundtland-report from 1987 where conflicts are masked in the abstract notion of intra- and inter-generational solidarity. The following conflict-generating problems have been *insufficiently addressed in global environmental govern-ance and in the sustainability discourse* – although all of them, finally, need to be addressed in conflict research:

1   Continuing older problems and forms of development

Continuing development gaps between the global North and South, the rich and the poor countries, the extracting and the processing economies
Incompatibility of continued (exponential) economic growth and sustainable use of natural resources

2   Accelerating and escalating new conflicts

Accelerating and conflicting race for natural resources through the late industrialisation in some big countries in the Global East and South
Intensifying and more violent resource conflicts after the collapse of East European socialism and the East–West confrontation in the cold war, for example, resource use conflicts related to global warming and climate change

3   Contrasts between proclaimed goals and practices

Contrasts between harmonistic global ethics and dividing consequences of sustainability policies and practices (e.g., environmentalism of the rich in contrast to environmentalism of the poor: Martinez-Alier, 2002)
Contrasts between the proclaimed goals of governmental sustainability policies and the lack of progress towards sustainability in most countries and the continuing intensification of resource use. Negative ecological trends described in the Millennium Ecosystem Assessment from 2005 have not changed much, as later analyses of ecological footprints and material and energy flow analyses show

With regard to the unsolved problems and environmental conflicts, global environmental governance is confronted with accumulating difficulties of how to deal with the complexity of systems, the limits of knowledge and increasing number of conflicts. When global social and environmental change appear as too complex to be managed, sustainable development as perspective of conflict analysis and resolution may be given up in favour of short-term perspectives and a process of 'muddling through'. The critical debate includes diagnoses that the sustainability discourse is stuck (Luks and Siemer, 2007), that the diffuse idea should be given up (Blowers et al., 2012, Benson and Craig, 2014) and replaced through the resilience concept connected with disaster management, or other concepts. Regarding resilience research (Folke, 2006; 2016), it seems sufficient to highlight its closeness to conflict research. Yet, the conflict term is not used in the functional and adaptive processes analysed in resilience research; it can be used as a complementary term to deal with the consequences of disturbance, catastrophes and disasters, when and where conflicts arise. It seems more important to discuss the blending of resilience and sustainability criticised and elaborated by various authors (e,g, Derissen et al., 2011; Bruckmeier, 2013; 2016). The ideas to replace sustainability as a long-term perspective are not more promising or less value-loaded, as exemplified by the concepts of conviviality (Illich, 1973), consilience (Wilson, 1998), environmental justice (Schlosberg, 2007).

More promising perspectives emerged in recent years: the rapidly developing debate about transition or transformation has meanwhile reached the global policy agenda, although without clarifying the transformation concept in relation to the interaction of social and ecological systems (United Nations, 2013). This debate includes critical reviews of illusionary ideas about sustainable development and ineffective policy programs, with the conclusion: sustainability as a long-term process of transition or transformation, as a new 'great transformation' (Polanyi, 1944) of society, needs to be rethought to include knowledge about conflicts on the way towards sustainability.

The Water Framework Directive of the European Union from 2000 aimed, under its overarching sustainability goal, at good ecological quality of all surface and ground waters in Europe until 2015, which was not achieved. This is less an example of bad policy, more for illusionary ideas: that sustainable water use and management can be achieved within a short time, without dealing with resource use conflicts, without changing the political and economic institutions of resource use and management, and insufficiently considering the complex interrelations between ecosystems and social systems.

Environmental conflicts need to be dealt with continually on the way towards sustainability, navigating through the processes of global environmental change, especially the disastrous consequences of climate change. Sustainability appears, more realistically, as a project of several generations or longer, of experience and learning how to build a new society: less through direct regulation and policy programs (or the meanwhile extended governance that includes civil society action and social movements), more through second order regulation, or other and indirect forms of influencing change and transformation of interacting social and ecological systems. However, the formulation of such principles and procedures is difficult; it requires elaborate theories of nature–society interaction, so far existing only in rudimentary forms in social and political ecology. Presently used notions show that the indirect processes are insufficiently understood and developed: 'navigating social-ecological systems''', 'second order regulation', 'multi-scale processes', 'hierarchical governance', 'governance of nested, embedded, networked systems', 'regulation of nature–society relations'.

Social-ecological systems – developing integrative perspectives of nature–society interaction for conflict research

The following summarising description, based on the analysis in Bruckmeier (2016, p. 183, cont.), refers to the theoretical construction of coupled social-ecological systems (SES). These concepts developed in social ecology, in a historically specified theory of nature–society interaction and human modifications of nature, especially in the debates of world ecology in the discourse of world systems theory (Wallerstein, 2000; Moore 2015), in the social-ecological research (Ostrom, 2009; Fischer-Kowalski and Haberl, 2007; Bruckmeier, 2016). That social and ecological systems are interconnected and co-evolving 'by necessity' is assumed in parts of resilience research (Folke, 2006; 2016), ignoring most of the differences between biological and sociocultural evolution, their heterogeneous principles, functions, processes and temporal scales. The normative idea to embed society in nature seems insufficient for interpreting the complex interactions between society and nature that changed throughout human history and include many different forms of coupling between social and ecological systems.

The complexity of SES needs to be analysed empirically and through theoretical analyses of modern society, modes of production and socio-metabolic regimes, to be able to identify the influencing factors and processes in the broader contexts. This context includes societal and ecological systems, forms of their reproduction, system structures that block or predetermine the long-term development of the systems. Societal structures affecting ecosystem management and environmental conflicts include social and class structures, societal division of labour, political and economic power relations, socially unequal appropriation and distribution of natural resources.

The historically specific forms of coupling of SES and interaction of nature and society cannot be read off from the empirical examples and case studies of resource use and the conflicts identified there. The present, functional as well as dysfunctional forms of coupling of SES result from the industrial socio-metabolic regimes in which *fossil energy resources* played a key role; first the coal regime, later the oil regime, still dominant but phasing out. The analysis of these regimes helps to find theoretical explanations for the unsustainable interaction between society and nature and resulting conflicts. This situation is accounting for systemic structures and bottlenecks of development, furthermore, supporting the consolidation of environmental conflict research. Interactions and feedback processes between social and ecological systems show that natural resource use conflicts are indicators of maladaptive change processes in modern society; conflict analysis needs to be complemented by analyses of the manifold and changing, loose or tight forms of coupling between social and ecological systems and their consequences for resource use. This analysis is guided by the question, how long can the present industrial forms of resource use and economic growth be maintained? Since the 1970s, when the discourse of limits to growth began, it has become evident that the overshoot of global resource use that has been achieved meanwhile cannot be maintained over a very long period of time.

Conclusions – interdisciplinary knowledge synthesis and its difficulties

Environment-related or natural resource use conflicts are not only political conflicts, although most of them are connected to public policies, policy programs, political controversies and political actors, unequal exchange and various forms of conflict resolution. The conflicts may originate in everyday practices of resource users, private persons or organisations that act in the institutionally channelled and regulated forms of cultural, political, economic and other specific forms of social systems. Conflict mitigation does not always require governmental or political institutions or decisions. Many resource use conflicts appear as multi-sectorial, multi-dimensional and multi-scale conflicts that are simultaneously economic, political, social, cultural, ethnic, conflicts between values, interests, user and property rights, and conflicts between the needs and interests of human and other resource users. In their multi-dimensionality they show the interconnections between different social spheres, social and ecological systems.

Assuming that resource use conflicts continue, inter- and transdisciplinary knowledge syntheses will become more important, to show the necessity and the forms of new development perspectives and improved procedures of conflict resolution. Knowledge about global social and environmental change – in which conflict mitigation and sustainability transformation are interwoven – makes the core of renewal. Interdisciplinary knowledge syntheses that require knowledge from the social and natural sciences are, however, badly developed. The scientific learning in the overarching process of social-ecological transformational is twofold: to learn how to integrate empirical research, theories and practical action, and to learn how to synthesise knowledge from social and natural scientific research. Both forms of knowledge integration imply methodological guidance, critical analysis, assessment, and learning from prior forms of policy and research, their misfits and their failures. Moreover, this seems necessary to prepare for more and intensifying conflicts as a consequence of global environmental change and the difficulties of conflict resolution. Such learning requires knowledge input from both ends: from the empirical and the theoretical research about the unsustainable state of nature–society interaction. Beyond the debate of transforming conflicts to cooperation to be able to solve them, more is to learn in conflict research: to advance from research about conflict transformation to research about social-ecological transformation towards sustainability.

Acknowledgements

I am grateful for comments and critique from the editors of the book and an anonymous reviewer who helped to improve the text.

References

Bächler, G. (1999) 'Environmental degradation and violent conflict', in Suliman, M. (ed.), *Ecology, politics, and violent conflicts*, Zed Books, New York, 76–112

Benson, M.H. and Craig, R.K. (2014) 'The end of sustainability', *Society and Natural Resources*, 27, 777–782

Blokhuis, H.J. (2008) 'International cooperation in animal welfare: The welfare quality project', *Acta Veterinaria Scandinavica*, 50, Suppl 1, S10, doi:10.186/1751–0147–50–S1-S10

Blowers, A., Boersema, J. and Martin, A. (2012) 'Is sustainable development sustainable?', *Journal of Integrative Environmental Sciences*, 9(1), 1–8

Brand, U. (2015) 'Sozial-ökologischen transformation als horizont praktischer kritik: Befreiung in zeiten sich vertiefender imperialer lebensweise', in Martin, D., MartinS. and WisselJ. (eds), *Perspektiven und konstellationen kritischer theorie*, Westfälisches Dampfboot, Münster, 166–182

Bruckmeier, K. (2009) 'Sustainability between neccessity, contingency and impossibility', *Sustainability*, 1(2), doi:10.3390/su10x000xwww.mdpi.com/journal/sustainability

Bruckmeier, K. (2013) *Natural resource use and global change: New interdisciplinary perspectives in social ecology*, Palgrave Macmillan, Basingstoke, UK

Bruckmeier, K. (2016) *Social-ecological transformation: Reconnecting society and nature*, Palgrave Macmillan, London

Cooper, D. and Palmer, J. (eds) (1995) *Just environments: Intergenerational, international and inter-species issues*, Routledge, London and New York

Cudworth, E. (2013) *Social lives with other animals: Tales of sex, death, and love*, Palgrave Mcmillan, Basingstoke, UK

Derissen, S., Quaas, M.F. and Baumgärtner, S. (2011) 'The relationship between resilience and sustainability of ecological-economic systems', *Ecological Economics*, 70, 1121–1128

Du Pisani, J. (2006) 'Sustainable development – historical roots of the concept', *Environmental Sciences*, 3(2), 83–96

Dyer, G. (2011) *Climate wars: The fight for survival as the world overheats*, Oneworld Publications

Fischer-Kowalski, M. and Haberl, H. (eds) (2007) *Socioecological transitions and global change*, Edward Elgar, Cheltenham, UK and Northampton USA

Folke, C. (2006) 'Resilience: The emergence of a perspective for social-ecological systems analyses', *Global Environmental Change*, 16, 253–267

Folke, C. (2016) 'Resilience (republished)', *Ecology and Society*, 21(4), Art. 44 https://doi.org/10575/ES-0908088-210444

Gleditsch, P. (2004) 'Beyond scarcity vs. abundance: A policy research agenda for natural resources and conflicts', in *Understanding environment, conflict, and cooperation*, United Nations Environment Programme

Haraway, D. (2008) *When species meet*, The University of Minnesota Press, Minneapolis

Hoffmann, J.P. (2004) 'Social and environmental influence on endangered species: A cross-national study', *Sociological Perspectives*, 47(1), 79–107

Homer-Dixon, T.D. (1999) *Environment, scarcity and violence*, Princeton University Press, Princeton, NJ

Illich, I. (1973) *Tools for conviviality*, Marion Boyars, London and New York

Klenke, R.A., Ring, I., Kranz, A., Jepsen, N., Rauschmayer, F. and Henle, K. (eds) (2013) *Human–wildlife conflicts in Europe: Fisheries and fish-eating vertebrates as a model case*, Springer, Berlin and Heidelberg

Leach, M., Rockström, J., Raskin, P., Scoones, I.C., Stirling, A.C., Smith, A., Thompson, J., Millstone, E., Ely, A., Arond, E., Folke, C. and Olsson, P. (2012) 'Transforming innovation for sustainability', *Ecology and Society*, 17(2), 11

Leal Filho, W., Brandt, N., Krahn, D. and Wennersten, R. (eds) (2008) *Conflict resolution in coastal zone management*, Environmental education, communication and sustainability, Vol. 28, Peter Lang GmbH, Internationaler Verlag der Wissenschaften, Fankfurt am Main

Luks, F. and Siemer, S.H. (2007) 'Whither sustainable development? A plea for humility', *GAIA*, 16(3), 187–192

Manderson, A.K. (2006) 'A systems framework to examine the multi-contextual application of the sustainability concept', *Environment, Development and Sustainability*, 8, 85–97

Martinez-Alier, J. (2002) *The environmentalism of the poor: A study of ecological conflicts and valuation*, Edward Elgar, Cheltenham, UK

Martinez-Alier, J. (2009) 'Social metabolism, ecological distribution conflicts, and languages of valuation', *Capitalism, Nature, Socialism*, 20(1), 58–87

Mason, S.A. and Muller, A. (2007) 'Transforming environmental and natural resource use conflicts', in CogoyM. and SteiningerK.W. (eds), *The economics of global environmental change*, Edward Elgar, Cheltenham, UK, 252–272

McCay, B.J. and Jentoft, S. (1998) 'Market or community failure? Critical perspectives on common property research', *Human Organization*, 7(1), 21–29

McCay, B.J. (2001) 'Community-based and cooperative fisheries: Solutions to fishermen's problems', in Burger, J., Ostrom, E., Norgaard, R.B., Policansky, D. and Goldstein, B.D. (eds), *Protecting the commons: A framework for resource management in the Americas*, Island Press, Washington, DC, 175–194

McCay, B.J. (2002) 'Co-management and crisis in fisheries science and management', *Marine Resources: Property Rights, Economics and Environment*, 14, Elsevier Science, 341–359

Meadows, D.H. and Meadows, D.L. (1972) *The limits to growth*, Universe Books

Mehta, M. and Quellet, E. (1995) *Environmental sociology: Theory and practice*, Captus Press, York, Ontario

Moore, J. (2015) *Capitalism and the web of life: Ecology and the accumulation of capital*, Verso, London

Myers, O.E. (2003) 'No longer the lonely species: A post-mead perspective on animals and sociology', *International Journal of Sociology and Social Policy*, 23(3), 46–68

Ohlsson, L. (1999) *Environment, scarcity and Conflict – a study of Malthusian concerns*, PhD thesis, Department of Peace and Development Research, University of Gothenburg, Sweden

Ostrom, E. (1999) 'Coping with the tragedy of the commons', *Annual Review of Political Science*, 2, 493–535

Ostrom, E. (2009) 'A general framework for analysing sustainability of social-ecological systems', *Science*, 325, (5939), 419–422

Polanyi, K. (1944) *The great transformation*, Farrar & Rinehart, New York

Princen, T. (2010) 'Speaking of sustainability: The potential of metaphor', *Sustainability Science, Practice, & Policy*, 6(2), 60–65

Rice, J. (2007) 'Ecological unequal exchange: Consumption, equity, and unsustainable structural relationships within the global economy', *International Journal of Comparative Sociology*, 48, 43–72

Schlosberg, D. (2007) *Defining environmental justice: Theories, movements, and nature*, Oxford University Press, Oxford

Schnaiberg, A. (1994) 'The political economy of environmental problems and policies: Consciousness, conflict and the environment', *Advances in Human Ecology*, 3, 23–64

Spillmann, K.R. and Bächler, G. (eds) (1995) *Environmental crisis: Regional conflicts and ways of cooperation*, Center for Security Studies and Conflict Research, Swiss Peace Foundation, Zürich and Bern

Stepanova, O. and Bruckmeier, K. (2013) 'The relevance of environmental conflict research for coastal management: A review of concepts, approaches and methods with a focus on Europe', *Ocean & Coastal Management*, 75, 20–32

Stepanova, O. (2015) *Conflict resolution in coastal management: Interdisciplinary analyses of resource use conflicts from the Swedish coast*, PhD thesis, Human Ecology, School of Global Studies, University of Gothenburg

Tedeschi, E. (2016) 'Animals, humans, and sociability', *Italian Sociological Review*, 6(2) http://www.questia.com/library/journal/q1P3-4208088321/animals-humans-and-so cialbility

United Nations (2013) *Global governance and the governance of global commons in the global partnership for development after 2015*, UN System Task Team on the Post-2015 UN Development Agenda

Wallerstein, I. (2000) 'Globalization or the age of transition? A long-term view of the trajectory of the world-system', *International Sociology*, 15(2), 249–265

Warlenius, R. (2017) 'Asymmetries: Conceptualizing environmental inequalities as ecological debt and ecologically unequal exchange', PhD thesis, Human Ecology, Lund University, Sweden

Welzer, H. (2008) *Klimakriege. Wofür im 21. Jahrhundert getötet wird*, S. Fischer Verlag, Frankfurt am Main

Wilson, E.O. (1998) *Consilience: The unity of knowledge*, Alfred A. Knopf, New York

Wittmer, H., Rauschmayer, F. and Klauer, B. (2006) 'How to select instruments for the resolution of environmental conflicts?', *Land Use Policy*, 23, 1–9

Wullweber, J. (2015) 'Global politics and empty signifiers: The political construction of high technology', *Critical Policy Studies*, 9(1), 78–96

14 The transformative potential of the food system concept

Sustainability conflicts or sustainability transitions?

E. Gunilla Almered Olsson

Introduction – global food systems and food security

Today, providing urban populations with food is dependent on the global food systems both in the Global North and Global South (Misselhorn et al., 2012). The instability of the global food system became evident during the 2007–2008 global food crisis with its spiking food prices and direct repercussions on global food security (Rosin et al., 2012). This process demonstrated the illusion of the idea of 'cheap food' as the solid pillar of global food security (ibid). The global food system is part of the liberalised global trade market and thus under the spell of the volatility of financial markets closely linked to the agro-industrial complex (Killeen et al., 2008; Feintrenie, 2014).

The effective functioning of the global food system demands the fulfilment of a number of preconditions, such as continuous access to land, energy, water and other resources, the absence of environmental disturbances and disasters such as droughts, floods, soil erosion or the contamination of air, water and soils and lack of disturbances resulting from political and military conflicts, or terror attacks (Sage, 2013; Porter et al., 2014; Dyball, 2015; Morgan, 2015; Olsson, 2018a). In a world of increasing uncertainty (Steffen et al., 2015), the above preconditions are not guaranteed. Therefore, dependence on the global food system is jeopardising human food security irrespective of the scale, be it international, national or local.

With growing insight into the consequences of the global food system for the environment, many cities in the Global North have implemented local/regional food strategies, food charters and other food system-related policies in an attempt to improve urban food security and encourage sustainable food system activities (Moragues-Faus et al., 2013; Ferguson, 2017; Olsson 2018b). Such activities include, for example, climate and ecosystem-friendly production methods, minimising the transportation of commodities in favour of food production located closer to consumers, and food systems driven by local participation and community actions (Blay-Palmer et al., 2018). There seems to be connection between several of the proposed food system activities and Transition Movement actions (IPBES, 2018). Could the development of a sustainable food system catalyse change/transitions towards sustainability? In order to explore this question, the aim of this chapter is to examine the link between sustainable food systems and pathways towards sustainability transitions.

The scope of food system issues and their connection to the Sustainable Development Goals

The food system encompasses the activities and processes of *producing food, processing and packaging food, distributing and retailing food, and consuming food* (Misselhorn et al., 2012) with the aim of securing food security at the scale in question. Globalisation has changed food security dynamics by involving food products and agricultural input commodities in the global trade market and global food system. At locations for large-scale export of agricultural commodities, local food production has been jeopardised by making land to produce local food unavailable. In parallel, food security is threatened in regions that depend on the long-distance transportation of food products from the global food system. This heavy dependence on distant landscapes and the global food system is illustrated by the case of pork production in Denmark, which is reliant on the import of soy cake from Brazil (Dyball, 2015). Apart from distant land use, the globalised food production results in increased transportation in order to transport products from the country of their production to the country of consumption (Kastner et al., 2014), which has a significant impact on the environment due to the resulting greenhouse gas emissions (McMichael et al., 2007).

The food system is a genuinely transdisciplinary topic as it has consequences for all social-economic, environmental and governance sectors, indeed, food issues cross all the United Nations Sustainable Development Goals (SDGs) (UN, 2015). This was recently demonstrated by Ilieva (2017) by finding connections to all SDGs in food strategy documents for five North American metropolitan regions. A larger study of food system policies in 15 urban regions (Sonnino, 2016) was used by Olsson (2018b) to identify connections between policy documents and the SDGs. An attempt to use food as an integrative approach for grouping the 17 SDGs into seven clusters was made by Blay-Palmer et al., (2018). These seven SDG-clusters are used in this chapter as a basis for further elaboration in order to encompass sustainable food systems (Fig. 14.1). The relevance of each cluster for the food system is outlined below. The SDGs 2, 10 and 16 are recurring in several clusters.

Cluster I: SDG2: No hunger, Food and nutrition security, Sustainable agriculture, Crop diversity. SDG 17: Multi-stakeholder partnership

Here are the core issues regarding food production methods whereby agro-ecological methods appear suitable as they have the potential to facilitate adaptation to local ecosystem conditions, embrace diversity in crops and land use, combine livestock raising with arable cultivation, thereby ensuring nutrient circulation and water conservation (Altieri, 2004; Auerbach et al., 2013; Mendez et al., 2013; Martin and Isaac, 2018) and promote climate-smart food production (Altieri et al., 2015). Food production that combines livestock raising with arable cultivation has the potential to

Figure 14.1 The clustering of the 17 Sustainable Development Goals (UN, 2015),
which illustrates how food system issues cross the different sustainability
dimensions. The relevant SDGs are given in each cluster. The figure is
modified from Blay-Palmer et al., (2018) and Olsson, (2018b).

use whole agricultural landscapes including using natural pastures for livestock grazing. This gives a potential for increased biodiversity and ecosystem services and the integration of food security with regional biodiversity
(Fischer et al., 2017).

Against the background of the debate on how to produce sufficient food to feed
the expanding human population, it is important to note that agro-ecological
methods are focused on diversification and multifunctionality. The use of multiple
crops with different life cycles and harvest seasons is central and in this way agro-
biodiversity can be used as a possibility for agricultural intensification (Caron et al.,
2014). Along these lines, agro-ecological methods comply with a majority of the
SDGs, which is in contrast to 'conventional' intensive methods that are based on
specialised technologies with the overall goal of obtaining high yields from
monocultures (Kuyper and Struik, 2014).

There is a positive correlation between human nutrition and crop diversity. However, since the 1960s, there has been a decline in biodiversity as well as in food product diversity, which is linked to the dominant global food system with negative implications for food security (Khoury et al., 2014). The privatisation and patenting of seeds, GMO technologies and the ties to agro-chemicals including pesticides along with the increasing dominance of multinational corporations within the agro-biochemical sector is counteracting local agro-biodiversity and resilient ecosystem functions and thereby threatening global food security. Developing multi-stakeholder partnerships, including public–private cooperation, to share knowledge, expertise, technology and financial support is suggested in SDG 17 as it would be beneficial for the application of agro-ecological methodologies at different levels and scales (Altieri et al., 2015) in order to promote food security.

Cluster II: SDG 2, 3: Health and well-being, Food and nutrition security. SDG 16: Peace, justice and strong institutions

Human health is significantly linked to nutrition security and diets (Gwatkin et al, 2007; Smith and Haddad, 2015; Otero et al., 2018). A food production system that is based on local resources in terms of crop diversity and crop cultivars is more likely to deliver both food and nutrition security compared to homogenised systems based on monocultures. Such diverse agro-ecosystems are referred to by Barthel et al. (2013) as 'biocultural refugia', and they are considered to have immense value in that they maintain food and nutrition security in a context of increasing uncertainty, of which climate change is just one factor. Of equal value is their reservoir of biodiversity, species, genetic varieties and landscapes and the local and traditional knowledge linked to the agricultural practices for maintaining such systems (Barthel et al., 2013). Further, such systems are rich sources of different innovatory methods and practices based on a combination of traditional and modern scientific knowledge (ibid.).

SDG3: Human health effects implying illness and deaths from hazardous chemicals, as well as soil, air and water contamination, have to be avoided in food production systems and practices. Agro-ecological methods striving to reduce such external inputs in the farming systems correspond to this urging (Mendez et al., 2013).

SDG 16: The development of effective and transparent institutions at all levels, that can maintain peace and justice and counteract corruption and ensure participatory decision making, are prerequisites for the functioning of the food system based in a local/regional context.

Cluster III: SDG 4, 5, 10: Equitable and lifelong learning, Intersectional equality, Improved economic equality. SDG 16: Peace, justice and strong institutions

A sustainable and resilient food system would have the potential of adaptation to changing conditions and unexpected disturbances. This implies capacity and agency for alterations along the food chain in terms of production methods,

Figure 14.2 Agro-ecological food systems, annual and perennial crop species. Bohol, The Philippines, October 2016. (Photo: E.G.A. Olsson)

crop diversity, etc. Here it is essential that traditional and local knowledge is maintained and applied in combination with modern scientific knowledge with transdisciplinary methodologies that can facilitate and stimulate innovations (Mendez et al., 2013; Altieri et al., 2015; Tengö et al., 2017). In this way, the food system issues will motivate lifelong learning and innovation efforts and could lead the way towards sustainability transitions (Barthel et al., 2013; Altieri et al., 2015; Auerbach et al., 2013).

The concept of *food justice* refers to '… the right to have access to these [foods, resources …] …. and to have the capacity to make one's voice heard so as to have access to food and resources …' (Hochedez and Le Gall, 2016). Food justice relates directly to social and intersectional inequalities and various forms of social, cultural, economic and spatial exclusion (Hope and Agyeman, 2011; Kolb, 2015; Hochedez and Le Gall, 2016). The dependence on distant landscapes in the global food system has an inevitable food justice dimension.

Related to this cluster are questions about food based on animal products, such as meat, dairy and eggs. In a sustainable food system, equity, justice, ethics and animal welfare issues related to the raising of animals for human food consumption are imperative and cannot be overlooked (Boscardin, 2017). This discussion is still in its infancy and considerable changes and regulations can be foreseen during the coming years. For this issue as well as for the food justice complex the link to SDG 16 – The development of effective and transparent institutions at all levels that can maintain peace and justice and counteract corruption and ensure participatory decision making – is crucial.

Cluster IV: SDG 1: No poverty. SDG 8, 9: Good work opportunities and sustainable economic growth, Innovations and infrastructure

The correlation between hunger and poverty (SDG 1) is manifest as is the link to poverty and unequal distribution of resources and equity (SDG 4, 5 – Cluster III). A sustainable food system with a high share of food produced locally implies shorter food chains and closer links between producers and consumers, which improves opportunities for providing consumers with the food products they demand. It also facilitates communication between producers and consumers about the food products and how they are marketed and delivered. This arrangement provides new job opportunities and improved preconditions for securing a decent income from food production due to a reduction in the number of intermediaries. An arrangement for local food production that is increasing in recognition in metropolitan regions, where agricultural land is very expensive, is Community Supported Agriculture (CSA) (Sharp et al., 2002). In general, this means an economic agreement between producers and consumers regarding the production and delivery of food products, which involves the sharing of risk between both groups. According to Bloemmen et al., (2015), the CSA model reflects a convergence of goals for the producer and the consumer and promotes a transition towards alternatives to GDP-growth[1] such as de-growth (D'Alisa et al., 2014). For the processing of local food products as well as the distribution systems, there is a demand for climate- and resource-smart innovations, which would also provide new job opportunities and develop small-scale process industries (Olsson et al., 2016).

Cluster V: SDG 7: Renewable and sustainable energy. SDG 13: Climate change mitigation and adaptation

Agriculture and food production along the 'productivist paradigm' with agricultural practices that are fuelled by access to cheap energy sources, mainly fossil fuel, is making a huge contribution to greenhouse gas emissions, not only as a result of the intensive use of vehicles and machinery and other inputs such as fertilisers (Pradhan et al., 2013), but also the continuous increase in agricultural area with expansion into grasslands and forests (Foley et al., 2011). Changing diets with an increase in meat and dairy consumption in wealthy countries and also by the middle-class in developing countries makes a significant contribution to global anthropogenic greenhouse gas emissions (Pradhan et al., 2013; Schader et al., 2015). Reducing the consumption of animal products and applying climate-smart methods and practices based on agro-ecology would reduce the impact of food production on the climate (Altieri et al., 2015; Graham and Abrahamse, 2017) and would also have a beneficial effect on human health (Tilman and Clark, 2015).

Cluster VI: SDG 6: Clean water and sanitation. SDG 14, 15: Life on land and below water (marine and fresh water) – biodiversity

Sustainable food production for the future must be able to handle the challenges of resource circulation and conservative use of land, water, nutrients and biodiversity in parallel with achieving the goal of food security at the global level. The current environmental impacts of agriculture on land, soils, climate, water and biodiversity are unprecedented and are completely unsustainable regarding future food security and seriously threaten human survival (Steffen et al., 2011; Foley et al., 2011). In order to reduce the impacts on terrestrial and aquatic biodiversity, the current agricultural paradigm based on maximising yields from monocultures (conventional intensification) has to be substituted by ecological, agro-ecological intensification methods (Kuyper and Struik, 2014). Such systems offer high yields in polyculture systems, which include perennial plants (trees and shrubs), that allow prolonged harvesting and promote diverse agricultural landscapes at the species and ecosystem levels (Altieri, et al., 2015; Martin and Isaac, 2018). Such systems, which are adapted to local conditions, e.g., choice of crop, and which are managed with traditional ecological knowledge, are in place in many smallholder farms at various locations in the Global South (Auerbach et al. 2013; Barthel et al., 2013). There is untapped potential in the Global North to introduce adaptations of such systems in combination with current biotechnological knowledge to achieve sustainable yields of food crops and simultaneously provide varied landscapes and viable livelihoods for people. There is a wealth of knowledge on the management of preindustrial agricultural landscapes in Europe, which could be used to develop innovations in food production and food systems for the future (Agnoletti and Emanueli, 2016; Olsson, 2018c).

Cluster VII: SDG 9, 10, 11: Improved urban–rural linkages with reduced urban–rural inequalities and improved infrastructure. SDG 12: Responsible consumption and production

There is potential for increasing both urban and rural viability via a sustainable food system based on local (urban and peri-urban) and regional (peri-urban and rural – regional) food production. This could be secured through, for example, new employment opportunities in food production, new food enterprises, and by reclaiming the value of produce from the region 'terroir' (Feagan, 2007; Sonnino, 2016). The establishment of CSAs (Community Supported Agriculture) will contribute to stabilising the urban–rural links as a result of their direct connection between (urban) consumers and peri-urban and rural producers and the creation of jobs. The territorial approach to food production has been put forward by several United Nations organisations based on the assertion that it is needed in order to achieve food security and improved nutrition policy (OECD, 2016). The regional and context-specific food systems have been overlooked in favour of global food systems. In order to implement 'multi-sectoral, bottom-up and place-based interventions' (OECD, 2016) there is a need for improved joint planning of urban and peri-urban regions (Olsson et al., 2016). How can this happen? Both locally and regionally, it is a requirement to identify pathways on *how* to organise the provision of food relying more on local food systems. Internationally, several activities on local food systems are going on, particularly in urban regions. The most important initiatives are summarised in a report on City Region Food Systems, which focuses on territorial approaches to food systems in order to support rural–urban linkages both in the Global North and Global South (Dubbeling et al., 2016; Blay-Palmer et al., 2018). The report emphasises that although very promising results have been achieved by local and regional food systems, there is still a lack of coherence in policies and planning initiatives for urban-rural regions (Blay-Palmer et al., 2018).

This survey of food system issues linked to the 17 SDGs reveals four recurring themes:

1   *Shift in agricultural production methods* from conventional intensive agriculture based on high inputs and favouring high yields from monocultures to agro-ecological intensification based on preconditions in the local ecosystem, polycultures and high agro-biodiversity
2   *Shift from dependence on the global food system* towards more reliance on local and regional food systems
3   *Combination of* scientific, agronomic and ecological *knowledge* with local and indigenous knowledge
4   *Different approach to governance*, from top-down governed agricultural systems to bottom-up organisation with the active involvement of local farmers and other stakeholders in the food system

Food, the Sustainable Development Goals and conflicts

The seven SDG-clusters outlined above all involve intrinsic and urgent conflicts but the overriding conflict is focused on how to solve the challenge of attaining global food security in 2050 when the global population is projected to be 9 billion people while at the same time addressing global environmental challenges. On one side is conventional agriculture along the 'productionist paradigm' (Lang and Heasman, 2015, p. 38), the aim of which is high-yielding monocultures with a drive to level out agro-ecosystem heterogeneities with external inputs driven by 'fewer entrepreneurial farmers mobilizing high levels of technical skills and financial fluxes' (ibid.). On the other side is the agro-ecological approach with methodologies and practices that are adapted to the local ecosystem and using agro-biodiversity rich polycultures. This approach is based on the view that agriculture is not only about food production, but also ensuring the delivery of ecosystem services in order to maintain the ecosystem as well as secure viable livelihoods for farmers and rich and diverse landscapes for all stakeholders. Most of the conflicts over food production are related to this overriding tension between the different approaches to agricultural production. However, some conflicts are not directly related to the above issue, such as the cultural context that influences methods for food production and processing and diets. There is a large unresolved and badly overlooked conflict on the ethics and welfare of animals used in food production. Surprisingly, in studies on local and regional food production in sustainable food systems the ethical and animal welfare dimension is also lacking (e.g., Conrad et al., 2016). A fundamental conflict in terms of food security is related to the unequal distribution of power and participation and access to basic resources for human well-being including land for food production.

What is a sustainable food system?

Is it possible to outline criteria for a sustainable food system?

All the dimensions listed under the seven clusters above would be included on the criteria list, but such a list must also encompass the resolution of the numerous conflicts that are currently connected to the various steps of the food system. The destabilising dimensions of a sustainable food system have been identified by Schipanski et al., (2016) as: 'Increased inequity and injustice; Environmental degradation; Exclusive reliance on global distribution networks; Homogenization of energy dense diets.' In contrast, dimensions that promote the transformation of a food system towards a more resilient/sustainable state are: 'Increased equity and justice; [Building on] Biodiversity through agro-ecological management; Increased diversity of distribution networks; Increased dietary diversity and reduced waste' (Schipanski et al., 2016). The destabilising dimensions are all characteristics of the global food system based on the conventional intensive agriculture paradigm, while the stabilising dimensions fit well with the food systems aspired to in local and sub-regional food strategies. It is noteworthy that in the seven food-related SDG-clusters described above, the governance of the food production is either absent, insufficiently developed or treated at a very general level. However, there are a number of studies that draw attention to local and regional food production that is driven by collective action and the participation of citizens in decisions about land use, organising livelihoods, local food production and cooperation between local (state) government and civil society (Moragues-Faus and Morgan, 2015; Blay-Palmer et al., 2016; 2018; Raffle and Carey, 2018). Such arrangement has been very successful in the city of Gothenburg, where the city administration offers land for urban and peri-urban food cultivation and provides support for Community Supported Agriculture (Olsson, 2018a).

A sustainable food system needs to include the application of local and traditional knowledge linked to the local ecosystem in combination with academic, agronomic and ecological knowledge in order to optimise the output of the system and build sustainability. Such knowledge can help to maintain local crop and animal varieties and their genetic diversity and accomplish adaptation to environmental changes such as climate change and local forms of sociocultural organisation related to food production (Altieri, 2004; Anderson, 2010; Altieri, 2015; Tengö et al., 2017; Olsson, 2018c). Such an approach to agricultural production would imply a rebalancing of power in favor of farmers so they would once again be actively contributing to the production and dissemination of knowledge, which would challenge the characteristic of expert specialisation inherent in the conventional agricultural model (Caron et al., 2014).

A sustainable food system must come to terms with the issue of the rearing of livestock for human consumption and include an in-depth, participatory discussion about the challenging issues of ethics and environmental justice related to human–animal relationships and animal welfare (Boscardin, 2017).

The urban–rural linkage via the food system is connected to the concept of the *Foodshed,* a geographic region that produces food for a specific human population (Peters et al., 2009).

According to Thompson et al., (in Sonnino, 2016), a foodshed can be interpreted as '… local food that takes into account not just territoriality, but also a series of quality attributes such as agricultural production methods, fair farm labor practices and animal welfare'. Hence, it seems that the foodshed concept will be vital for the realisation of sustainable food systems.

At the global level, in a document on food security, several United Nations agencies related to human development and food security (OECD, FAO, UNCDF) have proposed 'a shift in approach from sectoral, top-down and "one-size-fits-all" to one that is multi-sectoral, bottom-up and context-specific' (OECD, 2016). They stress the importance of a holistic 'territorial approach' to sustainable food systems and the achievement of food security (ibid.), which encompasses the consideration of local and regional ecosystems and their conditions for food production as well as the socio-cultural and economic conditions for local communities. The link to the 17 'indivisible' SDGs is emphasised. These recommendations correspond well with the elements of the sustainable food systems discussed above.

Figure 14.3 Agro-ecological food systems, local wine cultivation. Portugal, April 2017.
(Photo: E.G.A. Olsson)

On the transformative potential of food systems

Pathways towards sustainability transitions

Sustainability transitions seek to address critical challenges of contemporary societies by linking ecological integrity, societal viability and intergenerational justice (Markard et al., 2012; Luederitz et al., 2017). Such challenges include environmental degradation and climate change, growing inequality regarding resource accessibility and the need for participation between different groups and societies at the local, regional and global levels, which demands cross-sectoral and cross-scale societal changes. The transition pathways have been categorised into different narratives, which differ according to the diverging interpretations of sustainability (Luederitz et al., 2017; Hausknost et al., 2017).

An analysis of sustainability transition pathways related to the UN-SDGs was performed within the UN-IPBES framework (IPBES, 2018). The following different pathways were identified: *Green economy, Low carbon transformation, Ecotopian* and *Transition Movements*. Of these, the *Transition Movements* narrative matches best with the SDGs, while the other pathway narratives were strong in some dimensions, for example, climate and energy with carbon-reduction strategies, but weak in terms of the equity dimensions (IPBES, 2018). In contrast to the *Green Economy* and *Low Carbon Transformation* narratives, the *Transition Movements* narrative involves a change in values towards resource-saving lifestyles including, e.g., food and energy, while, in some cases, they explicitly emphasise non-GDP growth or de-growth (Muraca, 2012; Whitehead, 2013; IPBES, 2018). In the *Transition Movements* narrative, food system changes are important and involve the development of innovative forms of agriculture, combination of indigenous and local knowledge with scientific and technological knowledge to produce food based on methods from agro-ecology, agro-forestry and urban agriculture, and to implement transport and energy models that limit the impact on nature, climate and water. A focus on reduced social inequality and full employment (SDGs 8, 10) is included in the vision of enhancing quality of life in the *Transition Movements* narrative. The SDGs are achieved through new social models, which aim to reduce market globalisation and inter-regional flows, and support cultural identities, knowledge-sharing and transformative capabilities. Transformative capabilities are characterised here as individual and collective capacity to improve and enrich quality of life by changing factors that affect people's lives, of which the environment is central. Apart from education, the transformative capabilities include social capital, local leadership and empowerment, trust building, and collaboration and participatory decision making (IPBES, 2018).

Food systems and (pathways towards) sustainability transitions

Food-system activities can facilitate transcultural communication and stimulate new initiatives. Furthermore, they can cross borders between different stakeholder groups (local government, researchers, farmers, food stores, restaurants, etc.), socio-economic groups and generations. Central to the (urban) sustainability transition is the (re-)establishment of urban–rural linkages via the food system. The international overview of 'City region food systems linking urban and rural areas for sustainable and resilient development' (Dubbeling et al., 2016) provides examples from cities in the Global North and South of how food systems can generate political support for the wider urban–rural linkages through coalitions built on food. City Region Food Systems are vital for the implementation of the United Nations New Urban Agenda (UN, 2015) and, specifically, for linking SDG 2 (food security and sustainable agriculture), SDG 11 (sustainable cities and communities) and SDG 12 (sustainable production and consumption).

Recent studies have shown agreement between actions and goals suggested in the sustainable food system strategies and the elements of the Transition Movements (Olsson, 2018b). Such elements include food system impacts on, for example, lifestyle and consumption, diversified land use, agro-ecological production methods, decreased energy consumption, urban–rural planning, local empowerment, social cohesion, and livelihood strategies at the sub-regional scale. The necessary coupling between urban and rural regions will be achieved through changed policies, planning and reorientation of farm subsidies that reconnect the regions and by a number of new opportunities related to food system activities. This includes branding different food products as 'local' and development of the 'terroir' concept. Those activities will promote innovations in the food system, e.g., new distribution systems and consumer participation, and stimulate economic growth in the peri-urban and rural regions. Such actions would have broader implications for society as a whole which would not be limited to food issues.

Against this background, there are convincing arguments that the development of sustainable food systems and the Transition Movement have overlapping goals and ambitions. It is compelling that the achievement of sustainable food systems would pave the way to sustainability transitions.

Conclusion

From the preceding discussion of sustainable food systems that address not only the dual goals of increasing food production while minimising agriculture's contribution to global environmental degradation, but all the 17 SDGs, the following aspects emerge.

Characteristics of a sustainable food system

1   Shift from dependence on the global food system towards reliance on *local and regional food systems*
2   Shift from conventional intensive agricultural methods to *agro-ecological methods promoting water conservation, nutrient recirculation, biodiversity* at the levels of gene, crop, species, habitat
3   *Knowledge combination*: academic, scientific and local, traditional, ecological knowledge
4   *Changed approach to governance*: from top-down expert dominated to bottom-up decision making with the active involvement of local farmers and communities, intersectional
5   *Rebalancing of power* in favour of local farmers and producers, intersectional

6 Reconsideration of the *ethics and animal welfare* issues behind the ways of rearing animals for human consumption
7 Ensuring that food production generates a *reasonable income for farmers and producers*
8 Re-establishment of urban–rural linkages via local/regional food production, e.g., *foodsheds*

Finally, a majority of current food strategies and plans, which aim to contribute to sustainability, embrace a number of SDGs in terms of environmental, social, economic and equity dimensions. This is a characteristic of the Transition Movements pathway for sustainability transitions. The Transition Movement, which is found both in urban and rural contexts, is heterogeneous, complex and diverse, but participatory and community-based actions, in particular concerning food systems, are distinctive (see Chapter 2). In spite of the heterogeneity of the Transition Movement, it is possible that the range of participatory activities, which is also a characteristic of sustainable food systems, can act as 'seeds' for processes of change (Bennett et al., 2016), thereby stimulating transition.

Note

1 Non GDP-growth means alternatives to the market-driven economic growth paradigm; see
   Whitehead, (2013).

References

Agnoletti, M. and Emanueli, F. (eds) (2016) *Biocultural diversity in Europe*, Springer, Switzerland

Altieri, M.A. (2004) 'Linking ecologists and traditional farmers in the search for sustainable agriculture', *Frontiers in Ecology and Environment*, 2, 35–42

Altieri, M.A., Nicholls, C.I., Henao, A. and Lana, M.A. (2015) 'Agroecology and the design of climate resilient farming systems', *Agronomy for Sustainable Development*, 35, 869–890

Anderson, E.N. (2010) 'Food cultures: Linking people to landscapes', in Pilgrim, S. and Pretty, J. (eds), *Nature and culture – rebuilding lost connections*, Earthscan, London and New York, 185–194

Auerbach, R., Rundgren, G. and El-Hage Scialabba, N. (eds) (2013) *Organic agriculture: African experiences in resilience and sustainability*, FAO, Rome

Barthel, S., Crumley, C. and Svedin, U. (2013) 'Bio-cultural refugia: Safeguarding diversity of practices for food security and biodiversity', *Global Environmental Change*, 23, 1142–1152

Bennett, E.M., Solan, M., Biggs, R., McPhearson, T., Norström, A.V., Olsson, P., Pereira, L., Peterson, G.D., Raudsepp-Hearne, C., Biermann, F., Carpenter, S.R., Ellis, E.C., Hichert, T., Galaz, V., Lahsen, M., Milkoreit, M., Martin López, B., Nicholas, K.A., Preiser, R., Vince, G., Vervoort, J.M. and Xu, J. (2016) 'Bright spots: Seeds of a good Anthropocene', *Frontiers in Ecology and the Environment*, 14, 441–448

Blay-Palmer, A., SonninoR. and Custot, J. (2016) 'A food politics of the possible', *Agriculture and Human Values*, 33, 27–43

Blay-Palmer, A., Santini, G., Dubbeling, M., Renting, H., Taguchi, M. and Giordano, T. (2018) 'Validating the city region food system approach: Enacting inclusive, transformational city region food systems', *Sustainability*, 10, 1680

Bloemmen, M., Bobulescu, R., Tuyen Le, N. and Vitari, C. (2015) 'Microeconomic degrowth: The case of Community Supported Agriculture', *Ecological Economics*, 112, 110–115

Boscardin, L. (2017) 'Capitalizing on nature, naturalizing capitalism: An analysis of the "livestock revolution", planetary boundaries, and green tendencies in the animal-industrial complex', in Nibert, D. (ed.), *Animal oppression and capitalism*, 1, 259–276, Praeger, Santa Barbara and Denver

Caron, P., Bienabe, E. and Hainzelin, E. (2014) 'Making transition towards ecological intensification of agriculture a reality: The gaps in and the role of scientific knowledge', *Current Opinion in Environmental Sustainability*, 8, 44–52

Conrad, Z., Tichenor, N.E., Peters, C.F. and Griffin, T.S. (2016) 'Regional self-reliance for livestock feed, meat, dairy and eggs in the Northeast USA'. *Renewable Agriculture and Food Systems*, 32, 145–156

D'Alisa, G., Demaria, F. and Kallis, G. (eds) (2014) *Degrowth – a vocabulary for a new era*, Routledge, London and New York

Dubbeling, M., Bucatariu, C., Santini, G., Vogt, C. and Eisenbeiss, K. (eds) (2016) *City region food systems and food waste management: Linking urban and rural areas for sustainable and resilient development*, Deutsche Gesellschaft für Internationale Zusammenarbeit (GIZ) GmbH, Eschborn

Dyball, R. (2015) 'From industrial production to biosensitivity: The need for a food system paradigm shift', *Journal of Environmental Studies and Sciences*, 5, 560–572

Feagan, R., (2007) 'The place of food: Mapping out the 'local' in local food systems', *Progress in Human Geography*, 31, 23–42

Feintrenie, L. (2014) 'Agro-industrial plantations in Central Africa, risks and opportunities', *Biodiversity and Conservation*, 23, 1577–1589

Ferguson, C. (2017) *The development of local food strategies in the UK: Pathways to sustainability*, IDS, Brighton

Fischer, J., Abson, D.J., Bergsten, A., French Collier, N., Dorresteijn, I., Hanspach, J., Hylander, K., Schultner, J. and Senbeta, F. (2017) 'Reframing the Food–Biodiversity Challenge', *Trends in Ecology and Evolution*, 32, 335–345

Foley, J.A., Ramankutty, N., Brauman, K.A., Cassidy, E.S., Gerber, J.S., Johnston, M., Mueller, N.D., O'Connell, C., Ray, D.K., West, P.C., Balzer, C., Bennett, E.M., Carpenter, S.R., Hill, J., Monfreda, C., Polasky, S., Rockström, J., Sheehan, J., Siebert, S., Tilman, D. and Zaks, D.P.M. (2011) 'Solutions for a cultivated planet', *Nature*, 478, 337–342

Graham, T. and Abrahamse, W. (2017) 'Communicating the climate impacts of meat consumption: The effect of values and message framing', *Global Environmental Change*, 44, 98–108

Gwatkin, D.R., Rutstein, S., Johnson, K., Suliman, E., Wagstaff, A. and Amouzou, A. (2007) *Socio-economic differences in health, nutrition and population within developing countries*, Country reports on HNP and poverty, World Bank, September 2007

Hausknost, D., Shriefl, E., Lauk, C. and Kalt, G. (2017) 'A transition to which bioeconomy? An exploration of diverging techno-political choices', *Sustainability*, 9, 669–691

Hochedez, C. and Le Gall, J. (2016) 'Food justice and agriculture', *Spatial Justice*, 9, 1–31

Hope, A.A. and Agyeman, J. (2011) *Cultivating food justice*, The MIT Press, Cambridge, MA

Ilieva, R.T. (2017) 'Urban food system strategies: A promising tool for implementing the SDGs in practice', *Sustainability*, 9, 707–1742

IPBES (2018) *Summary for policy makers of the regional assessment report on biodiversity and ecosystem services for Europe and Central Asia of the Intergovernmental Science-Policy Platform on Biodiversity and Ecosystem Services*, IPBES Secretariat, Bonn

Kastner, T., Erb, K-H. and Haberl, H. (2014) 'Rapid growth in agricultural trade: Effects on global area efficiency and the role of management', *Environmental Research Letters*, 9, 034015

Khoury, C.K., Bjorkman, A.D., Dempewolf, H., Ramirez-Villegas, J., Guarino, L., Jarvis, A., Rieseberg, L.H. and Struik, P.C. (2014) 'Increasing homogeneity in global food supplies and the implication for food security', *Proceedings of the National Academy of Sciences*, 111, 4001–4006

Killeen, T.J., Guerra, A., Calzada, M., Correa, L., Calderon, V., Soria, L., Quezada, B. and Steininge, M.K. (2008) 'Total historical land-use change in Eastern Bolivia: Who, where, when, and how much?' *Ecology and Society*, 13(1), art. 36 http://www.ecologyandsociety.org/vol13/iss1/art36/

Kolb, V. (2015) *Geographical analysis of environmental and ecological inequalities in coastal urban territories*, PhD thesis, University of La Rochelle and CNRS, France

Kuyper, T.W. and Struik, P. (2014) 'Epilogue: Global food security, rhetoric, and the sustainable intensification debate', *Current Opinion in Environmental Sustainability*, 8, 71–79

Lang, T. and Heasman, M. (2015) *Food wars: The battle for mouths, minds and markets*, 2nd edition, Earthscan, London and New York

Luederitz, C., Abson, D.J., Audet, R. and Lang, D.J. (2017) 'Many pathways towards sustainability: Not conflict but co-learning between transition narratives', *Sustainability Science*, 12, 93–407

Markard, J., Raven, R. and Truffer, B. (2012) 'Sustainability transitions: An emerging field of research and its prospects', *Research Policy*, 41, 955–967

Martin, A.R. and Isaac, M.E. (2018) 'Functional traits in agroecology: Advancing description and prediction in agroecosystems', *Journal of Applied Ecology*, 55, 5–11

McMichael, A.J., Powles, J.W., Butler, C.D., and Uauy, R. (2007) 'Food, livestock production, energy, climate change, and health', *The Lancet*, 370, 1253–1263

MendezV.E., Bacon, C.M. and Cohen, R. (2013) 'Agroecology as a transdisciplinary, participatory and action-oriented approach', *Agroecology and Sustainable Food Systems*, 37, 3–18

Misselhorn, A., Aggarwal, P., Ericksen, P., Gregory, P., Horn-Phathanothai, L., Ingram, J. and Wiebe, K. (2012) 'A vision for attaining food security', *Current opinion in environmental sustainability*, 4, 7–17

Moragues-Faus, A., Morgan, K., Moschitz, H., Neimane, I., Nilsson, H., Pinto, M., Rohracher, H., Ruiz, R., Thuswald, M., Tisenkopfs, T. and Halliday, J. (2013) *Urban food strategies: The rough guide to sustainable food systems*, Document developed in the framework of the FP7 project FOODLINKS (GA No. 265287) http://www.foodlinkscommunity.

Moragues-Faus, A. and Morgan, K. (2015) 'Reframing the foodscape: The emergent world of urban food policy', *Environment and Planning A*, 47, 1558–1573

Morgan, K., (2015) 'Nourishing the city: The rise of the urban food question in the Global North', *Urban Studies*, 52, 1379–1394

Muraca, B. (2012) 'Towards a fair degrowth-society: Justice and the right to a "good life" beyond growth', *Futures*, 44, 535–545

OECD (2016) *Adopting a territorial approach to food security and nutrition policy*, OECD/FAO/UNCDF,OECD Publishinghttps://doi.org/10.1787/9789264257108-en

Olsson, E.G.A., Kerselaers, E., Søderkvist Kristensen, L., Primdahl, J., Rogge, E. and Wästfelt, A. (2016) 'Peri-urban food production and its relation to urban resilience', *Sustainability*, 8, 1340

Olsson, E.G.A. (2018a) 'Peri-urban food production as means towards urban food security and increased urban resilience', in Zeunert, J. and Waterman, T. (eds), *Routledge handbook of landscape and food*, Routledge, London and New York, 197–212

Olsson, E.G.A. (2018b) 'Urban food systems as vehicles for sustainability transitions', *Bulletin of Geography. Socio-economic Series*, 40, 133–144

Olsson, E.G.A. (2018c) 'The shaping of food landscapes from the Neolithic to Industrial period: Changing agro-ecosystems between three agrarian revolutions', in Zeunert, J. and Waterman, T. (eds), *Routledge handbook of landscape and food*, Routledge, London and New York, 24–40

Otero, G., Gürcan, E.C., Pechlaner, G. and Liberman, G. (2018) 'Food security, obesity, and inequality: Measuring the risk of exposure to the neoliberal diet', *Journal of Agrarian Change*, 18, 536–554

Peters, C.J., Bills, N.L., Wilkins, J.L. and Fick, G.W. (2009) 'Foodshed analysis and its relevance to sustainability', *Renewable Agriculture and Food Systems*, 24, 1–7

Porter, J.R., Dyball, R., Dumaresq, D., Deutsch, L. and Matsuda, H. (2014) 'Feeding capitals: Urban food security and self-provisioning in Canberra, Copenhagen and Tokyo', *Global Food Security*, 3, 1–7

Pradhan, P., Reusser, D.E. and Kropp, J.P. (2013) 'Embodied greenhouse gas emissions in diets', *PLOS ONE*, 8, e62228

Raffle, A.E. and Carey, J. (2018) 'Ten years in one city's food story – Bristol, England', in WatermanT. and ZeunertJ. (eds), *The Routledge Handbook of Landscape and Food*, Routledge, London and New York, 500–513

Rosin, C., Stock, P. and Campbell, H. (2012) *Food system failure: The global food crisis and the future of agriculture*, Earthscan, London and New York

Sage, C. (2013) 'The interconnected challenges for food security from a food regimes perspective: Energy, climate and malconsumption', *Journal of Rural Studies*, 29, 71–80

Schader, C., Muller, A., El-Hage Scialabba, N., Hecht, J., Isensee, A., Erb, K-H., Smith, P., Makkar, H.P.S., Klocke, P., Leiber, F., Schwegler, P., Stolze, M. and Niggli, U. (2015) 'Impacts of feeding less food-competing feedstuffs to livestock on global food system sustainability', *Journal of Royal Society Interface*, 12, 20150891http://dx.doi.org/10.1098/rsif.2015.0891

Schipanski, M.E., Macdonald, G.K., Rosenzwig, S., Chappell, M.J., Bennett, E.M., Bezner Kerr, R., Blesh, J., Crews, T., Drinkwater, L., Lundgren, J.G. and Schnarr, C. (2016) 'Realizing resilient food systems', *BioScience*, 66, 600–610

Sharp, J., Imerman, E. and Peters, G. (2002) 'Community Supported Agriculture (CSA): Building community among farmers and non-farmers', *Journal of Extension*, 40(3) https://www.joe.org/joe/2002june/a3.php

Smith, L.C. and Haddad, L. (2015) 'Reducing child undernutrition: Past drivers and priorities for the post-MDG era', *World Development*, 68, 180–204

Sonnino, R. (2016) 'The new geography of food security: Exploring the potential of urban food strategies', *The Geographical Journal*, 182, 190–200

Steffen, W., Persson, Å., Deutsch, L., Zalasiewicz, J., Williams, M., Richardson, K., Crumley, C., Crutzen, P., Folke, C., Gordon, L., Molina, M., Ramanathan, V., Rockstrom, J., Scheffer, M., Schellnhuber, H.J. and Svedin, U. (2011) 'The Anthropocene: From global change to planetary stewardship', *AMBIO*, 40, 739–761

Steffen, W., Richardson, K., Rockström, J., Cornell, S.E., Fetzer, I., Bennett, E.M., Biggs, R., Carpenter, S.R., de Vries, W. and de Wit, C.A. (2015) 'Planetary boundaries: Guiding human development on a changing planet', *Science*, 347, art. 1259855

Tengö, M., Hill, R., Malmer, P., Raymond, C.M., Spierenburg, M., Danielsen, F., Elmqvist, T. and Folke, C. (2017) 'Weaving knowledge systems in IPBES, CBD and beyond—lessons learned for sustainability', *Current Opinion in Environmental Sustainability*, 26–27, 17–25

Tilman, D. and Clark, M. (2015) 'Global diets link environmental sustainability and human health', *Nature*, 515, 518–522

UN (2015) *Transforming our world: The 2030 agenda for sustainable development* (A/RES/70/1), New York, United Nationshttps://sustainabledevelopment.un.org/content/documents/UN (Accessed: 26 January 2018)

Whitehead, M. (2013) 'Degrowth or regrowth?' *Environmental Values*, 2, 141–145

Index

Note: bold page numbers indicate tables; italic page numbers indicate figures; numbers preceded by n refer to chapter endnotes.